COMPUTER CONCEPTS and APPLICATIONS FOR THE MEDICAL OFFICE

Kathy Bonewit-West

B.S., M.Ed., CMA-C
Coordinator and Instructor
Medical Assistant Technology
Hocking College
Nelsonville, Ohio

Member of the
Curriculum Review Board
of the American Association
of Medical Assistants
(1985 - 1991)

W.B. SAUNDERS COMPANY
A Division of Harcourt Brace & Company

Philadelphia London Toronto Montreal Sydney Tokyo

W.B. SAUNDERS COMPANY
A Division of
Harcourt Brace & Company
The Curtis Center
Independence Square West
Philadelphia, PA 19103-3399

Library of Congress Cataloging-in-Publication Data
Bonewit-West, Kathy
Computer concepts and applications for the medical office / Kathy Bonewit-West. — 1st ed. p. cm.
Includes index.
ISBN 0-7216-4945-9
1. Medical offices—Data processing. 2. Medical offices—Automation. I. Title.
[DNLM: 1. Practice Management, Medical. W 26.5 B712c 1993]
R864.B65 1993
651.9'61—dc20
DNLM/DLC 93-9263

COMPUTER CONCEPTS AND APPLICATIONS FOR THE MEDICAL OFFICE
First Edition ISBN 0-7216-4945-9

Printed in the U.S.A.

Last digit is the print number: 9 8 7 6 5 4

For Mom and Trissy

Preface

With the advent of the microcomputer, most medical offices now use a computer to perform administrative procedures which were previously performed manually. Yet, because of a shortage of truly computer literate medical office personnel, computers may not be used to their full potential even in those offices where they have already been installed. Instead, partially trained individuals with limited applications skills and lacking an understanding of basic computer concepts are unable to make complete use of their computer systems. Thus, there is a demonstrated need for individuals fully trained in medical office management computer applications, not only to perform administrative tasks on the computer, but also to instruct other staff members in computer operations. This text has been designed and organized to meet that need by providing students and educators with a comprehensive, yet understandable base in computer concepts and applications for the medical office. Once this foundation in theory has been laid, the text provides students with a practical applications approach that is generalized enough that the student can anticipate few surprises when confronted with any medical management program in the actual workplace.

Chapter 1 presents a thorough discussion of computer concepts beginning with a basic definition of the computer, proceeding through how computers work to how they are operated. The goal of this chapter is to provide students with an understanding adequate to demystify computer operations and yet not burden them with information better left to hardware and software specialists. Chapter 1 presents a related set of concepts and is divided into sections each of which focuses on one concept at a time. Each subsequent section builds on the previous one as the student progresses from the simple to the complex. Wherever practical, examples from the medical office have been used for purposes of illustration.

Chapters 2 and 3 are organized similarly to Chapter 1 and introduce the student to applications commonly used in the medical office. Chapter 2 presents word processing, the most common application of microcomputers. Again, the chapter is divided into sections which guide the student through the basics to the more complicated uses of word processing programs. Chapter 3 introduces basic medical office management applications theory. This chapter specifically discusses the most common functions performed by computers in the medical office, how they are performed and the computer equipment needed to perform them.

At the beginning of the introductory chapters (Chapters 1 through 3) are a chapter outline, learning objectives, and computer terminology. The chapter outline provides a quick reference for review of the information included in that chapter. The learning objectives address the cognitive knowledge required in order to master the chapter. The computer terminology designates the terms and definitions to be mastered for each chapter. Numerous illustrations have been employed in Chapters 1 through 3 to assist in comprehension of text material. Review questions (Checkpoint) and practical applications exercises (Critical Literacy) are integrated into the chapters to assist student comprehension and retention to text material.

Throughout this text emphasis has been placed on a practical applications approach to facilitate the transition from classroom to workplace. This approach is best illustrated by the unique simulated medical office management program (entitled the *Medical Practice Manager*) which constitutes Chapters 4 through 10. In these chapters students are carefully guided, on paper, through a generic medical office management program which highlights the most common aspects of commercially available medical management programs now in use. The purpose of the *Medical Practice Manager* is to illustrate both menu screens and data entry screens which the student could expect to encounter when operating a medical management program in the medical office. Furthermore, the *Medical Practice Manager* demonstrates the relationship of the various menu screens and data entry screens to each other, so that when the student begins to train on the computer, he/she is prepared for and able to anticipate how the computer will respond. This feature of the text makes it particularly useful as either a lead-in for a program-based course or as a course in itself.

The following leading manufacturers of medical management software programs served as consultants for this project by providing program user manuals, reference information, and in some cases, demonstration software:

Alcon Systems, Inc.
4221 Forest Park Boulevard
St. Louis, MO 63108-2810
Program Name: Ivy Practice Management System
(800) 289-1991

Articulate Publications
Division of CyCare Systems, Inc.
21201 Oxnard Street
Woodland Hills, CA 91367-5094
Program Name: Medicalis
(818) 716-8080

Calyx Corporation
150 North Sunnyslope Road
Brookfield, WI 53005
Program Name: MDX
(414) 782-0300

CMA Micro Computer
55888 Yucca Trail
Yucca Valley, CA 92286-2080
Program Name: Medical Office Management
(619) 365-9718

Health America Systems
404 North Milwaukee Avenue
Libertyville, Illinois 60048
Program Name: Patient Management System-Plus
(708) 362-3730

Pacific Medsoft Inc.
3080 North Lake Boulevard
Tahoe City, CA 95730
Program Name: Medical Practice Manager
(916) 583-2994

The Small Computer Company
1211 Streets Run Road
Pittsburgh, PA 15236
Program Name: Medical Office System
(412) 885-7100

Systems Plus, Inc.
500 Clyde Avenue
Mountain View, CA 94093
Program Name: The Medical Manager
(415) 969-7047

Wallaby Software Corporation
10 Industrial Avenue
Mahwah, NJ 07430
Name of Program: The Resident
(201) 934-9333

Contents

1 COMPUTER CONCEPTS FOR HEALTH PROFESSIONALS

CHAPTER OUTLINE

COMPETENCIES

After completing this chapter, you should be able to perform the following:

1. Insert a floppy disk into a disk drive.
2. Load an application program using a warm start and a cold start.
3. Boot the operating system.
4. Format a floppy disk.
5. Make a backup copy.
6. Shut down the computer.

LEARNING OBJECTIVES

After completing this chapter, you should be able to:

Introduction

1. Define the terms presented in Computer Terminology.
2. State the purpose and advantages of a computer.
3. Describe the difference between a mainframe computer, a minicomputer and a microcomputer.

Data Processing

1. Explain the difference between data and a program.
2. Explain the purpose of each of the following parts of the data processing sequence: input, processing, and output.
3. List four examples of input devices.
4. List two examples of output devices.
5. Identify five types of processing functions performed on data by a computer.

Components of the Computer System

1. Explain the difference between hardware and software.
2. Explain the difference between system software and application software.
3. State the four hardware components required for a basic operational computer system in the medical office.
4. Explain the function of the following three parts of the CPU: control unit, ALU, and primary storage.
5. Describe the care and maintenance of the main computer unit.

Computer Monitor

1. State the two main functions of the computer monitor.
2. Explain why resolution is an important consideration in the selection of a monitor.
3. Describe the difference between a monochrome monitor and a color monitor.
4. List and describe the function of the monitor controls.
5. Describe the care and maintenance of the computer monitor.

Computer Keyboard

1. Identify the differences between a typewriter keyboard and a computer keyboard.
2. Describe the care and maintenance of a computer keyboard.

Printers

1. Explain the difference between letter quality print and near-letter quality print.
2. Identify examples of the following classifications of printers: impact and nonimpact.
3. Explain how the following printers form characters on paper: dot-matrix, daisywheel, and laser printers.
4. Describe the following paper-feeding methods: tractor-feeding, friction feeding, and cut-sheet feeding.
5. Identify the guidelines to follow in the care and maintenance of a printer.
6. Explain the function of the following printer controls: on/off, on-line, line-feed, and form-feed.

Internal Memory and Operating Systems

1. Explain the function of RAM.
2. Describe how the capacity of a computer's memory correlates with the programs that can be used with it.
3. Explain the function of ROM.

Secondary Storage Devices

1. Explain the function of a secondary storage device.
2. Explain the purpose of tracks and sectors.
3. Explain the difference between a double-density and a high-density disk.
4. Identify and explain the function of each of the following openings on a floppy disk jacket: hub, data access area, index hole, write-protect notch.
5. Identify the guidelines which should be followed in caring for a floppy disk.
6. State the function of a disk drive.
7. Explain the difference between read and write.
8. List the advantages offered by a hard disk.
9. Identify the primary use of magnetic tape.

Basic Computer Procedures

1. Explain when the cold start and warm start methods should be used to start the computer.
2. State the purpose of formatting a disk.
3. Explain why a backup copy of important disks should be made.
4. Explain the purpose of write-protection.

COMPUTER TERMINOLOGY

ALU (arithmetic/logic unit)—The part of the CPU that executes the program's instructions by performing mathematical computations and logical operations.
application software —Software designed to accomplish a specific task (e.g., word processing). Also called application program and software program.
backup copy—A duplicate copy of a program or data kept for reference in case the original is damaged, lost, or destroyed.
byte—A unit of computer storage capacity. One byte is approximately equal to one character.
computer—An electronic machine which has the ability to process data according to a program in order to produce a desired result.
computerphobia—The fear of computers.
control unit—The part of the CPU that coordinates the entire computer system.
CPU (central processing unit)—The "heart" of the computer housed in the main unit. The CPU consists of the control unit, the ALU, and primary storage.
CRT (cathode ray tube)—A monitor similar to a television screen that permits the visual display of input and output.
data—Raw, unorganized facts about subject matter presented to the computer for processing.
data disk—A disk that has been formatted and prepared to receive and store data from an application program.
data processing—The changing of raw facts or data into usable information following a three part sequence: input, processing, output.
directory—A special area on a disk which contains the names and location of all the items stored on the disk. The computer uses the directory to locate items on the disk.
disk drive—A mechanical device which rotates a floppy disk and uses a read/write head for the purpose of data transmission.
DOS (Disk Operating System)—A term commonly used to refer to the following operating systems: PC-DOS and MS-DOS.
double-density disk—A disk that can hold twice as much information as a single-density disk.
double-sided disk—A disk that can store information on both sides of the disk.
floppy disk—A secondary storage device consisting of flexible mylar plastic coated with iron oxide and encased in a square jacket.
formatting (initializing)—The process of marking track and sector numbers on a disk so that it can be used by the computer to store and retrieve information. Formatting erases any information previously stored on the disk.
hard disk—A secondary storage device consisting of one or more rigid, nonflexible magnetic platters encased in a permanently sealed, air-tight container.
hardcopy—Printed output from a computer.
hardware—The physical devices making up the computer system (e.g., CPU, keyboard, monitor, printer).
impact printer—A type of printer that forms characters using a print element that strikes an inked ribbon against the paper (e.g., dot-matrix, daisywheel).
information—Data that has been processed into a usable form by the computer.
input—1. (noun) Data that has been entered into the computer. 2. (verb) The transfer of data to the computer for processing.
input device—A device for entering data into the computer (e.g., keyboard, scanner, mouse).
K (kilobyte)—A unit of computer storage capacity. Once kilobyte is equal to 1024 bytes (characters).
keyboard (computer)—An input device which converts data into an electronic code for processing by the computer.
letter quality (LQ)—Print that is characterized by sharp, crisp, high-quality, fully formed characters similar to the characters produced by a typewriter.
load—The process of transferring information into computer memory from a secondary storage device such as a hard disk or floppy disk.
MB (megabyte)—A unit of computer storage capacity. One megabyte is equal to a little over one million bytes.
magnetic tape—A secondary storage device consisting of a thin, plastic material which has a magnetic surface for storing data. Magnetic tape is most often used to back up a hard disk.
near-letter quality (NLQ)—Print that is of a slightly lesser quality than that of letter quality print.

nonimpact printer—A type of printer that forms characters without making a striking motion against the paper, but rather through the use of laser beams, ink-jet spraying, or heat (e.g., laser printer, ink-jet printer, thermal printer).

operating system—A group of programs which serve as a manager to control computer operations not controlled by ROM.

output—1. (noun) Information that has been generated by the computer. 2. (verb) The transfer of processed data back to the user.

primary storage—The part of the CPU that is responsible for temporarily storing information until it is needed for processing by the computer. Primary storage in a microcomputer is known as RAM.

printer—An output device that produces hardcopy output.

processing—The manipulation and reorganization of data according to the instructions in a program.

program—A set of instructions organized in a logical step-by-step sequence which tells the computer how to perform a specific function.

program disk—A floppy disk that contains an application program.

RAM (random-access memory)—Primary storage in a microcomputer which is used to temporarily store items until needed by the computer. Also known as computer memory.

read—The transfer of information from a storage medium, such as a floppy disk or a hard disk, to computer memory.

resolution—The sharpness of the image displayed on the screen of a computer monitor.

ROM (read-only memory)—A type of memory found in microcomputers which can only be read. ROM is permanently installed by the manufacturer and holds instructions that the computer needs to manage itself.

secondary storage device—A storage device used to permanently store information for later retrieval by the computer.

single-sided disk—A disk which can store information on only one side of the disk.

softcopy—The visual display of information on the display screen of a computer monitor.

software—A general term for the programs or instructions that tell a computer what to do.

system disk—A floppy disk that contains an operating system.

user—The individual using the computer.

write—The transfer of information from computer memory to a storage medium such as a floppy disk or hard disk.

write-protect—To protect the information on a disk. When a disk is write-protected, the computer cannot make changes to information, erase any information or write new information on the disk.

Introduction

Computers are designed to perform tasks that would otherwise be performed by hand; however computers perform these tasks more efficiently. Because of their complex circuitry, computers are intimidating to some individuals, but they need not be. In fact, a computer is no more difficult to operate than an electronic typewriter, an electrocardiograph machine, a blood chemistry analyzer or other devices used in the medical office. All are devices that react to what you tell them to do, and with each a solid foundation in theory should first be acquired for you to feel confident during hands-on operation.

This chapter has been designed to provide you with the theoretical foundation necessary to effectively use computers in the medical office. Because most offices use a microcomputer (as opposed to a minicomputer or a mainframe computer), this chapter focuses on the theory and techniques of microcomputer systems.

It is important that you carefully read the information in each section and answer all of the review questions before proceeding to the next section. Having completed this chapter, you should find computers less mysterious and discover that any *computerphobia* you may be experiencing has been eliminated.

COMPUTERS

A *computer* is a device consisting of electronic components which has the ability to process data according to a program in order to produce a desired result. The primary advantage of using a computer to perform administrative procedures in the medical office is that these tasks are performed with greater speed and accuracy than with other types of devices such as a typewriter, pegboard system, calculator and so on. In addition, computers are versatile: rather than performing only one function (e.g., typing, posting a payment, math calculations), a computer can perform a variety of administrative procedures.

Another unique feature of the computer is its ability to communicate or *interact* with the user. When you use an electronic typewriter, you do not expect a response from it to any of your actions. With a computer, however, you are involved in constant back-and-forth communication. Each time you communicate with the computer you receive a response.

Computers are useful tools because they are capable of performing the same tasks repeatedly while maintaining the same level of efficiency. It should always be remembered however, that the computer does not have a mind of its own. You are always in complete charge, and the computer will never do anything without your direction.

Types of Computers

Based upon size and capability, computers can be classified into three main categories: mainframe computers, minicomputers and microcomputers.

A *mainframe computer* consists of a large central computer system to which numerous terminals are attached. The advantage of a mainframe system is that it can process an enormous amount of data at a very high rate of speed and serve the needs of up to 500 users at a time. Disadvantages include high cost and the necessity that it be housed in a specially-constructed, air-conditioned room. Mainframe computers are used primarily by large corporations, hospitals, universities and other facilities with large processing requirements. Exceptionally large medical clinics may use a mainframe, but cost and space requirements make its use in the private-practice medical office impractical.

A *minicomputer* is a midsize system typically used by engineering firms, large medical clinics, and academic institutions. The minicomputer has the same components as the mainframe, but has less memory and fewer capabilities. It is able to support between 10 and 100 users at a time.

A *microcomputer*, also called a personal computer, is a small, general purpose computer that relies on a tiny microprocessor chip to perform its processing functions. Although they do not have the capability or memory of the larger computers, microcomputers are smaller and less expensive than mainframe or minicomputers. Microcomputers are used in the medical office to perform front office procedures, and continuing advances in technology are allowing them to perform an expanding array of more difficult and sophisticated tasks. It should be noted that, although this chapter focuses on the microcomputer, most of the theory presented here applies to mainframe computers and minicomputers as well.

Data Processing

Data processing is the term applied to changing raw facts or data into usable information. To fully comprehend data processing, it is important to have a thorough understanding of the terms data and program. *Data* is a general term used to describe the raw, unorganized facts presented to the computer for processing. Patients' names, addresses and telephone numbers are examples of data frequently entered into the computer in the medical office.

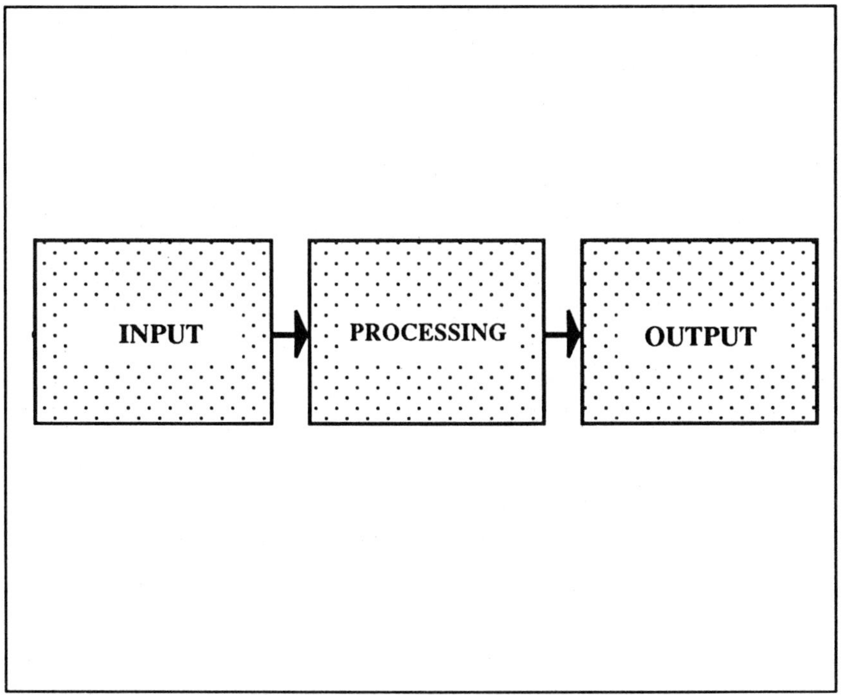

FIGURE 1 - 1. The Data Processing Cycle.

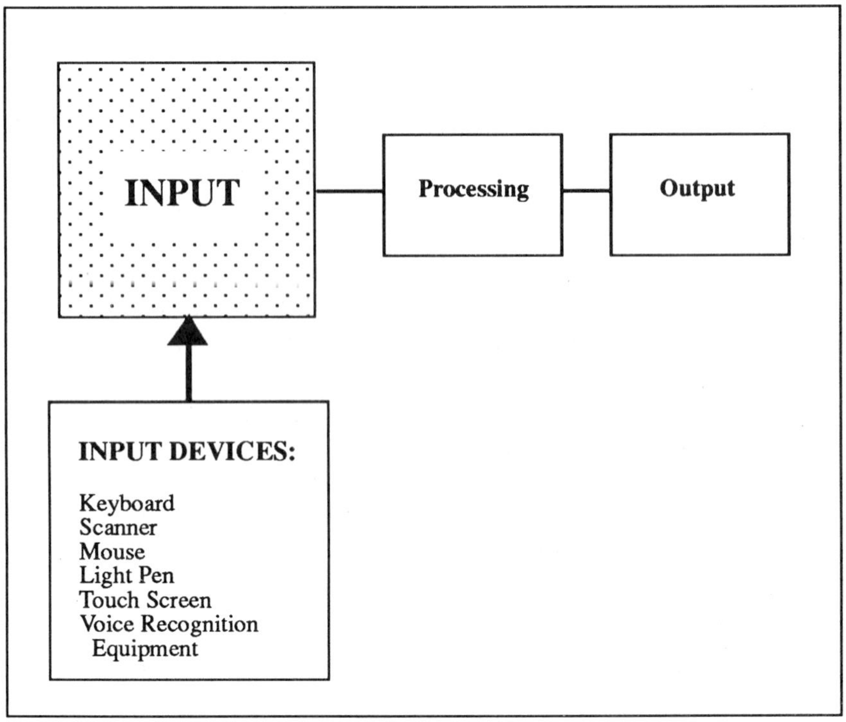

FIGURE 1 - 2. Input Devices.

A *program* is defined as a set of instructions organized in a logical step-by-step sequence which tells the computer how to perform a specific function. In order to process data, you must have a program to tell the computer what to do with the data. Just as in baking, a recipe is required to tell you how to mix ingredients, a computer requires a program to tell it how to process data.

Computers process data into useful information in a logical three part sequence, the phases of which are: input, processing and output (Fig. 1-1). Each phase of the data processing cycle contributes to the desired result and involves a specific activity which is described below. It should be noted that the terms input and output have slightly different meanings depending on how they are used. When referring to the data processing cycle, they are used from the "computer's point of view" as verbs to describe the transfer of information. Input and output are also used as nouns to describe the data that has been entered into the computer (input) and the information that has been generated by the computer (output). As these terms appear throughout this chapter you will become familiar with their different meanings.

Input

The *input* of data is the transfer of data to the computer for processing. Input includes both the entering of data into the computer and the conversion of it into an electronic form which can be understood by the computer. Because computers cannot understand the "written word" in the form used in communication by humans, the data must first be translated into an electronic code which can then be processed by the computer. Once the computer is finished working on the "electronic" data, it must be converted back into a form that can be understood by the *user*, the individual using the computer.

Data must be entered into the computer through an *input device* (Fig. 1-2). The most common example of an input device is the computer keyboard. The computer keyboard converts data into a series of electronic signals which can then be understood and processed by the computer. Other less frequently used types of input devices include the scanner, the mouse, the light pen, the touch screen, and voice recognition equipment.

Processing

The *processing* of data is the computer's handling and arranging of the electronic data according to a program; in other words, the data undergoes some type of manipulation or change to produce useful information. Depending upon the result, the processing phase may include one or more of the following: classifying, sorting, calculating, summarizing or listing of the data (Fig. 1-3).

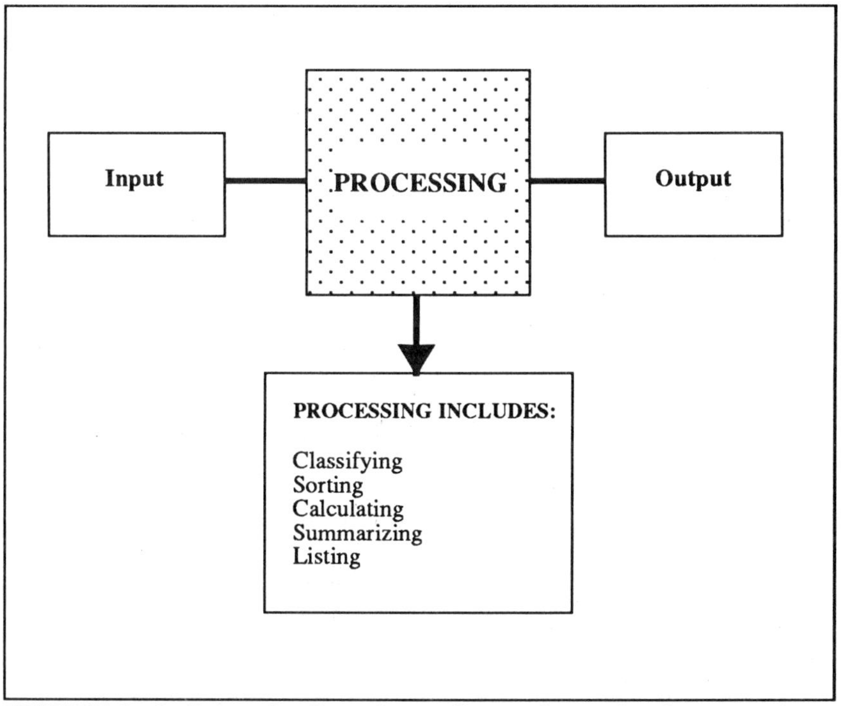

FIGURE 1 - 3. Processing Data. Depending on the results, the processing phase may include one or more of the following: classifying, sorting, calculating, summarizing or listing of the data.

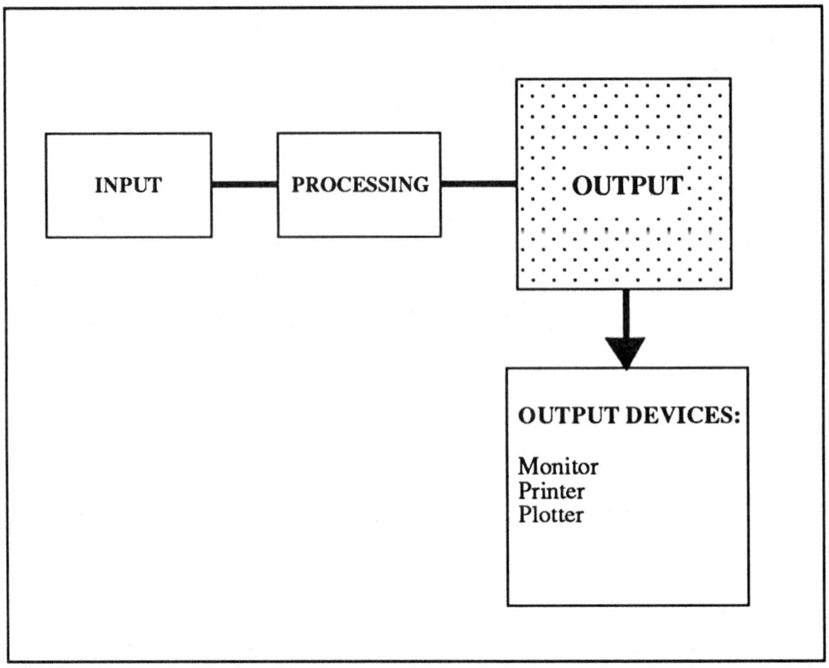

FIGURE 1 - 4. Output Devices.

Output

The final phase of the data processing sequence is the *output* of the processed data. Output is the transfer of usable information back to the user. Because the computer only deals with electronic signals, an output device must be used to communicate with the user. The *output device* converts the electronic signals of information into a form which can be understood by the user. The most common output devices are the monitor and the printer (Fig. 1-4).

The following is a specific example of how a computer is used for data processing. In this example, the terminology presented above is described using a simulated computer task.

Simulated Task: Enter one-hundred medical terms into the computer for the purpose of arranging them in alphabetical order on a printed list.

Data: (Also called input) The list of one-hundred medical terms.
Input: Entering the one-hundred medical terms into the computer.
Input Device: Computer keyboard.
Program Instructions: Place the data in alphabetical order.
Processing Function: The actual arranging of the medical terms in alphabetical order (sorting and listing).
Output: The transfer of the alphabetical list of medical terms back to the user.
Output Device: Printer.
Usable Information: (Also called output) The printed alphabetized list of medical terms.

CHECKPOINT

1. What is a computer? ______________________________

____

2. What are the principle advantages of using a computer to perform administrative procedures in the medical office?

____

____

3. List two examples of facilities in which you might find a mainframe computer.

____

4. What type of computer is used most often in a private practice medical office?

____

5. Define the following term: data processing.

____

6. What is the term used to describe raw, unorganized facts presented to the computer for processing?

____

7. What is the term to describe a set of instructions organized in a logical step-by-step sequence which tells the computer how to perform a specific function?

____

8. List and define the three phases included in the data processing sequence.

____

9. Why must a computer convert data into an electronic code?

____

10. What is the term to describe an individual using a computer?

____

11. List four examples of input devices. ______________________________

____

____

12. List five types of processing functions performed on data by the computer.

____

____

13. List two examples of output devices. ______________________________

____

14. What is the term used to describe data that has been entered into the computer?

____

15. What is the term used to describe information that has been generated by the computer?

____

CRITICAL LITERACY

Data Processing Assignment: A simulated computer task is described below. Using this description, complete the following categories with the required information.

Simulated Task: Enter 400 CPT codes and descriptions into your computer for the purpose of arranging them in numerical sequence by code number to produce a printed copy of these codes.

____________________ 1. Data

____________________ 2. Input

____________________ 3. Input Device

____________________ 4. Program Instructions

____________________ 5. Processing Function

____________________ 6. Output

____________________ 7. Output Device

____________________ 8. Usable Information

COMPONENTS OF THE COMPUTER SYSTEM

All the components making up the computer are collectively known as the *computer system*. Computer systems are classified according to the instructions (software) and equipment (hardware) needed to operate them.

Software is a general term for the programs or instructions that tell a computer what to do. Software tells the computer how to perform specific tasks in a series of step-by-step instructions organized in a logical sequence. There are two categories of software: system software and application software. *System software* is made up of a group of special programs, the most important of which is the *operating system*. The operating system performs "housekeeping chores" required by the computer system to operate itself. Specifically, the operating system is responsible for coordinating all the hardware components and application programs and for interpreting and executing commands entered from the keyboard. A thorough discussion of operating systems is presented later in this chapter.

Software designed to accomplish a specific task is known as *application software* and constitutes the greatest proportion of the software used on computers. Other terms used to refer to application software are *application program* and *software program*. WordPerfect is an example of application software that provides instructions to the computer for word processing. Other examples of commercially available application software include Microsoft Word, FoxPro, and Lotus 1-2-3. (*Note*: This text will refer to a medical office management application software program as a medical management program in the remaining chapters.)

Hardware is the term for the equipment making up the computer system; that is, the tangible computer parts. Hardware includes the CPU, the keyboard, the monitor, the printer, hard disks, floppy disks, magnetic tape, the mouse, and so on. While a computer system may include a variety of hardware, four devices are necessary to form a basic operational system in the medical office: a CPU, a monitor, a computer keyboard, and a printer (Fig. 1-5). The CPU is discussed in this section while the remaining computer components (monitor, keyboard and printer) are presented in the following sections.

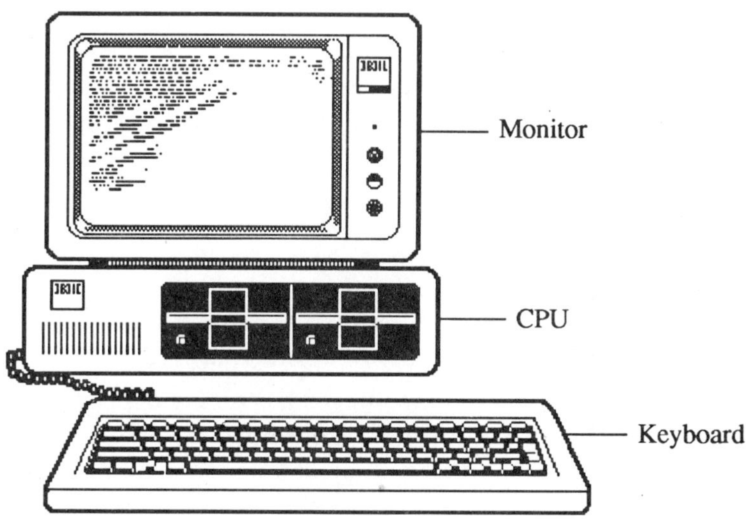

FIGURE 1 - 5. Four types of hardware are necessary to form a basic operational system in the medical office: a CPU, a monitor, a computer keyboard, and a printer.

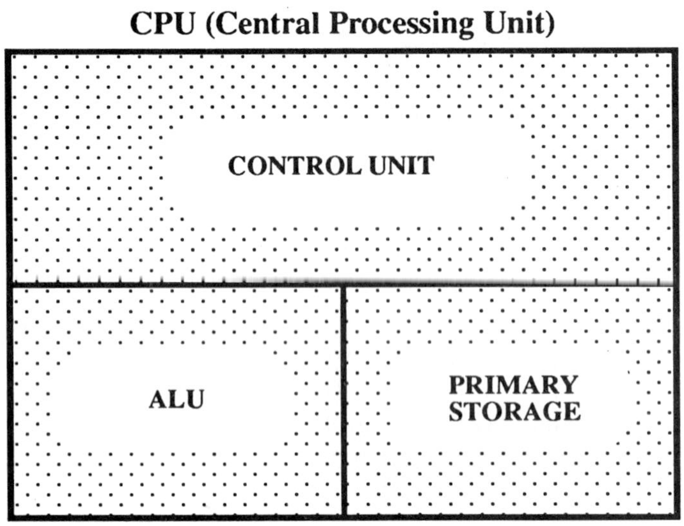

FIGURE 1 - 6. The CPU consists of three separate parts: the control unit, the arithmetic/logic unit and primary storage.

CPU (Central Processing Unit)

The *CPU* or *central processing unit*, is the functional core or "heart" of the computer and is the most complex computer system component. The CPU is contained on small silicon chips and resides on an electronic circuit board which is housed in the main unit of the computer. The CPU consists of three separate parts: 1) the control unit; 2) the arithmetic/logic unit; and 3) primary storage (Fig. 1-6). Each of these performs a specific function which is described in the following paragraphs.

Control Unit

The *control unit* coordinates the entire computer system functioning as a "traffic patrolman" to direct the step-by-step operation of all the processing functions. Specifically, the control unit reads and interprets the pre-set instructions of a program and tells the other components of the computer system what to do. During the processing phase, it keeps track of which steps of the program have been performed and which remain. Finally, the control unit collects the output and directs it to the designated output device (e.g., the printer). It is important to note that the control unit does not execute instructions or process any data itself, but directs the computer in how to carry out these functions.

ALU

The *arithmetic/logic unit* (abbreviated ALU) performs the actual processing functions within the computer, executing the program's instructions through a series of mathematical computations and logical operations. Mathematical computations include addition, subtraction, multiplication, and division. Logical operations involve making comparisons between items and performing a function based on the results. Items are compared by the ALU to determine if they are equal or if one has a greater or lesser value than the other. These compared values may be either numeric or alphabetic. An example of an alphabetic operation would be alphabetizing a list of patient's names. All processing of data performed by a computer relies on either arithmetic computations, logical comparisons, or a combination of the two. Thus, computers would not be able to perform most of the tasks we find useful without the ALU.

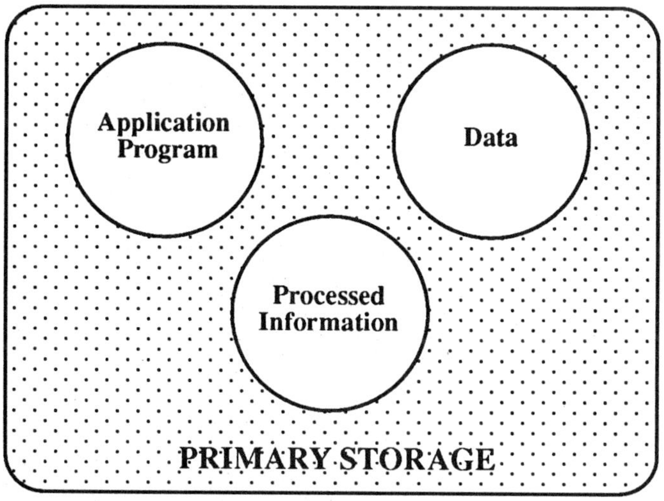

FIGURE 1 - 7. Items commonly held in the primary storage unit are the application program, data waiting to be processed, and information ready for output.

Primary Storage

Primary storage, also called internal memory, is responsible for temporarily storing information until ready for use. Primary storage can be compared to a holding tank in which items are placed for immediate access and use when needed for processing. Among those items commonly held in the primary storage unit are the application program, data waiting to be processed, and information ready for output (Fig. 1-7). In a microcomputer system, primary storage has a special name known as RAM, which is an acronym for random-access memory. RAM is vital to microcomputer systems and is discussed in detail later in this chapter.

Care and Maintenance of the Main Computer Unit

The CPU is housed in a hard plastic case that is usually rectangular in shape. This casing and its contents is known as the *main computer unit,* or simply the main unit (Fig. 1-8). The main unit also houses other hardware components such as floppy disk drives and the hard disk.

The main unit should be placed on a flat, stable surface to prevent excessive vibration during operation which could loosen the electronic circuit boards. Most main units are designed so that they can be placed in either a horizontal or a vertical position. Information on proper positioning is always indicated in the instruction manual accompanying the computer.

Computers operate best in a moderately cool temperature environment. Extreme heat and inadequate ventilation increase the chance of malfunction. As a precautionary measure, the main unit should not be placed near a window or other areas that receive direct sunlight. In addition, to prevent overheating, the ventilation slots on the main unit should not be obstructed.

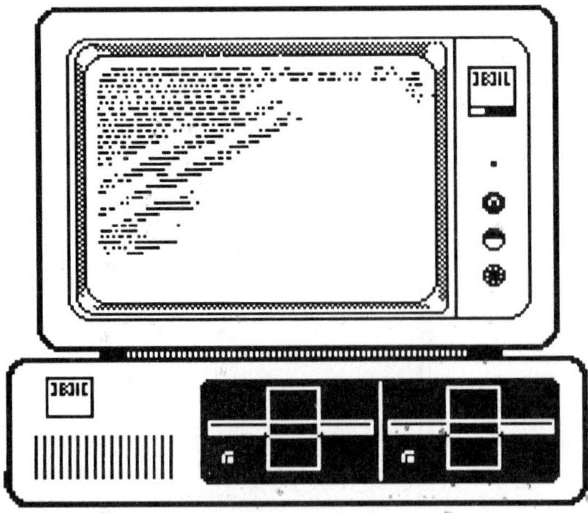

FIGURE 1 - 8. The CPU is housed in a hard plastic case that is usually rectangular in shape. This casing (including its contents) is known as the main computer unit.

The primary cause of improper functioning of the computer is exposure to environmental contaminants such as dust, dirt, and smoke. For this reason, the "computer room" should be kept clean and individuals should be encouraged not to smoke. Commercial dust covers are available to protect the computer from contaminants when it is not in use. The casing of the main unit should periodically be wiped with a slightly damp, lint-free cloth to remove dust and dirt. Aerosol sprays, solvents, and abrasives should never be used to clean the casing as they can damage the finish.

Liquids should be kept away from the computer. A liquid spilled into the main unit can cause irreparable damage to the electronic circuit boards. In addition, an electrical short may occur which could result in a fire or a small explosion.

The main unit is attached by cables to the other computer components (i.e., monitor, keyboard, printer). The cables should be checked on a regular basis to ascertain that they are secure. A loose or disengaged cable can result in temporary malfunctioning of the computer system.

CHECKPOINT

1. What is a computer system? ______________________________

____

2. Explain the difference between hardware and software.

____

____

3. What is the function of system software? ______________________________

____

____

4. What other terms are used to refer to application software?

5. List two examples of application software (brand names).

6. List four examples of hardware.

7. What components are necessary to form a basic operational computer system in the medical office?

8. What is the meaning of the following abbreviation: CPU?

9. What three parts make up the CPU?

10. What is the function of the control unit?

11. What is the function of the ALU?

12. What is the function of primary storage?

13. Explain how to prevent overheating of the computer.

14. How can environmental contaminants be kept away from the computer?

15. What can happen if a liquid spills into the main computer unit?

CRITICAL LITERACY

Computer Systems Assignment: Observe a computer system and complete the following questions.

1. What is the brand name of the computer?

2. What hardware is included in this computer system?

3. What application software is used with this computer system? Indicate the function performed by each brand of software listed.

4. What input devices are included with this computer system?

5. What output devices are included with this computer system?

Application Software Selection Assignment: You have just purchased an IBM computer system. Listed below are the brand names of commercially available application software programs along with a description of the functions performed by each. From this list, you may select five programs for your computer system. In the space provided, indicate the programs you selected and what you plan to do with each of them.

SOFTWARE PROGRAMS:

PrintPower: A powerful and flexible print program for home, office and school. It lets you print your own personalized creations—from invitations and announcements to flyers, letterhead, notepaper, greeting cards, posters—even multi-line banners! Six typefaces are included, each with seven variations (plain, bold, italic and others) and three type sizes to accommodate everything from poster size to stationery. A library of graphics images and decorative border increases your design options.

WordPerfect: A powerful word processing program which includes automatic formatting and pagination, mail merge, indexing, vertical text centering, footnoting, spell checking and outlining.

Create A Calendar: A fun and powerful tool for designing daily, weekly, monthly or annual calendars in just moments. Includes over 100 graphics, borders and typefaces to jazz up just about every occasion. Add detailed notes and graphics to any date on the calendar and automatically schedule regular events as they repeat throughout the year.

Joshua's Reading Machine: Joshua the Giraffe and his Reading Machine use Mother Goose rhymes, children's songs and Aesops' fables to help develop word recognition skills. Joshua also helps children develop vocabulary and sentence context skills, which improves reading comprehension. Features colorful graphics and fun music. Ages 3-6.

Quicken: Quicken is truly easy-to-use software that automates routine financial tasks for any home or small business. Features check writing, tax recordkeeping, financial reporting, budgeting and cash management. Quicken works just like the paper checkbook you use now. There's no accounting jargon to learn, no "debits" or "credits".

Star Wars: At last—The Force is with your computer! Pilot an agile X-wing fighter as you attack the Empire's Death Star. Based on the movie and arcade classics. May the Force be with you!

Stock Portfolio: Lets you easily compute the difference between buy and sell, evaluate market changes, consider stock splits and compute profit and loss. Great for the beginner and the experienced stockbroker.

Great Chefs: Make meals more exciting with Great Chefs—Master Collection. This collection includes seven full disks with over 800 wonderful recipes. Great Chefs also features a wealth of cooking tips, personal anecdotes and wine suggestions from some of the great chefs themselves.

Home Inventory: An easy-to-use data base for keeping track of all the important items in your home such as stereo equipment, jewelry or other valuables. Excellent for insurance and tax record keeping.

The Games—Summer Edition: You've been waiting your whole life to play on this team. Imagine facing the world's greatest athletes in eight demanding, nerve-racking, sweat-inducing events. It's the opportunity—and challenge—of a lifetime. Participate in events such as sprint cycling, pole vaulting, hammer-throwing, uneven parallel bars, rings, archery and springboard diving.

Grandslam Bridge: Now you can play a challenging game of bridge no matter how many players you have. Play solitaire, practice communication skills with a partner, or play with three humans and a computer fourth. Your computer opponents can be set at three different levels of aggressiveness.

One-Write Plus Payroll: Enables you to cost effectively do your own payroll in-house and on time. The system handles all aspects of issuing a payroll, including calculating taxes and generating tax forms and reports such as W-2's and 1099's.

Math Blaster: An award-winning program that helps students in grades 1 through 6 master basic math facts using 600 problems. This easy, fun and effective program includes animation, color and sound and an arcade-style game that provides a fun and challenging format for students. For ages 6-11.

Nutri-Fit: An exciting new way to keep fit through proper nutrition! Charts your daily intake of over 30 essential nutrients and itemizes your calorie, protein, fat and carbohydrate intake.

Typing Tutor IV: Get the most out of your computer by learning to type quickly and easily—the most effective typing instruction program ever developed. The program automatically adjusts to personal abilities and progress.

Speller Bee: Speller Bee, the incredible talking spelling coach, encourages students in three exciting, challenging word games that help improve spelling skills. Students move at their own pace, while reinforcing letter-sound-word relationships and independent problem-solving. A 150-word spelling list is built in, or you may construct lists from school assignments, most-often misspelled words, or subjects of interest.

List the five programs you selected and the reason for selecting each of them.

____

____

____

____

____

____

____

COMPUTER MONITOR

A computer monitor is a bulky and fragile visual display device similar to a television screen. The type of monitor most often used in a microcomputer system is a cathode-ray tube (or CRT). A cathode-ray tube works by spraying electrons onto a viewing screen, under the direction of a magnetic field, to form characters on the screen.

The monitor permits the user to view both a) input and, or more specifically, the data entered into the computer, and b) output, the information produced by the computer as a result of processing. Viewing the input displayed on the monitor allows the user to check the data for accuracy as it is entered. As an output device the monitor is often used to review information that needs to be viewed briefly and for which a printed copy (hardcopy) is not needed. For example, if a forgetful patient calls your office to inquire when his next appointment is scheduled, you can quickly call up this information, view it on the display screen, and relay it to the patient. The term used to describe the visual display of information on the screen of the monitor is *softcopy*. In summary, softcopy is useful when information is needed immediately and a permanent printed record is not required.

The typical computer monitor used in a medical office has a screen size from 10 to 14 inches across measured diagonally with the range of available screen sizes falling between 5 to 20 inches. Most screens are capable of displaying 80 characters of data horizontally and 25 lines vertically (Fig. 1-9) which provides ample space for working on data and displaying information on the screen.

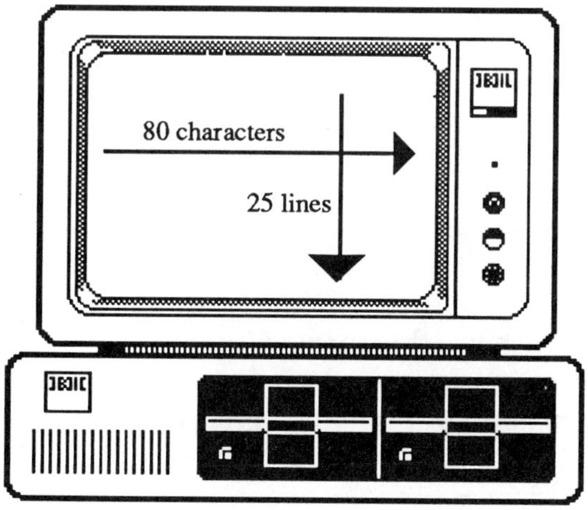

FIGURE 1 - 9. Most screens are capable of displaying 80 characters of data horizontally and 25 lines vertically.

Resolution

An important area of consideration when working with a computer system is the resolution of the monitor. The term *resolution* refers to the sharpness of the image displayed on the screen. A computer monitor with high resolution produces crisp, clear, easy-to-read characters, while images on a low resolution monitor appear somewhat blurry. As a result, individuals working for a prolonged period of time on a low resolution monitor frequently experience eyestrain and headaches. Resolution is measured in units called picture elements or *pixels*. Pixels are "dot" locations on the screen that can be lit up as needed to display characters and other images. Low resolution monitors are lower in cost and display approximately 320 pixels horizontally and 200 pixels vertically on the screen (320 x 200). High resolution monitors are more expensive but typically display 720 x 350 pixels or more, and are usually preferred for use in the medical office.

Types of Monitors

The CRT may be either a monochrome monitor or a color monitor. A *monochrome monitor* is a display device that exhibits a single-color. Depending upon the brand of monitor, text is displayed in either white, green, or amber characters on a black background. The best color to use for displaying characters is a matter of individual preference; some individuals prefer working with white characters, while others may prefer green or amber. Monochrome monitors are preferred for those tasks involving the entry of text because they provide better resolution for letters and numbers than do color monitors. In addition, color monitors are much heavier and more expensive than monochrome monitors of the same size. *Color monitors*, on the other hand, display text and graphics in a variety of colors, which is particularly useful when working with charts, graphs, and pictures. It is important to understand, however, that the colors displayed on the screen can be only printed in color if the computer system includes a color printer.

Monitor Controls

Located on either the front or side of the monitor are three important controls which are used to operate and adjust the display screen. The first of these is the *on/off switch*, either a pull-knob or a push-button. When the monitor is turned on, an indicator light comes on denoting that the monitor is receiving power and is ready for use.

There are two controls for adjusting the viewing screen: the brightness control and the contrast control. These controls work much like the same controls on a television set. The *brightness control* allows you to increase or decrease the intensity of the images on the screen. This control should be adjusted until the background just disappears, which provides a good balance between screen and character brightness. If a monitor is left on for long periods of time while not being used, images on the screen will start to "burn in" and the screen may be permanently damaged. To prevent this from happening, the brightness control should be turned down when you are not using the computer, but leaving it on for long periods.

The *contrast control* is used to adjust the screen for comfortable viewing. Contrast refers to the degree of difference between the light and dark areas on the display screen. For example, if you are working with a monochrome monitor that displays white characters on a black background, the contrast would be the amount of difference that exists between the characters (light area) and the background (dark area).Too much contrast makes it uncomfortable to look at the characters on the screen, while not enough contrast results in difficulty in viewing the characters. Because of individual viewing preferences, you should adjust both the brightness and contrast control when first beginning work on the computer to find the setting that works best for your viewing comfort.

Care and Maintenance

The monitor should rest on a flat, stable surface, such as a table or on top of the main computer unit itself. The monitor should be placed so the top of the screen is at eye level or just below eye level to prevent back and neck tension. To avoid glare, the monitor should be positioned so that the screen does not reflect bright light which could result in eye strain. For example, positioning the monitor directly in front of a bright window causes a distracting reflection on the screen. Subdued overhead lighting is considered best for computer use because it causes the least amount of glare. Glare filters are available to help reduce unavoidable reflections such as from bright overhead fluorescent lights. A glare filter is a transparent covering that fits over the front of the screen similar to placing a camera filter over the lens of a camera.

There are a number of ventilation slots on the top of computer monitors which allow heat to escape. To prevent overheating, never place anything (not even a piece of paper) on top of the monitor.

Monitors collect dust and dirt over a period of time and therefore, must be properly maintained. The screen should be cleaned with a household glass cleaner applied with a clean, lint-free cloth or paper towel. The glass cleaner should *not* be sprayed directly on the screen as it may run down into the inside of the case and damage the electrical circuits. The outside casing of the monitor should periodically be wiped with a damp, lint-free cloth to remove dust and dirt. Aerosol sprays, solvents, and abrasives should not be used to clean the casing as they can damage the finish.

CHECKPOINT

1. Why is a computer monitor often referred to as a CRT?

2. Why is it important to be able to view both input and output on the screen of a monitor?

3. What is softcopy?

4. How many characters do most screens display horizontally? How many lines are usually displayed vertically?

5. What type of visual display is produced by a high resolution monitor?

6. Explain the difference between a monochrome monitor and a color monitor.

7. Explain the function of each of the following monitor controls:

   a. on/off switch

   b. brightness control

   c. contrast control

8. What can be done to minimize glare on the screen of the monitor?

9. Why should you avoid placing anything on top of a computer monitor?

10. Describe the maintenance procedures that should be followed in caring for the screen and casing of a computer monitor.

____

____

CRITICAL LITERACY

Computer Monitor Assignment: Observe a computer monitor and complete the following questions.

1. What is the screen size (in inches) of this monitor?

____

2. Is this a monochrome monitor? If so, what color is used to display text?

____

3. On what type of surface is the monitor resting?

____

4. Where are the ventilation slots located? _______________________

____

5. Where are the following controls located?

   a. on/off switch _______________________________

   b. brightness control ___________________________

   c. contrast control _____________________________

6. Adjust the brightness and contrast controls to find the setting that works best for your viewing comfort.

COMPUTER KEYBOARD

The *computer keyboard* is similar to an ordinary typewriter keyboard in both appearance and function. Because of this, you should not experience much difficulty when first beginning to work on one.

The keyboard may be integrated as part of the main unit of the computer or, more commonly, it may be separate from the main unit and attached by a cable (Fig. 1-10). The latter arrangement allows the user to position the keyboard according to his/her preference and comfort. As previously explained, computers can only work with electronic data. When a key is pressed on a computer keyboard, an electronic code is generated which is passed along to the CPU for processing. At the same time, the computer displays the input as words and symbols on the monitor.

Because of their electronic components, computer keyboards can be damaged if liquids spill into them, particularly those that are sweet or sticky such as soft drinks. Therefore, it is best not to place beverages close to the keyboard. If a liquid is accidentally spilled into the keyboard, the computer should immediately be turned off and the keyboard taken to an authorized computer dealer.

Different brands of computer keyboards vary in size, shape, and layout, however all contain the same basic elements (Fig. 1-11). Computer keyboards include all the keys normally found on a typewriter keyboard. The composition of the keyboard is alphanumeric; that is, it consists of both alphabetic and numeric keys. The keys are located in the same place as on the standard typewriter keyboard and are used for the same purpose. Computer keyboards produce both upper and lowercase letters and have the standard typewriter "QWERTY" layout, named for the first row of letters.

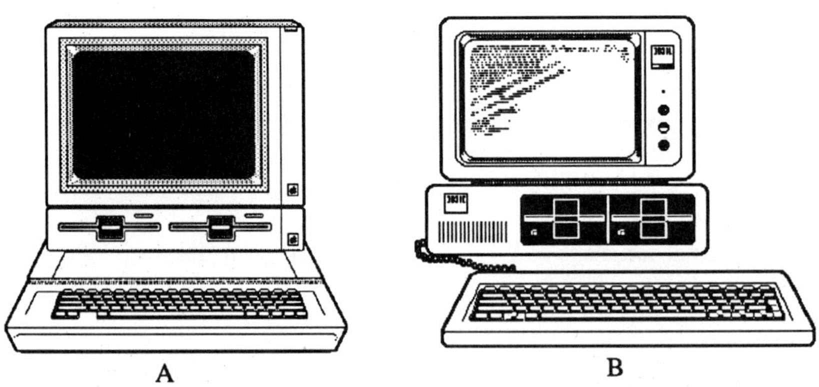

Figure 1 - 10. The keyboard may be integrated as part of the main unit of the computer (A) or it may be separate from the main unit and attached by a cable (B).

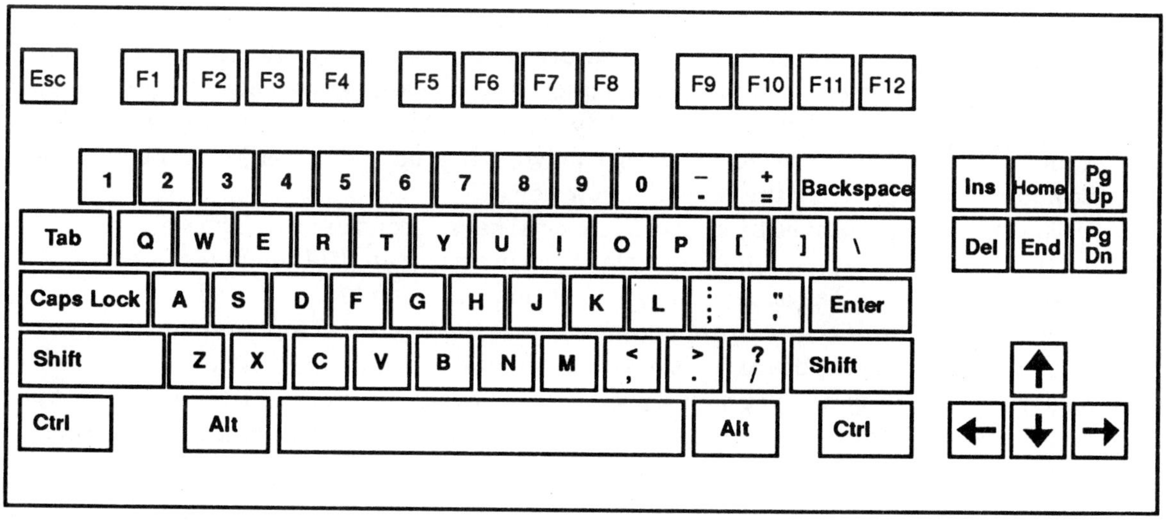

Enter Key: Pressing the Enter key tells the computer to act on the instructions which have been given to it.

Arrow Keys: Arrow keys permit the user to move around the screen as needed (also known as cursor movement keys).

Function Keys (F1 - F12): Software programs use these keys to issue commands. The function performed by each key is based on the software program being used.

Esc Key: This key is generally used to move out of a command that the user does not want to be in.

Ctrl Key: This key is pressed along with another key to issue commands. The key combinations and the functions performed are based on the software program being used.

Alt Key: This key is pressed along with another key to issue commands. The key combinations and the functions performed are based on the software program being used.

FIGURE 1 - 11. Computer Keyboard. A computer keyboard is similar to a typewriter keyboard. The most significant difference is the presence of special keys which are identified in white in this illustration and described above.

Special Keys

The most significant difference between a computer keyboard and a typewriter keyboard is the presence of additional keys known as *special keys* (Fig. 1-11). Special keys issue commands to the CPU to perform specific functions on the information displayed on the screen. Pressing a special key does not cause a character to be typed on the screen, nor does the command appear on printed copy. Instead these keys allow the user to perform such tasks as selecting text, saving text, printing text, centering text, moving a block of text, repagination, obtaining help, and so on.

Examples of special keys that function the same, regardless of the type of computer or program being used are the Enter key and the arrow keys. The Enter key (called the Return key on some keyboards) is the most frequently used special key. Pressing the Enter key tells the computer to act on the instructions which have been given to it. In simple terms, it gives the computer the "okay" to go ahead with a function. For example, if you have given the computer the Print command, the Enter key must then be pressed to tell the computer to go ahead with this instruction. If you forget to press this key, the computer will not do anything, causing many first-time users to erroneously conclude that the computer is broken. A set of four *arrow keys* permit the user to move the insertion point, or *cursor*, around the screen as needed. These keys move the cursor up, down, right or left without it having any effect on the information displayed. For example, if you need to move the cursor down a line on the screen, it can easily be accomplished by pressing the "down" arrow key (↓).

The functions performed by most of the special keys depend upon the type of computer and the program being used. For example, if you are using an IBM computer, the special keys include a set of F keys. The F keys are termed *function keys* and consist of 12 keys labeled F1 to F12 which are usually located above the top row of alphanumeric keys or on the left side of the keyboard. To issue the command to print text with the WordPerfect word processing program, you would press F7; however, to perform this same task with the Microsoft Word program, you would press F8. Additional information on special keys is presented in Chapter 2: Word Processing.

Care and Maintenance

To prevent muscle fatigue of the upper extremities, the computer keyboard should be placed at a level that is lower than that of a conventional desk or table. The feet should be flat on the floor and the hands should rest comfortably at the keyboard with the elbow flexed at a 90 degree angle. An adjustable chair with good back support is often used to attain the proper typing height for each individual working with the computer. An adequate working space should be available to position the material being entered into the computer. The material should be placed so that it is either lying flat on the work surface or being held vertically in a copy holder.

If with extended use a residue builds up on the keyboard, it should be cleaned with a slightly damp (not wet), lint-free cloth. Aerosol sprays should never be used to clean the keyboard because a drop of liquid may drip down into the keyboard, damaging its electrical components. The keyboard interior can be "dusted" by using a compressed inert gas which comes in a pressurized can and is available from computer supply stores. Alternatively, a vacuum cleaner with a small brush attachment may be used to clean the keyboard interior.

CHECKPOINT

1. List the similarities between a computer keyboard and a typewriter keyboard.

   ____

   ____

2. Why are computer keyboards easily damaged by liquids spilling into them? What should be done if this occurs?

   ____

   ____

3. List three examples of tasks performed by special keys. ____________________

   ____

   ____

4. What special function is served by the Enter key on a computer keyboard?

   ____

5. What function is served by the arrow keys on the computer keyboard?

   ____

6. How should the computer keyboard be positioned to prevent muscle fatigue?

   ____

   ____

7. Describe the maintenance procedures that should be followed in caring for a computer keyboard.

   ____

   ____

   ____

CRITICAL LITERACY

Computer Keyboard Assignment: Observe a computer keyboard and answer the following questions.

1. Is the keyboard separate from the computer or part of the computer housing?

   ____

2. Where is the Enter key located?________________________

   ____

3. Where are the arrow keys located?

   ____

4. If possible, obtain the reference information accompanying an IBM word processing program (e.g., WordPerfect, WordStar, Microsoft Word) and indicate the function(s) performed by the each of the F keys for that program.

   Name of program: ________________________

   F1 ________________________________

   F2 ________________________________

   F3 ________________________________

   F4 ________________________________

   F5 ________________________________

   F6 ________________________________

   F7 ________________________________

   F8 ________________________________

   F9 ________________________________

   F10 _______________________________

PRINTERS

A printer is an output device capable of printing characters, symbols and sometimes graphics on paper. Printers convert processed data from a combination of electronic impulses into a printed form called *hardcopy*. In the medical office, a hardcopy of the computer output is frequently required; examples include superbills, patient statements, insurance claims and status reports.

The speed of a printer, that is, how quickly it creates hardcopy, is often expressed in characters per second (cps). To provide an example of how this translates into the more familiar words-per-minute typing speed, a printing speed of 60 cps is equivalent to 720 words per minute. Speed is an important consideration when selecting a printer for the medical office because a slow printer can adversely affect the smooth and efficient operation of the office.

Printers are classified as either letter quality or near-letter quality, depending upon the quality of the print produced. *Letter quality* (abbreviated LQ) consists of print that is characterized by sharp, crisp, high-quality fully formed characters similar to the characters produced by a typewriter. *Near-letter quality* (abbreviated NLQ) refers to print that is of a slightly lesser quality than that of letter quality print, often resembling the characters produced by a cloth-ribbon typewriter. Thus, a document produced by a letter quality printer is more pleasant to look at and easier to read because of its better print quality.

Types of Printers

Printers can further be classified as impact printers and nonimpact printers. The classification is based on the method used to form characters on paper. *Impact printers* form characters with a mechanical print element which strikes an inked ribbon against the paper. The character is imprinted on the paper in a method similar to the formation of characters by a typewriter. Dot-matrix and daisywheel printers are the most commonly used impact printers. Because the print element is constantly making contact with the paper, impact printers, and particularly daisywheel printers, are noisy. Sound suppressing accessories such as acoustic table pads, acoustic covers, and sound suppressing cabinets are available to reduce the racket caused by a noisy printer.

Nonimpact printers form characters without making a striking motion or impact against the paper. Rather, characters are formed through the use of laser beams, ink-jet spraying, or heat. Examples of nonimpact printers include laser printers, ink-jet printers and thermal printers. Because no contact with paper occurs, these printers generate much less noise than impact printers.

Dot-matrix, daisywheel and, to a growing extent, laser printers are more commonly used in medical offices. All are discussed in more detail on the following pages.

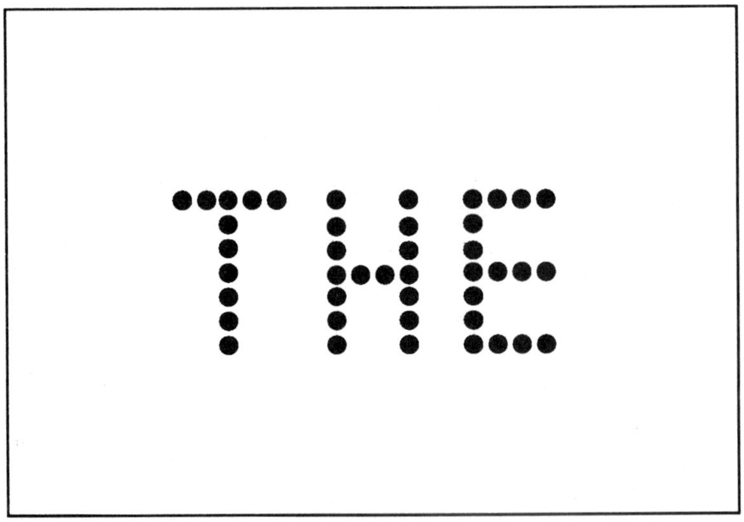

FIGURE 1-12. The dot-matrix printer prints characters as formations of tiny dots similar to the numbers produced on a football or basketball scoreboard.

Dot-Matrix Printers

Dot-matrix printers are used most often in the medical office because they offer greater speed, more flexibility and a lower cost than other types of printers currently available. This type of printer prints characters as formations of tiny dots similar to the numbers produced on a football or basketball scoreboard (Fig. 1-12). The print element consists of a rectangular printhead made up of small hammers that look like the heads of pins. Electronic signals from the computer activate these pins which, in turn, strike the ribbon against the paper in a pattern of closely-spaced dots making up each character. A specific combination of pins must be properly activated to form each character.

The printhead moves across the page in both directions to produce the hardcopy. That is, it moves from left to right—and then from right to left (printing backwards)—until the end of the document is reached. Because of this back-and-forth motion (known as *bidirectional printing*), dot-matrix printers are fairly fast, ranging from 60 cps to 300 cps.

The quality of the print produced by a dot-matrix printer is directly related to the number of pins in the printhead. Dot-matrix printers are available with either a 9-pin or a 24-pin printhead. Because of its greater number of pins, the 24-pin printer is able to produce a much more precise and better quality image on the paper. In fact, some of the newer 24-pin printers produce such a heavy concentration of dots that the resulting print is termed letter quality.

Most dot-matrix printers have two print speed settings: a faster draft setting and a slower, but better print-quality setting (either NLQ or LQ). For example, the Epson LQ-510 produces a rough draft copy at a printing speed of 180 cps and a letter quality copy at 60 cps. The user guide accompanying the printer always specifies the printing speed for both the draft and better print-quality settings. When the printer is set on draft mode, the printhead moves across the page at a rapid rate producing a hardcopy in a short period of time, however the print produced has a rough or "dotty" appearance. With the NLQ or LQ mode, the printer operates at a slower rate in order to produce a hardcopy with a better print quality. In the medical office, the draft setting is used when print quality is not an important consideration such as when printing out an inventory list of supplies for office use. On the other hand, the better letter quality setting is preferred for reports and professional correspondence such as referral letters.

Daisywheel Printers

A daisywheel printer is an impact printer which uses a rotating print-wheel, called a *daisywheel* to form characters. The daisywheel consists of a flat, metal or plastic device with 96 radiating spokes resembling the "petals of a daisy". An alphabetic or a numeric character is positioned at the outer edge of each spoke (Fig. 1-13). To print a specific character, the daisywheel rotates to the appropriate character slot, which is then struck with a hammer. The hammer action causes a fully formed character to be pressed against the inked ribbon to form a clear, crisp impression on the paper. Because the characters are fully formed when they hit the paper, the print is letter quality and comparable to that produced by a good carbon-ribbon typewriter. Compared with other types of printers, however, the speed of a daisywheel printer is relatively slow, ranging between 15 to 90 cps. The longer print time is required for the rotation of the daisywheel to take place.

The principal advantage of a daisywheel printer is its superior print-quality which is ideal for professional correspondence. Unfortunately, the disadvantages of daisywheel printers often outweigh this attribute. These include slow printing speed and the distracting amount of noise generated. As dot-matrix printers continue to improve technologically—particularly in print quality—the popularity of the daisywheel printer appears to be declining.

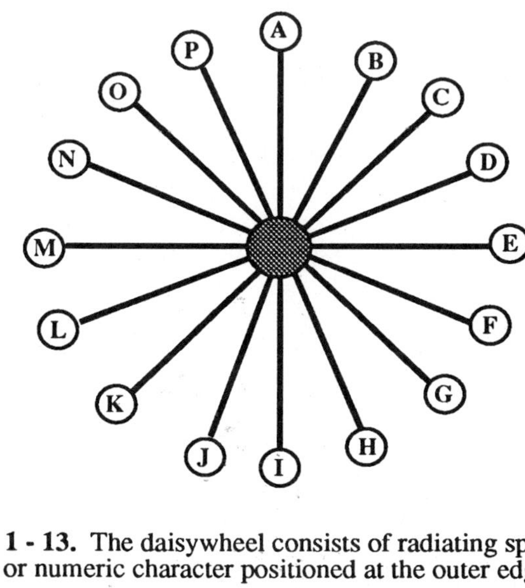

FIGURE 1 - 13. The daisywheel consists of radiating spokes with an alphabetic or numeric character positioned at the outer edge of each spoke.

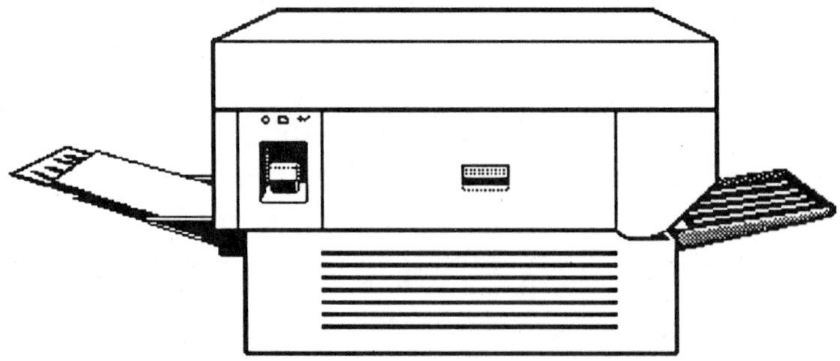

FIGURE 1 - 14. Laser Printer. Laser printers use a beam of light, electric charges and a black toner powder to produce each page of text.

Laser Printers

The most significant feature of a laser printer (Fig. 1-14) is that it has a "computer" of its own to direct its functioning. Laser printers use a micro-thin beam of light (laser beam), electric charges, and a black toner powder to produce each page of text. Under direction of the printer's computer, the laser beam is bounced off of a series of mirrors onto a positively charged rotating drum. The pulses of the beam correspond to the characters making up the document being printed. The areas where the laser beam hits the drum become neutral which enables the black toner to stick to them and form characters. Finally, the characters are transferred from the rotating drum to paper with the use of pressure and heat to solidify the toner powder on the paper. This process is similar to that of a photocopy machine.

The print quality of laser printers is better than that of the best daisywheel printers, nearly attaining the quality of typesetting which is the kind of print used in textbooks. Other advantages of laser printers include their quiet operation and printing speed. The printing speed of laser printers is expressed in pages per minute (ppm). Depending on the model of laser printer, the printing speed ranges from 6 to 10 ppm, which is equivalent to 300 to 400 characters per second. In addition, laser printers do not have as many mechanical moving parts as other types of printers which usually reduces the frequency of repair.

Because of their expense, laser printers are currently used in only a small number of medical offices. However, as advances are made in their manufacture, laser printers are becoming much more affordable, and their use in medical offices should increase over the next decade.

*Nonetheless, b*ecause impact printers (dot-matrix and daisywheel) are currently used more often in the medical office, the remaining information in this section refers solely to impact printers.

Printer Paper

The type of paper used with a printer is classified as either continuous paper or cut sheets. *Continuous paper* (also called "computer paper") consists of a continuous length of sheets joined with perforations and folded in a zig-zag fashion. Columns of small sprocket holes on its outer edges serve to automatically feed the paper through the printer, thus avoiding the time consuming hand-feeding of individual sheets of paper into the printer. Continuous paper is available in a number of formats: blank sheets, professional letterhead, envelopes, mailing labels, index cards and preprinted forms such as patient statements and insurance claim forms. Continuous preprinted forms are also available in multiple-parts, consisting of an original and one or more copies. This is useful when more than one person needs a copy of the same document (e.g., insurance claims).

After feeding through the printer, continuous paper must be separated at its perforated margins to remove the sprocket holes. Removing the margins of standard continuous paper leaves the edges slightly ragged. A more expensive paper with smaller perforations resulting in much cleaner edges is available and is suitable for professional correspondence.

Cut-sheet paper refers to single sheets of paper as commonly used with a typewriter. This type of paper is also available in a number of formats such as letterhead, bond paper, preprinted forms, envelopes, and so on.

Paper Feeding

Paper feeding refers to the way in which paper is fed into and out of the printer. Impact printers use one or more of the following methods to move paper: a) tractor feeding b) friction feeding c) cut-sheet feeding. Each of these methods is described below.

A *tractor feeder* is a mechanism that uses a set of gears to push (push-feeder) or pull (pull-feeder) continuous paper through the printer. In the medical office, tractor feeders are especially useful for the batch processing of insurance claim forms and patient statements. The sprocket holes on the sides of the paper fit over the teeth of the tractor feeder gears which guide the paper as it moves through the printer. Most tractor feeders are adjustable, and the gears can be moved closer together or further apart to accommodate use of continuous paper of different widths.

Occasionally a paper jam will occur with a tractor-feeder. Paper jams are caused by a physical obstruction such as an accumulation of paper behind the printer or by a problem with the paper position in front of the printer. When a paper jam occurs, turn off the printer, remove the obstructing paper, and realign the paper in the tractor feeds.

Friction feeders rely on the pressure and rotation of the print roller (or *platen*) to move paper through the printer in a manner similar to moving paper through a typewriter. As with a typewriter, each sheet must be individually inserted and positioned in the printer by hand; however, once the printing begins, the paper is automatically advanced by the platen. Friction feeders are useful for printing single sheets of paper such as office letterhead and envelopes.

Cut-sheet feeders are available as an accessory to friction-feed printers and take the place of having to manually insert paper into the printer. A cut-sheet feeder consists of a feed tray attached to the printer which holds a stack of up to 150 single sheets. Each sheet is automatically grabbed by the platen and fed through the printer. The result is the fast and efficient printing of many copies or pages of finished quality.

Medical offices often use a dot-matrix printer that is equipped with both tractor feed and friction feed. In this way, continuous preprinted forms can be used for the generation of such documents as superbills, patient statements, and insurance claims, and single sheets of office letterhead can be printed when required for professional correspondence.

Printer Controls

Printer controls are used to select printing options. The type and location of the controls varies based on the printer being used. It is important to learn the location and use of the printer controls to avoid unnecessary problems such as paper jams and improper paper positioning. This can be accomplished by thoroughly reading the printer's user manual.

Some basic controls found on most printers are described below. These controls consist of buttons for selecting the option desired as well as corresponding indicator lights to designate the status of each of the various settings (Fig. 1-15).

On/Off: This control is used to turn the printer on or off and is often located on the back or the side of the printer. When this control is turned to the "on" position, power is supplied to the printer. Turning it to the "off" position removes the power supply. As a safety precaution, this control should always be in the "off" position when you are performing maintenance procedures such as changing the ribbon.

On-Line: The on-line control, also called the *select* control, is used to put the printer in direct communication with the computer. When this control is activated, the printer is able to accept data for printing. If this control is deactivated, the printer is not in communication with the computer, or is *off-line,* and unable to print. Many first-time users erroneously think the printer is broken when, in fact, it is only off-line.

Line-Feed: The line-feed control (abbreviated LF) is used to advance paper in the printer. Before this control can be activated, the computer must be placed off-line. Pressing this control once advances the paper forward by one line. Holding this control down advances the paper continuously—one line at a time—until the control is released.

Form-Feed: The form-feed control (abbreviated FF) is also used to advance paper in the printer, but in a much larger increment. Again the printer must be off-line in order to activate this control. Pressing form-feed advances continuous paper to the top of the next page. Pressing this control when a single sheet of paper is in the printer, causes it to be ejected. The printer should always be placed back on-line after using the line-feed and the form-feed control.

Care and Maintenance

Proper maintenance keeps the printer operating at its best and prolongs its life. Some important guidelines which should be followed to properly care for and maintain the printer are presented below.

1. Place the printer on a flat, stable surface to prevent excessive vibration during operation which could damage it.
2. Avoid placing the printer in a location that would expose it to direct sunlight, excessive heat, moisture, or dust.
3. Sufficient room should be left around the printer to allow for easy access for such tasks as changing the paper.
4. Continuous form paper must be positioned properly to prevent paper jams. The paper supply should be in direct alignment with the tractor so that the paper feeds smoothly into the printer.
5. After turning off the printer, wait at least 5 seconds before turning it back on. Rapid switching of the power off and on can damage the printer.

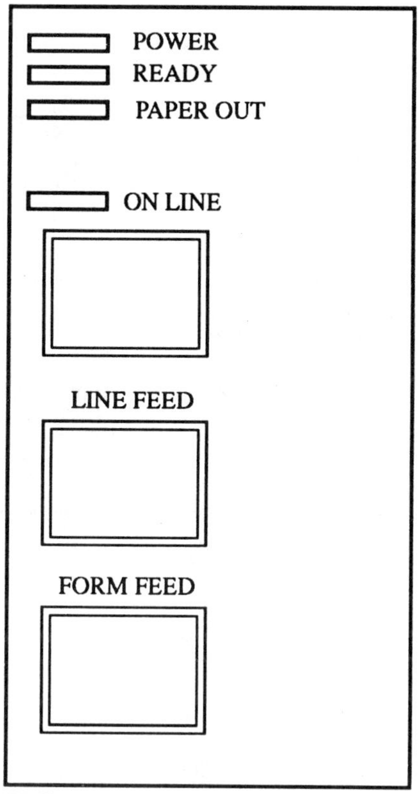

FIGURE 1 - 15. Printer Controls.

6. The print element can be damaged if it is allowed to print directly on the platen. Therefore, always operate the printer with paper and make sure that printing does not exceed the paper width.
7. Change the ribbon when the printing becomes faint. The power should always be turned off before performing this task. The printhead of dot-matrix printers becomes quite hot during use. Therefore, to avoid a burn, you should first let the printhead cool before changing the ribbon in this type of printer. Most printer ribbons consist of cartridges which are designed to easily snap in and out of the printer. The printer's user manual identifies the type of ribbon needed. Once the ribbon has been replaced, check to make sure it is not twisted or creased.
8. The printer should be cleaned every six-months to remove accumulated dust and dirt. This is accomplished by first unplugging the printer from the power supply and removing the ribbon cartridge. A dry, clean, soft brush should be used to dust the area around the carriage shaft and platen, being careful not to damage any of the parts inside the printer. Any loose particles of paper should be removed by vacuuming or simply blowing them away. The outside case should be cleaned with a soft, clean cloth dampened with a mild detergent solution. Never use strong detergents or solvents on the casing as these could damage the finish.

CHECKPOINT

1. What is the term used to describe printed output from a computer?

    ____

2. What is the difference between letter quality print and near-letter quality print?

    ____

    ____

3. What is the difference between an impact printer and a nonimpact printer?

    ____

    ____

4. List two examples of impact printers. ______________________________

    ____

5. List two examples of nonimpact printers. ______________________________

    ____

6. How are characters produced with a dot-matrix printer?

    ____

7. What is the printing speed range for dot-matrix printers?

    ____

8. What are the two print speed settings on a dot-matrix printer?

    ____

9. What type of print is produced by a daisywheel printer?

    ____

10. What is the printing speed range for daisywheel printers?

    ____

11. What are the two main disadvantages of daisywheel printers?

    ____

12. What type of print is produced by a laser printer?

    ____

13. What is the printing speed range of laser printers?

    ____

14. List six formats available for continuous paper. ______________

    ____

    ____

15. List and describe the three methods used to move paper through an impact printer.

    ____

    ____

16. What is the function of the on-line printer control? ______________

    ____

17. When should a printer be placed off-line? ______________

    ____

18. What is the function of the line-feed printer control? ______________

    ____

19. What is the function of the form-feed printer control? ______________

    ____

20. List five guidelines which should be followed in caring for a printer.

    ____

    ____

    ____

CRITICAL LITERACY

Printer Assignment: Observe a printer and complete the following questions.

1. What type of printer is this (e.g., dot-matrix, daisywheel)?

 ____

2. Is this an example of an impact or nonimpact printer?

 ____

3. What is the printing speed of this printer?

 ____

4. What type of print is produced by this printer?

 ____

5. What type of paper feeding is used with this printer?

 ____

6. What type of paper is used with this printer?

 ____

7. What are the names of the controls found on this printer and where is each located?

 ____

 ____

 ____

 ____

 ____

 ____

 ____

INTERNAL MEMORY AND OPERATING SYSTEMS

Internal memory and operating systems play key roles in a computer system. Microcomputer systems have two types of internal memory: RAM and ROM. Both RAM and ROM are contained on small silicon chips that reside on an electronic circuit board in the main computer unit. As will be described below, each has specific functions important to the efficient operation of the microcomputer.

In the section on Computer Components (Page 13), you learned about a type of software called system software which holds an operating system. An operating system is a group of programs which provides instructions for performing computer "housekeeping chores". As you will see, without an operating system, application programs are useless.

Although internal memory and operating systems can be confusing and difficult to understand, this section attempts to present them in a way that is easily comprehended.

Random-Access Memory

RAM is an acronym for *random-access memory* and, as you have already learned, is the primary storage unit of a microcomputer. This type of memory is called random-access because the computer can get to any part of the information stored in its memory directly, rather than having to look through all of the rest of its stored information. This is in contrast to *sequential-access memory* in which all stored data must be searched sequentially from beginning to end to locate the desired information. The difference between random-access and sequential-access memory can be illustrated by comparing a cassette-tape recorder and a compact disk player. To locate a particular song on a cassette-tape, you must sequentially hunt through the tape, song by song, until you locate the one desired (sequential-access). Some CD players, however, have the ability to randomly-access the disk, and go directly to the desired song without having to hunt through all the rest of the songs on the disk. As you can see, much less time is involved in locating information using random-access, and it is one of the factors which allows computers to perform tasks very quickly.

Purpose of RAM

The purpose of RAM is to temporarily store items until they are needed by the computer. Because of this, RAM is often referred to as "computer memory". Among those items commonly held in RAM are application programs and data (Fig. 1-16). When you turn on the computer, RAM is empty; therefore, you must first place the items you want to work with in RAM. A copy of the application program is transferred into RAM from a secondary storage device such as a floppy disk or a hard disk, and, as you already know, data is transferred into RAM through an input device such as a keyboard. Once these items are in RAM, they are easily accessible and can be quickly retrieved when needed by other parts of the CPU such as the control unit or the ALU. After the data has been processed according to the instructions in the program, the resulting usable information is then placed back in RAM for temporary storage.

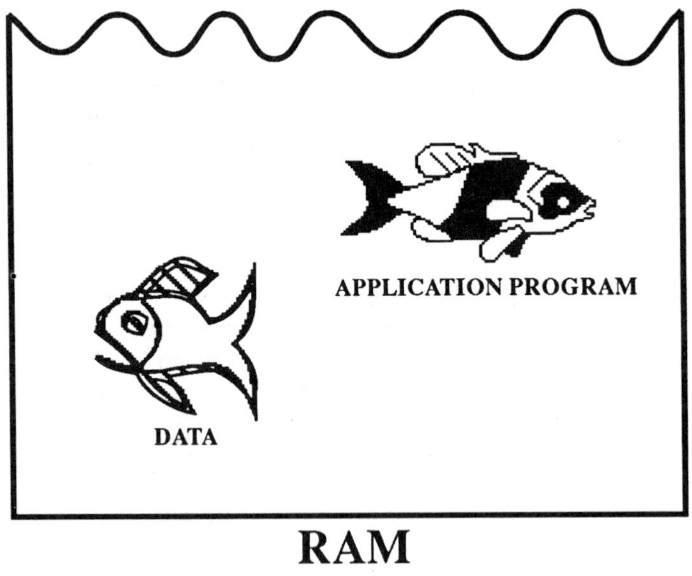

FIGURE 1 - 16. The purpose of RAM is to temporarily store items until they are needed by the computer; examples include application programs and data.

One very important aspect of RAM is that it provides only *temporary* storage, not permanent storage. When the computer is turned off, all of the items stored in RAM are "dumped out"; in other words, RAM will be empty when the computer is turned back on and therefore, ready to accept more storage items. Because of this, you *must be sure* to permanently store information that you do not want to lose before turning off the computer (Fig. 1-17). In the medical office, this information is almost always stored on a hard disk, whereas individuals using a home computer usually store information on a floppy disk. It should be mentioned that the application program is already stored on a permanent storage device (e.g., floppy disk or hard disk), and, therefore, you need only be concerned with storing your processed data.

Storage Capacity

Random-access memory has a storage capacity which refers to the number of items of data that can be stored at any one time. The capacity of RAM is measured in units of storage known as *bytes* (Fig. 1-18). One byte is approximately equal to one character, such as a letter or a number. Stating the capacity of RAM in bytes, however, results in astronomically-high numbers. Therefore, it is more convenient to use larger units such as kilobytes and megabytes. A *kilobyte* (K) is equal to 1,024 bytes and a *megabyte* (MB) is equal to a little over one million bytes. As you would imagine, the larger the capacity of RAM, the more information it can hold at one time. For example, a computer with a RAM of 640 K has the ability to hold 655,360 bytes (640 x 1,024), whereas a computer with 1 MB of RAM can hold well over a million bytes. These units of measurement (K, MB) are also used to indicate the capacity of hard disks, floppy disks, and the size of application programs.

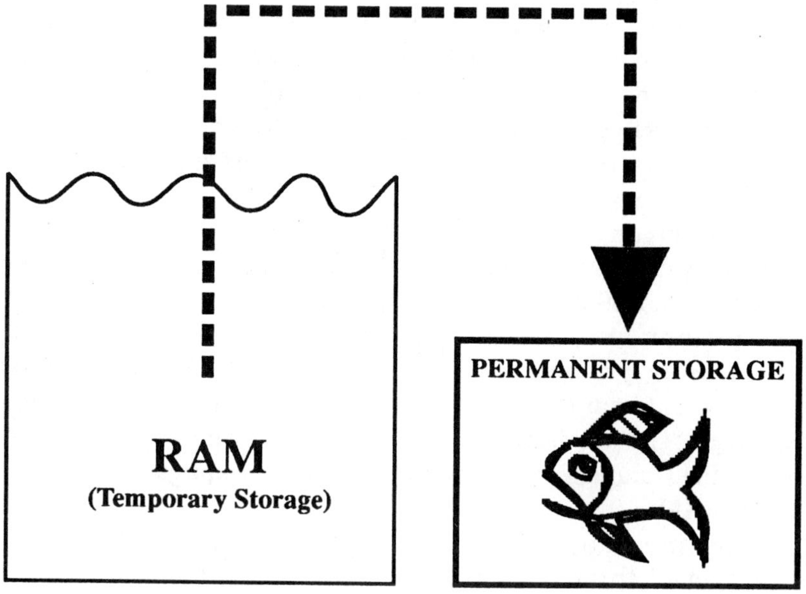

FIGURE 1 - 17. RAM provides only temporary storage. Therefore, needed information must be permanently stored before turning off the computer to prevent its loss.

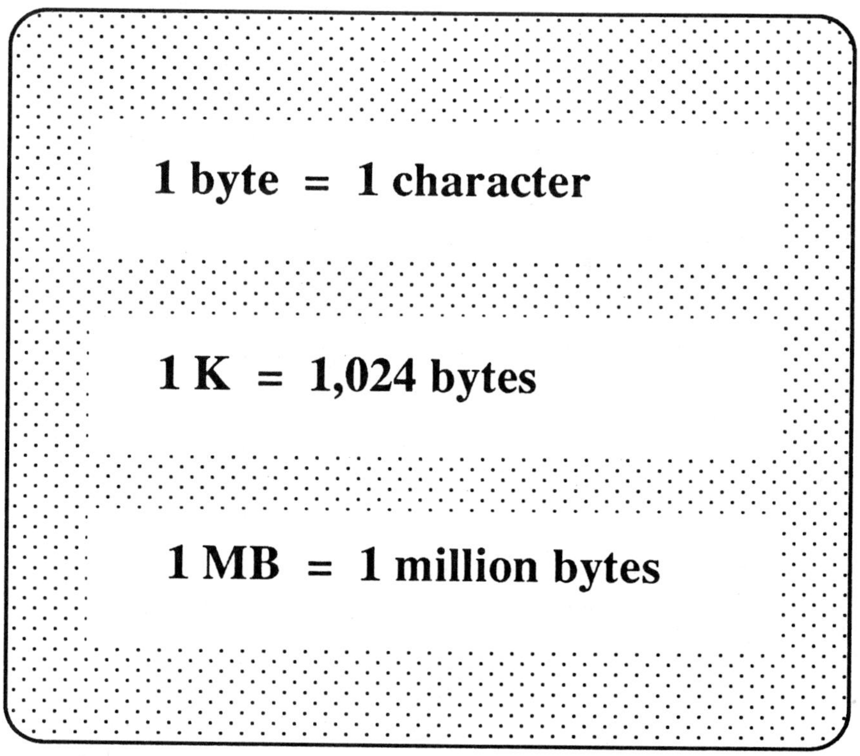

FIGURE 1 - 18. The capacity of RAM is measured in units of storage known as bytes.

The capacity of a computer's memory (RAM) correlates directly to the level of sophistication of the programs it can use. Just as a tropical fish occupies a certain amount of space in a fish tank, a program occupies a certain amount of space in RAM. A small fish takes up much less space in the tank than a large fish, and similarly, small and simple, programs that perform a limited number of tasks take up much less space in RAM than large, sophisticated and powerful programs that perform numerous tasks. For example, a simple word processing program, such as Bank Street Writer, requires only 128 K of RAM to operate, while a sophisticated and complex word processing program such as Microsoft Word requires 320 K of RAM (Fig. 1-19).

The capacity of RAM is an important criterion to consider when working with, or purchasing a computer. Just as you could not put a big fish in a small tank, a computer with less than the required memory for a particular program would not have enough storage space to hold that program. For example, a program requiring 450 K of RAM could not be loaded into a computer with only 256 K of RAM (Fig. 1-20). Because medical management programs are complex and perform a multitude of tasks, their storage requirements are quite large. The medical software vendor will specify the RAM requirements; however, medical management programs usually require a computer with a minimum of 1 MB of RAM.

In summary, RAM provides necessary storage space for placing items until they are needed by the computer. Best of all, this space is reusable; once you are finished working with one program, you can remove it and place a different program in RAM.

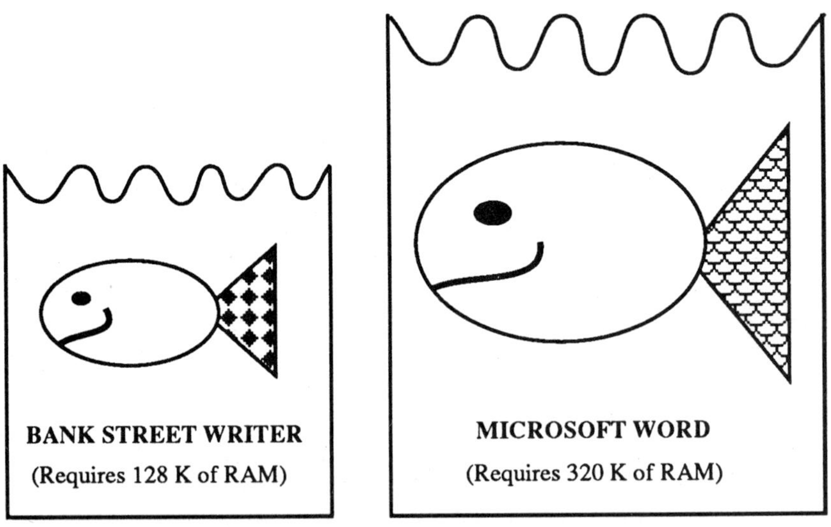

FIGURE 1 - 19. The capacity of a computer's memory is directly correlated to the level of sophistication of the programs it can use. For example, Bank Street Writer requires a computer with less RAM than Microsoft Word.

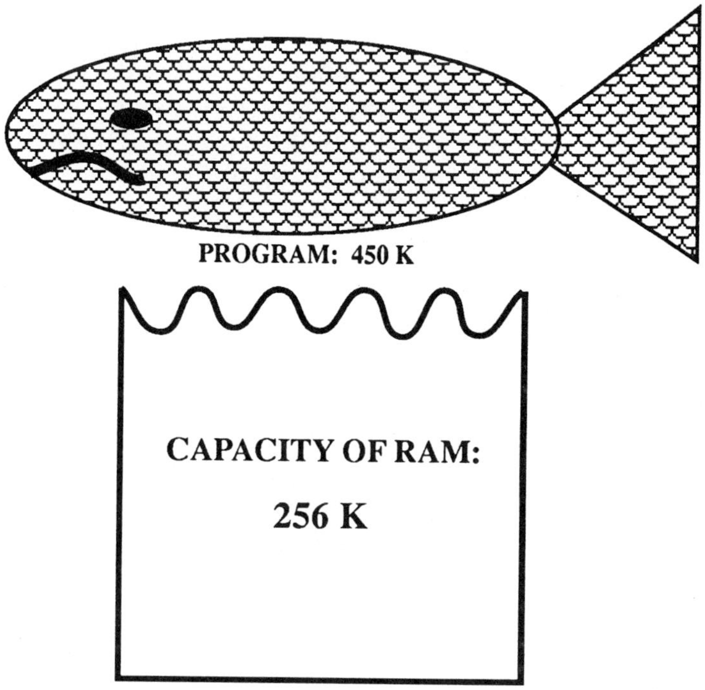

FIGURE 1 - 20. A computer with less than the required memory for a particular program would not have enough storage space to hold that program. For example, a program requiring 450 K of Ram could not be loaded into a computer with only 256 K of RAM.

Read-Only Memory

The second type of internal memory found in microcomputers is ROM which is an acronym for *read-only memory*. It is called read-only because its information can be read and used only. It cannot be changed or deleted, nor can it be used for temporary storage of programs or data. ROM is permanently installed by the computer manufacturer and is automatically activated when the computer is turned on. Its purpose is to hold important instructions needed by the computer to prepare itself to receive programs and data. ROM retains its information after all power has been removed from the computer. In other words, the instructions in ROM are permanent and remain intact after the computer is turned off and are ready for use again when the computer is turned back on.

ROM can be compared to a maintenance manager who prepares a school building for use by teachers and students by unlocking the doors, turning on the lights, making sure the heating system is working, and so on. Specific examples of functions performed by ROM include a) providing instructions on how to start the computer when the power is turned on; b) checking the hardware for problems when the computer is turned on; c) interpreting input from the keyboard; d) providing instructions on how to send characters to the monitor and e) providing instructions on how to accept programs into RAM from a secondary storage device such as a floppy disk. Without ROM, nothing would happen when you turn on the computer, all characters and commands entered through the keyboard would be ignored by the hardware, and the computer would not know how to load an application program into RAM.

OPERATING SYSTEMS

In addition to ROM, the computer requires an "assistant manager" to perform ongoing "housekeeping chores". This assistant resides on a floppy disk and is known as an *operating system*. The term used to describe the floppy disk containing the operating system is the *system disk*. The system disk label always identifies the name of the operating system stored on that disk (e.g., MS-DOS, Version 3.2). There are four key operating systems for microcomputers:

1. PC-DOS and MS-DOS (Commonly known as DOS)
2. Apple DOS and ProDOS
3. OS/2
4. UNIX

The operating system you use depends upon the computer system you have and your "housekeeping" requirements. For example, Apple DOS is the operating system developed for use on the Apple II computer, whereas PC-DOS is the operating system for use on the IBM Personal Computer (PC). Because the operating system is so closely integrated with the hardware, computer manufacturers usually recommend and often supply the operating system best suited for their products.

In order to use an operating system it must be first loaded into the computer's memory. This process is called *booting the system*. Once loaded, the operating system must have a way of telling you it is ready to accept a "housekeeping" command. This is accomplished by the display of a *system prompt* on the screen. The system prompt for DOS, when using a floppy disk drive, is the "A prompt" which appears on the screen as follows: A >. The system prompt for DOS, when using a hard disk drive, is "C prompt" (C >). Once displayed, the user can give commands to DOS on what needs to be done (e.g., loading an application program, formatting a disk, making a backup copy, and so on).

History of Operating Systems

To understand operating systems, it is helpful to know how they evolved. In the early years of personal computers operating systems were permanently etched onto ROM chips and were automatically activated whenever the computer was turned on. However, as the demand for more storage led to the development of floppy disks (and ultimately hard disks), it was necessary to supplement the built-in operating systems in order to take care of the floppy disk "housekeeping" functions. This led to the development of the disk operating system which provides a means of communication between the computer and disk drives.

One of the earliest operating systems on disk was PC-DOS (Personal Computer Disk Operating System) developed by the Microsoft Corporation for the IBM PC. Microsoft also developed MS-DOS (Microsoft Disk Operating System) which is the generic equivalent of PC-DOS for use with both IBM and IBM-compatible computers. (An IBM compatible computer is not manufactured by IBM but uses the same operating system and will, therefore, run any software programs that will run on an IBM computer). DOS (pronounced *dawss*) is the shortened term that is commonly used to refer to PC-DOS and MS-DOS. DOS is currently the most widely used operating system in the world.

TABLE 1 - 1. Versions of DOS

Since its introduction, DOS has undergone numerous revisions to keep pace with changes in computer technology. A brief summary of these revisions and their characteristics follows:

Versions 1.0 and 1.1:	The basis of all PC operating systems in use today, supporting standard devices and hardware of its time; 1.1 has added support for 5.25-inch floppy disk drives.
Versions 2.0 and 2.1:	Designed for the IBM XT, 2.0 has added support for hard drives.
Version 3.0:	Developed for the IBM AT, 3.0 supports high-density floppy drives.
Version 3.1:	Added support to run PC hardware and software.
Version 3.2:	Provides support for 3.5-inch floppy drives.
Version 3.3:	Introduced with the IBM PS/2 series, 3.3 has become the predominant operating system in use today.
Versions 4.0 and 4.01:	Supports large hard disks and text-based menus that make iteasier to access programs and execute DOS commands.

Since its introduction, DOS has undergone numerous revisions to keep pace with changes in computer technology. Each subsequent level or version of DOS is more powerful and able to perform more operating system functions. A brief summary of these revisions and their characteristics is presented in Table 1-1.

Apple DOS is an operating system developed by Apple Computer, Inc. for the Apple II computer. ProDOS (Professional Disk Operating System) is an enhanced version of Apple DOS that offers considerably more capabilities and power. In general, Apple DOS is limited to floppy disk systems while ProDOS supports hard drives. Like other operating systems, ProDOS has undergone numerous revisions over the years to keep pace with new developments in Apple technology.

The OS/2 operating system was developed for the newer IBM computers (e.g., IBM Personal System/2) to perform a variety of higher-level operations including multitasking operations. UNIX is an operating system for use on a variety of computers, all the way from mainframes to microcomputers. UNIX is a powerful operating system which performs complex multitasking functions. It is primarily used in settings which have complex processing requirements such as large medical clinics, colleges and universities, large corporations and research facilities.

Operating System Functions

The most important function performed by an operating system is to serve as an intermediary to tell the hardware how to run an application program. Hence, application programs are useless without their operating system. In order to start an application program, the operating system must first be loaded into computer memory. There are four methods for starting an application program which are outlined in Table 1-2. The manufacturer of each application program makes the decision as to which method (or methods) is best for use with that program. The program user manual always specifies this information under a section entitled *Start-Up Procedures* located at the beginning of the manual. Regardless of the method used, the end result is always the same—the operating system is loaded into computer memory, followed by the loading of the application program.

Another very important function performed by operating systems is to interpret and execute commands entered from the keyboard. Examples of commands executed by DOS include the FORMAT command used to format a data disk and the COPY command used to make a backup copy.

Specific procedures for performing DOS functions are presented later in this chapter and include: a) booting DOS; b) formatting a data disk; and, c) making a backup copy.

Table 1 - 2. Application Program Start-Up Methods

There are four methods for starting an application program. The manufacturer of each application program makes the decision as to which method (or methods) is best for use with that program. The program user's manual specifies this information under a section entitled *Start-Up Procedures* located at the beginning of the manual. These four methods include:

1. **Initial Loading**: The initial loading method requires the loading of the operating system into computer memory followed by the loading of the application program. The system disk is inserted into drive A and the operating system is loaded into computer memory (Refer to Booting the System, page 74). Next, the program disk is inserted into drive A and a special command is entered at the system prompt which is usually an abbreviation of the name of the program (such as WP for WordPerfect). Entering this command instructs the computer to load the application program. This entire procedure must be repeated each time the application program is used.

2. **One-Time Installation**: The user may need to perform a one-time installation procedure which involves copying the operating system onto the program disk. Thereafter, the operating system automatically loads whenever the program is loaded. Thus, the same disk can be used to load both the operating system as well as the program. This eliminates having to get out the system disk each time you want to use the application program, as is required in the method presented above. The program's user manual specifies the instructions to follow to copy the operating system onto the application program. These instructions must be followed exactly, otherwise the computer will not be able to perform the copying procedure.

3. **Manufacturer Installation:** The software manufacturer may install the operating system on the program disk and, as a result, it will already be there when you purchase the application program. When you load the application program, the operating system is automatically loaded as well. The program's user manual will specify if the pre-installation procedure has been performed.

4. **Hard Disk Installation**: The operating system can be transferred from the system disk and onto a hard disk. Once the operating system has been installed on the hard disk, it automatically loads into computer memory whenever the computer is turned on making the computer ready for an application program to be loaded.

CHECKPOINT

1. Where are RAM and ROM located? ____________________

2. What is the difference between random-access and sequential-access?

3. What is the function of RAM? ____________________

4. What term is frequently used to refer to RAM? ____________________

5. What items are commonly held in RAM? ____________________

6. What happens to information in RAM when the computer is turned off?

7. One byte is equivalent to how many characters?

8. How many bytes are in a kilobyte (K)?

9. How much RAM is usually required to run a medical management program?

10. What is the function of ROM? ____________________

11. What happens to the information in ROM when the computer is turned off?

12. Who has access to ROM? ______________________________

____

13. What is an operating system? ______________________________

____

14. What is a system disk? ______________________________

____

15. How does an operating system tell you it is ready to perform its "housekeeping chores"?

____

16. Explain why application programs are useless without an operating system.

____

____

17. List two examples of commands executed by DOS. ______________________________

____

____

CRITICAL LITERACY

Computer Memory Assignment: The following are examples of situations you may encounter when working with a computer system. Using your computer knowledge, respond to each situation in the space provided.

1. You have entered two pages of text into your computer using the WordStar word processing program. A thunderstorm suddenly occurs and the power goes out temporarily.

   a. Where did the computer place the text you entered (before the thunderstorm occurred)?

   ____

   b. Where did the computer place the word processing program (before the thunderstorm occurred)?

   ____

c. What happened to your text when the power went out?

____

d. What happened to your program when the power went out?

____

e. What happened to the information in ROM when the power went out?

____

f. What must you do to recover your text? ____________________

____

g. Have you permanently lost your word processing program? Explain your answer.

____

____

2. You have an IBM PC computer with 256 K of RAM. Listed below are the names of application programs along with their RAM requirements. Place a check mark next to each program that you would be able to use with your computer.

_______ a. BankStreet Writer for IBM
RAM requirement: 128 K

_______ b. Microsoft Word for the Apple Macintosh
RAM requirement: 256 K

_______ c. PageMaker for IBM
RAM requirement: 640 K

_______ d. The Medical Office Manager for IBM
RAM requirement: 1 MB

_______ e. Flight Simulator for IBM
RAM requirement: 64 K

_______ f. Microsoft Word for IBM
RAM requirement: 256 K

_______ g. Apache Strike for IBM
RAM requirement: 128 K

_______ h. Calendar Maker for Apple
RAM requirement: 64 K

________ i. Label Maker for IBM
RAM requirement: 128 K

________ j. Resume Writer for Apple Macintosh
RAM requirement: 64 K

DOS Assignment: Listed below are two descriptions of Start-Up Procedures for the following word processing programs: Bank Street Writer (BSW) and Microsoft Word (MSW). Both programs require an IBM computer and the PC-DOS operating system. After reviewing these descriptions, complete the corresponding questions for each.

A. Getting Started With Bank Street Writer:

The first time you use Bank Street Writer, you will have to copy PC-DOS onto your Bank Street Writer disk. Once this is done, the Bank Street Writer program will automatically start when you turn on your computer (with the BSW disk in drive A). You only need to install PC-DOS the first time the disk is used. The following steps should be followed to perform the copying procedure:

a. Start up your computer with PC-DOS in drive A.
b. After the A > appears on the screen, insert the BSW program disk in drive B.
c. To copy PC-DOS onto the BSW disk, type the following at the system prompt:
(A > B:INSTALL2
d. Press the Enter key.
e. The disk drive indicator light will come on telling you that PC-DOS is being copied onto the BSW program disk.

1. What is the purpose for placing a copy of PC-DOS on the BSW program disk?

____

2. What command is required to perform the PC-DOS copying procedure?

A > ______________________________________

3. How many times does the copying procedure have to be performed?

____

____

4. Which of the four Start-Up Procedures is used to start Bank Street Writer? (Use Table 1-2 as a reference.)

____

B. Getting Started With Microsoft Word:

If you have a floppy disk drive system (without a hard drive), you will need to load DOS before loading Microsoft Word. This must be done each time you use the program. The following steps should be followed to start Microsoft Word:

a. Start up your computer with DOS in drive A.
b. After the A > appears on the screen, remove DOS, and insert the MSW program disk in drive A.
c. To start MSW, type the following at the system prompt:
(A >) word
d. Press the Enter key. Once the program loads into memory, the MSW title screen will appear on the monitor.

1. What must be done before Microsoft Word can be loaded?

____

2. What command is required to start Microsoft Word?

A > ____

3. Will you need to get DOS out the next time you use this program? Explain your answer.

____

____

4. Which of the four Start-Up Procedures is used to start Microsoft Word? (Use Table 1-2 as a reference.)

____

SECONDARY STORAGE DEVICES

The two types of storage used by computers are primary storage and secondary storage. As discussed earlier in this chapter, primary storage (RAM) is used to hold items *temporarily* for ready access and use by the computer. Secondary storage, on the other hand, includes all of the storage devices that are used to *permanently* store and retrieve information. Unlike RAM, secondary storage devices retain their information after the power has been removed. The filing cabinets of the computer system, they are used to store both programs and data that can then be brought back into RAM as needed. Secondary storage devices available for microcomputer systems include floppy disks, hard disks, and magnetic tape, all of which are discussed in detail on the following pages.

Floppy Disks

Floppy disks are the most widely used secondary storage devices for microcomputers. Their principal advantages are low cost, portability and ease of mailing. They are often referred to by other names such as diskettes, floppies, or simply disks. A floppy disk is a circular, thin, platter-like storage medium with a flexible, bending quality which gives rise to the term "floppy". It is not possible to view the actual floppy disk first-hand because it is almost entirely enclosed and sealed in a permanent protective covering known as the *disk jacket*. Thus, the round disk appears square because of its enclosure in the disk jacket. The inside of the disk jacket is lined with white felt that has been specially treated to reduce friction and static and to keep the disk clean. The disk is never removed from the jacket, even when inserting it into the disk drive, where it must be placed in order to store or retrieve information.

Sizes and Types of Disks

Floppy disks are available in two sizes: 5.25-inch diameter and 3.5-inch diameter. The 5.25-inch disk is sometimes called a minidiskette, while the 3.5-inch disk is also known as a microdiskette or a microfloppy. The jacket of the 5.25-inch disk is made of flexible vinyl, while the jacket of the 3.5-inch disk consists of hard plastic. Because of their smaller size and more durable jackets, 3.5-inch disks are less susceptible to contaminants and damage and therefore, are much easier and safer to mail and carry around.

Disks which are identical in their physical make-up are called by different names depending on the information which they contain. Thus, a disk used to store program instructions is known as a *program disk*, while a disk used to store data for an application program is termed a *data disk*. Most programs do not allow data to be stored on the program disk itself. As you have already learned, a disk used to store an operating system is termed a *system disk*. Because program and data disks wear out after approximately 25 to 40 hours of use, backup copies of these important disks should be made, as is discussed later in this chapter.

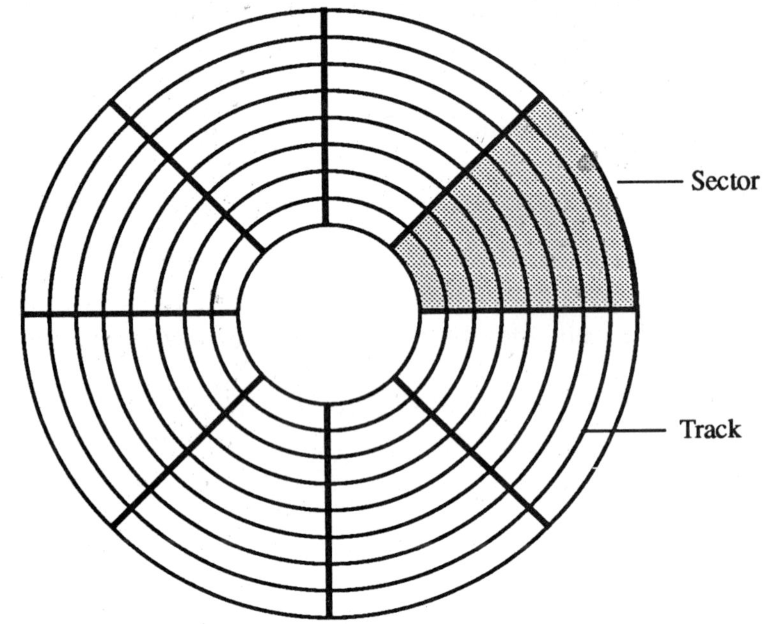

FIGURE 1 - 21. The surface of a floppy disk is divided into a set of concentric circles known as tracks. Tracks are further divided into sectors which resemble the wedge-shaped pieces of a pie. Tracks and sectors provide a method of organization for the storage and retrieval of information.

Tracks and Sectors

The composition of a floppy disk is designed to maximize its important functions: the storage and retrieval of information. To accommodate the storage of information, disks are made of mylar plastic that has been coated with iron oxide, a magnetically sensitive material. The iron oxide gives the disk its characteristic rust-brown color. Data is stored on the disk as magnetic particles in a manner similar to that used to record voice on a cassette tape.

To store and retrieve the information on the disk as quickly as possible, a method of organization is used which divides the disk into designated areas similar to the division of a piece of property into housing lots. The disk surface is divided into a set of concentric circles; each of these circles is called a *track* (Fig. 1-21). Data is stored on these tracks in the form of magnetized particles. Tracks are further divided into *sectors* which resemble the wedge-shaped pieces of a pie (Fig. 1-21). A typical 5.25-inch floppy disk contains 40 tracks and 8 or 9 sectors. Tracks and sectors are not visible with the eye when looking at a floppy disk. Through a process called *formatting*, (discussed later in this chapter), the tracks and sectors are numerically marked to facilitate the location of information stored on the disk.

The following example provides a comparison of how the arrangement of tracks and sectors assists in locating information stored on the disk. Let's say that a friend invites you to her house at 102 Sunnyside Drive in Greenfield Village. You arrive at Greenfield Village and first locate the proper street and then you look for the house number. But just think how difficult and time consuming it would be to locate your friend's house without a street name or house number. Comparing this example to the organization of floppy disks, tracks and sectors are comparable to the division of Greenfield Village into streets and housing lots, and the formatting process which numerically marks each track and sector is comparable to the street names and house numbers.

Storage Capacity

The amount of data that can be stored on a floppy disk varies based on several factors. The first of these is the recording density of the disk. *Recording density* is the amount of information that can be placed on the surface of the disk. The recording density of floppy disks falls into two categories: double-density and high-density. (Single density disks are no longer available and are seldom used today.) If a disk is a *double-density* (DD) disk, it can hold approximately twice as much information as the former single-density disk. A *high-density* (HD) disk has twice as many sectors as a double-density disk, enabling it to store twice again as much data. If a disk is labeled *double-sided* (DS), information can be stored on both sides of the disk. This is in contrast to the original single-sided disk which stores data on only one side of the disk. Based on the above information, disks are classified as either double-sided/double-density (DS/DD) or double-sided/high-density (DS/HD).

The amount of data that can be stored on a floppy disk also depends on the size of the disk. Although smaller in size, a 3.5-inch DS/DD disk has twice the storage capacity (720 K) of a 5.25-inch DS/DD disk (360 K). Translated into printed data, 2 K is approximately equal to one double-spaced page of text. Therefore, 360 K is approximately equal to 180 double-spaced pages of text and 720 K is approximately equal to 360 pages of text. Of all floppy disks, high-density disks can store the greatest amount of data. A 5.25-inch DS/HD disk has a storage capacity of 1.2 MB, while a 3.5-inch DS/HD disk has a storage capacity of 1.4 MB, equivalent to a 500-page textbook.

The Disk Jacket

The effect of placing a floppy disk into a disk drive is similar to playing a record on a phonograph system. The disk is rotated at high speed while a read/write head, comparable to a phonograph arm, moves over the surface of the spinning disk. When a disk drive is operating, information is either being stored or retrieved as directed by the user. To assist in the transmittal of information, the disk jacket has several openings and notches (Fig. 1-22) described as follows. The round opening in the center of the floppy disk is called the *hub*. It fits over a mount or spindle on the disk drive similar to a record fitting

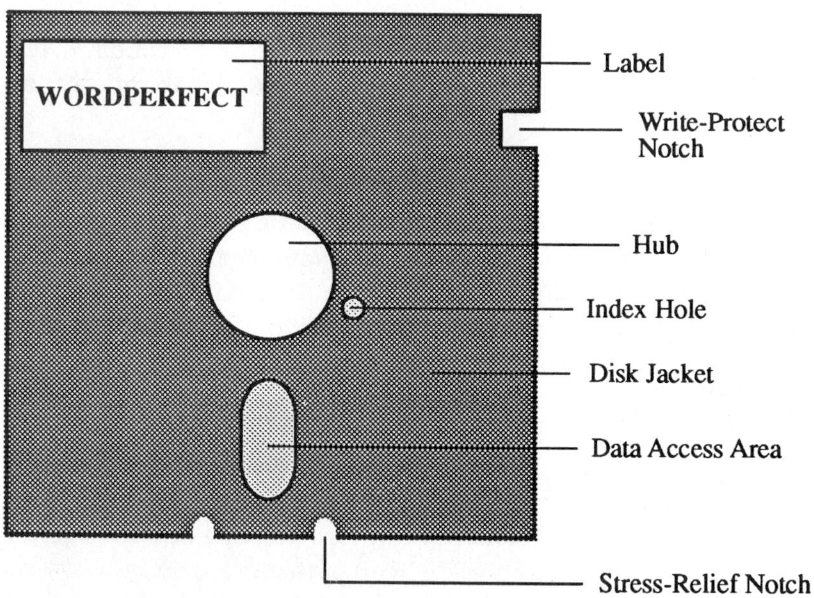

FIGURE 1 - 22. Disk jacket of a 5.25-inch disk.

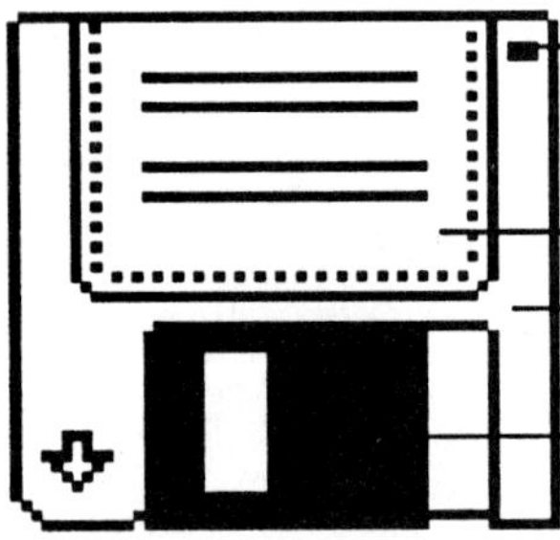

FIGURE 1 - 23. Disk jacket of a 3.5-inch disk.

over a phonograph spindle. This holds the disk in place while it is spinning. The large oblong opening is called the *data access area*; it provides access for the read/write head of the disk drive to come into contact with the magnetic surface of the disk. The last opening in the jacket is a small round reference hole, known as the *index hole*. Its purpose is to indicate to the read/write head where the disk is in its rotation. Located on the opposite end to the disk label are two small notches known as *stress-relief notches* . Their function is to protect the jacket from warping and to assist in lining up the disk when it is placed in the disk drive. Finally, the large square notch located on the side of the disk is known as the *write-protect notch*. Its function is discussed later in this chapter.

The jacket of a 3.5-inch disk has openings with similar functions; however they differ in appearance (Fig. 1-23). The hub opening is almost completely covered by a hub piece. The disk jacket has a data access area, but it is completely covered by a spring-loaded sliding metal cover. The metal covering protects the magnetic surface when the disk is out of the disk drive. Inserting the disk into the disk drive causes the metal cover to slide to one side, allowing the read/write head to access information. It is important never to slide the metal covering to the side when the disk is out of the disk drive. Doing so exposes the data access area to dust and fingerprints which could lead to the loss of data. The write-protect notch of a 3.5-inch disk consists of a small sliding plastic tab rather than a notch in one corner of the disk.

Care and Handling of Floppy Disks

Floppy disks must be handled carefully because their magnetic coatings are vulnerable to damage and wear. Because information is stored as magnetic particles on a disk, destruction of the magnetic material results in loss of data. In addition, proper disk handling is essential to the reliable operation of a computer system. Improper handling is the cause of most computer problems. To ensure the integrity of floppy disks, the following guidelines should be followed for both 5.25-inch and 3.5-inch disks.

1. Make sure the computer environment is clean and "pollution-free". Contaminants in the air, such as dust, smoke, and machinery pollutants can be extremely hazardous to floppy disks. In addition, these contaminants can also damage other computer components such as the CPU and the read/write head of the disk drive.
2. Label each disk to identify its contents (e.g., WordPerfect Data Disk). This avoids having to determine the information stored on a stack of unidentified disks.

3. Keep the disk away from electromagnetic fields which can erase information contained on it. Examples of electromagnetic fields include the computer monitor, typewriters, magnetized paper clip holders, telephone receivers, and kitchen appliances.
4. Store disks in a dry, cool area. Do not expose the disk to extremely hot or cold temperatures or direct sunlight. Intense heat (above 120 degrees F) or cold (below 41 degrees F) can result in loss of data.
5. Do not allow the disk to come in contact with food or liquids. Food particles can scratch the surface of the disk and permanently damage it. Liquids, such as soft drinks or coffee, can leave a residue which renders the disk useless. This residue can also permanently damage the disk drive, and therefore, it is best not to use or even keep a disk that has gotten wet.
6. Do not use an eraser to erase a disk label. Residue from an eraser may work its way onto the disk surface and damage it.
7. Store the disks in a clean area to protect them from exposure to dust and dirt. Floppy disk storage cases are commercially available for this purpose. Do not overcrowd the disks in their storage case because the pressure exerted could damage them.
8. Do not lay anything heavy on the disk. The weight can damage the disk surface resulting in loss of data.
9. Keep disks out of reach of small children and pets.

Because 5.25-inch disks are enclosed in a vinyl rather than a hard plastic jacket they are more susceptible to harm, and some additional precautions must be followed as listed below.

1. Always complete the label before attaching it to the disk jacket. If information needs to be modified on an affixed label, a felt tip pen must be used. Using a ball point pen or pencil causes pressure on the disk surface which could damage it. (*Note*: Because of their hard plastic jacket, a ball point pen or pencil can be used to write on an affixed label of a 3.5-inch disk.)
2. Each 5.25-inch disk comes with a paper or cardboard envelope. The disk envelope must be removed before the disk is inserted into the disk drive. Always return the disk to its envelope *immediately* after use to protect it from dust and dirt. Leaving an unprotected disk lying out is courting disaster.
3. Handle the disk so that the data access area does not come in contact with anything other than the disk drive head. Touching this exposed area may cause body oils to be transferred to it resulting in dust particles sticking to its mylar surface. Dust particles can scratch the surface of the disk when the read/write head moves over them leading to loss of data. The proper method for holding a 5.25-inch disk is to place the thumb of the right hand on top of the label with two fingers supporting the underside of the disk directly below the label.
4. Do not bend or fold the disk. The disk is able to withstand a certain amount of flexing, however, excessive bending or flexing could cause the magnetic material coating the disk to flake off resulting in loss of data.
5. Do not use rubber bands or paper clips on the disk.

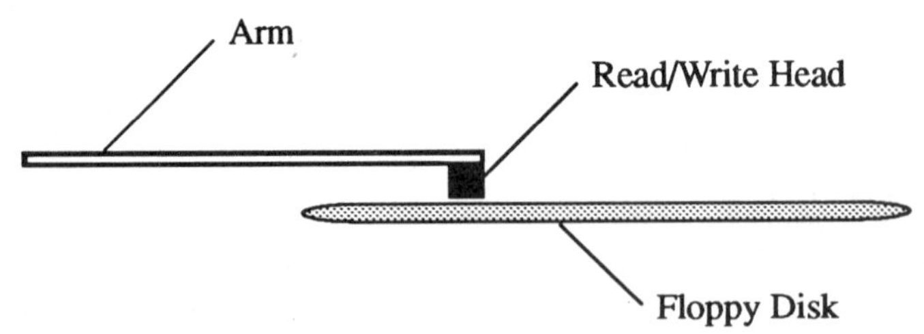

FIGURE 1 - 24. Read/write head of a floppy disk drive. The purpose of the read/write head is to store information onto and retrieve information off of a floppy disk.

Floppy Disk Drive

A *disk drive* is a mechanical device which rotates a floppy disk in contact with a magnetic read/write head mounted on an arm (Fig. 1-24). The purpose of the read/write head is to a) store information onto and b) retrieve information from the floppy disk. Information stored on a floppy disk is located through random-access; that is, the computer can retrieve specific information directly without having to look through all of the stored information.

Two important computer terms are used to express the storage and retrieval of information by the disk drive. The term used to describe the storage of information onto a disk is *write*, while the term used to describe the retrieval of information from a disk is *read* (Fig. 1-25). When information is *written*, it is transferred from RAM to the disk. On the other hand, when information is *read*, a copy of the information is transferred from the disk into RAM. For example, if a program disk is placed in the disk drive, the read/write head reads the program and transfers a copy of it into RAM. On the other hand, when you have entered data into your computer that you want to save, it is transferred from RAM and *written* onto a data disk.

Types of Disk Drives

Disk drives are available in two types: 5.25-inch disk drives and 3.5-inch disk drives. As you would surmise, 5.25-inch floppy disks must be used with the former type of disk drive, while 3.5-inch disks must be used with the latter type of disk drive. The type and number of disk drives depends upon the computer system. For example, an Apple IIe comes with two 5.25-inch disk drives while an IBM PS/2, Model 30 computer comes with one 3.5-inch disk drive (and a hard disk drive).

Computer systems with a hard disk drive must have at least one floppy disk drive so that application programs can be transferred from floppy disks onto the hard disk. Computer systems *without* a hard drive almost always have two floppy disk drives

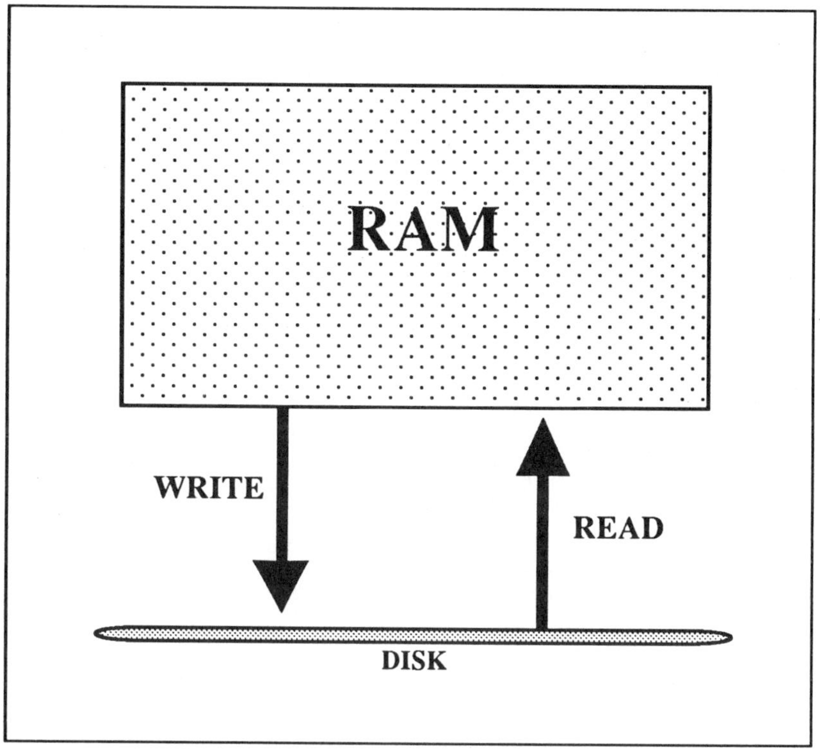

FIGURE 1 - 25. Read and Write. When information is written, it is transferred from RAM (computer memory) to a disk. When information is read, a copy of the information is transferred from the disk and into RAM.

because using one drive with such a system requires the user to change disks more frequently. In addition, most application programs require that the program disk be located in one drive and the data disk in another.

With a two-drive system, the disk drives are identical in mechanical structure but have different functions. The first disk drive is identified as drive A and the second as drive B. Drive A is the *default drive*; it is the drive automatically chosen by the computer when looking for disk information. Because of this, the operating system disk and program disks must be inserted into Drive A to be loaded into the computer's memory. Drive B is generally used for saving data on a data disk and making backup copies.

The floppy disk drives are positioned either a) one on top of the other or b) side by side in the computer housing (Fig. 1-26). In the former arrangement, Drive A is always located on the top, whereas with the latter arrangement, drive A is always on the left.

Operation of the Disk Drive

To operate the disk drive, a floppy disk is first inserted into the slot opening of the drive. The user then activates the disk drive which causes the read/write head to rest on the surface of the disk while the disk drive spins the disk inside its jacket at a speed of approximately 300 rpm. The read/write head moves back and forth over the data. A small indicator light on the disk drive identifies when the drive is spinning. It is extremely important *not* to remove the disk while the light is on as this could result in damage to the surface of the disk. This would be comparable to removing a spinning record from a phonograph system while the needle is in contact with the record. Based upon directions from the user, information is read from or written onto the disk. When the indicator light goes out, this means the disk drive has completed its operation.

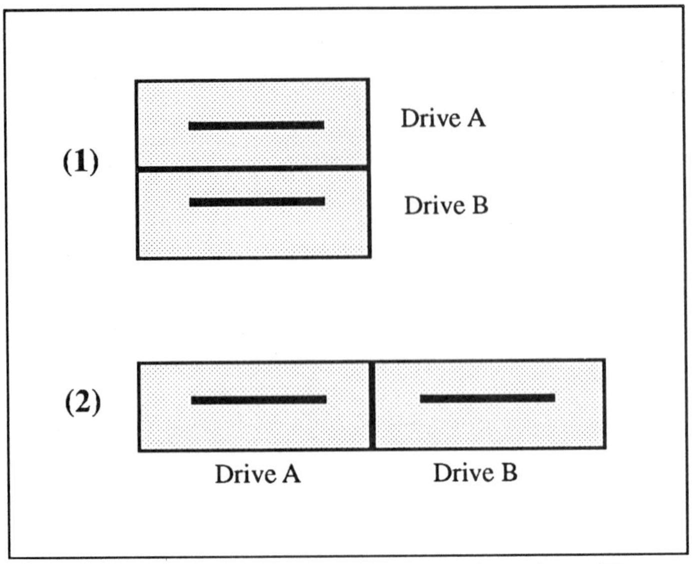

FIGURE 1 - 26. Arrangement of floppy disk drives. Floppy disk drives are positioned either one on top of the other (1) or side by side (2).

Disk drives are sensitive mechanical devices. Therefore, you should be careful to avoid shocks and vibrations to the disk drive which could result in misalignment of the read/write head. One of the worst enemies of a disk drive is dust and dirt. Because of this, the read/write heads should be cleaned on a regular basis to eliminate these contaminants. Special head-cleaning kits are commercially available for this purpose.

Hard Disks

Although floppy disks are the most popular secondary storage device for microcomputer systems, even the floppy with the highest storage capacity (3.5-inch double-sided, high-density) has a maximum capacity of 1.4 megabytes. Thus, to accommodate a large amount of information, numerous floppy disks are required. To avoid the necessity of working with a number of floppy disks, as well as having to continuously switch disks in the disk drive, a type of secondary storage device known as a hard disk is often used.

Hard disks are able to store between 20 and 160 megabytes or more, depending on the size of the disk. A 20 MB hard disk can store 20 million characters which is the equivalent of sixty 5.25-inch floppy disks. Thus, all programs and data can be stored in one place which eliminates having to sort through a stack of floppy disks. In addition to their greater storage capacity hard disks work much faster than floppy disks, both in storing and retrieving data. Finally, hard disks are virtually "wear-free". Unlike floppy disks, they can store and retrieve data for an unlimited period of time without wearing out. Although a hard disk significantly adds to the expense of a computer system, most users agree that the added cost is offset by the advantages.

A hard disk (also known as a fixed disk) derives its name from the fact that it consists of a thin, rigid metal platter coated with a magnetic material. To increase their storage capacity, most hard disk units consist of two or more disks. Both sides of the disk are used to store information and each side of the disk has its own read/write head (Fig. 1-27). Because hard disks are very sensitive to dirt, dust, and smoke, the entire disk unit is

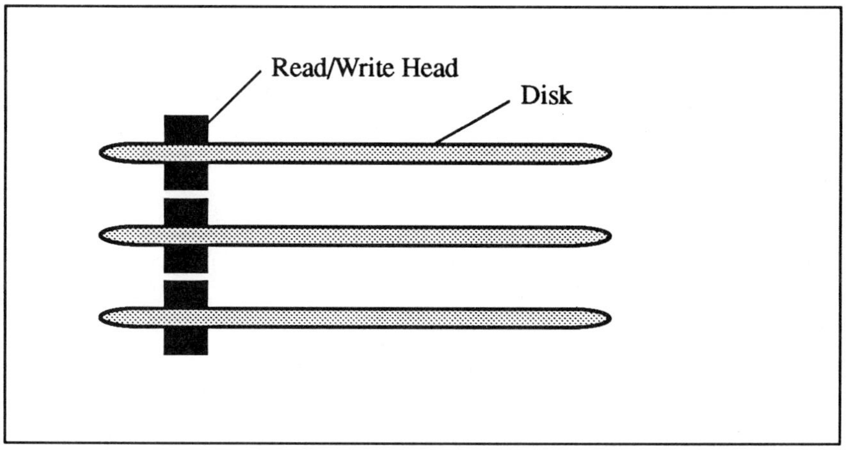

FIGURE 1 - 27. Hard disk drive consisting of three disks (side view).

encased in a permanently sealed, air-tight container to protect it from these contaminants. The computer term for a disk unit (consisting of the hard disks and read/write heads) is a *hard disk drive*.

Hard disk drives are usually internal, meaning they are located inside the main computer unit. Unlike a floppy disk, an internal hard disk cannot be removed from the computer. This arrangement is considered a disadvantage, since any time information needs to be transported (either by hand or through the mail), it must first be copied onto a floppy disk(s).

As with a floppy disk, information is stored and retrieved on a hard disk through the use of tracks and sectors and random-access. However, the hard disk spins at 3600 rpm, more than ten times faster than a floppy disk, which allows for the storage and retrieval of information to take place at lightning speed.

Medical management programs almost always require a hard disk for operation of the program. An initial, one-time installation procedure must be performed to transfer a copy of the medical management program from a number of floppy disks onto the hard disk. The installation procedure is usually performed by a technical staff member from the medical software company. Installing the program on the hard disk makes it readily available for immediate use when the computer system is turned on each day. (*Note:* Should you ever need to transfer a copy of a program from a floppy disk onto a hard disk, you will find detailed program installation instructions in the program user manual.)

Magnetic Tape

Magnetic tape is a low-cost secondary storage device for microcomputer systems which is used as a back-up medium. It consists of a thin, plastic material which has a magnetic surface for storing information. The most commonly used type of magnetic tape comes in the form of a tape cassette. A magnetic tape cassette consists of a reel of magnetic tape housed in a plastic container which has a very similar appearance to an audio-cassette tape. Information is stored and retrieved using a tape drive which is similar in both appearance and function to a cassette tape-recorder. The tape drive is either housed in the main computer unit itself or is external to the main unit and attached by a cable (Fig. 1-28).

Magnetic tape stores and retrieves information through sequential-access, rather than random-access. Because sequential-access takes considerably longer, magnetic tape is impractical for actively storing and retrieving information in daily computer operations. Hard disks and floppy disks which use random-access to store and retrieve information have a much faster access time. This is why magnetic tape is used as a backup medium, rather than as a main storage device.

Magnetic tape can store a tremendous amount of information. Because of this, it is often preferred over floppy disks for making a backup copy of the contents of a hard disk. To back up an entire hard disk using floppy disks requires numerous disks as well as the constant changing of them in the disk drive. For example, to back up a 20 MB hard drive requires approximately twenty-five 3.5-inch DS/DD floppy disks. On the other hand, one tape cassette can easily back up the contents of a 40 MB hard disk. In addition, a previously used magnetic tape can be used over again to make another backup copy, much the same as recording over a previously recorded audio-tape.

The care and handling of magnetic tape is the same as that of floppy disks. Refer to Care and Handling of Floppy Disks (pages 58-59) to review this information. Each magnetic tape cassette comes with a storage case, very similar in appearance to the storage case for an audio-tape cassette. When not in use, the magnetic tape cassette should always be stored in its case to protect it from environmental contaminants such as dust and dirt. The case is also designed to lock the cassette tape wheels in position to prevent the tape from loosening up.

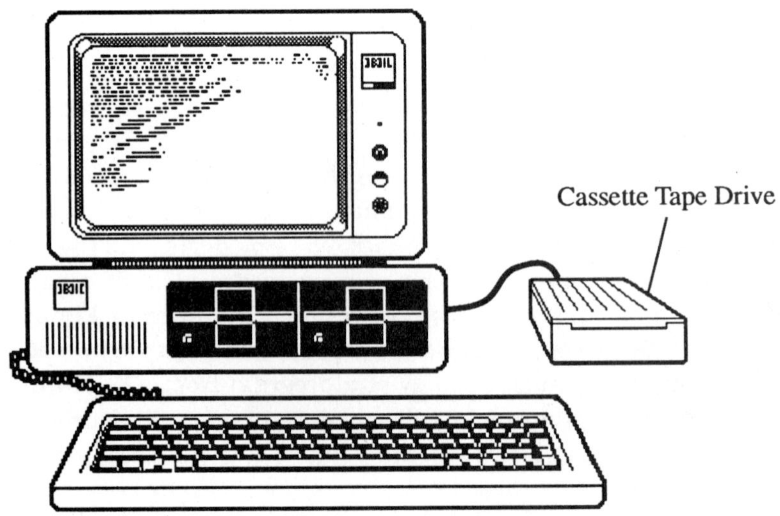

FIGURE 1 - 28. An example of a cassette tape drive that is attached to the computer by a cable.

CHECKPOINT

1. What is the difference between primary storage and secondary storage?

____

____

2. List three examples of secondary storage devices used with microcomputer systems.

____

3. What other terms are used to refer to floppy disks?______________

____

4. What is the shape of a floppy disk? Why can't a floppy disk be viewed first hand?

____

____

5. Why is a 3.5-inch floppy disk less susceptible to damage than a 5.25-inch disk?

____

____

6. What is the difference between a program disk and a data disk?

____

____

7. What is the purpose of tracks and sectors?______________

____

____

8. What is the function of each of the following openings of a 5.25-inch disk jacket?

   a. hub______________________________

   b. data access area ______________________

   c. index hole ______________________________

   d. write-protect notch ______________________

9. List five guidelines which should be followed in the care and handling of floppy disks.

____

____

____

____

10. What are the two main functions of a floppy disk drive? _______________

____

11. Explain the difference between read and write.

____

____

12. What type of floppy disk must be used with a 5.25-inch disk drive? With a 3.5 inch disk drive?

____

13. What is the definition of the default drive?

____

____

14. Why is it important not to remove a floppy disk from the disk drive when the indicator light is on?

____

15. How do you know when a disk drive has completed its operation?

____

16. What are the advantages of using a hard disk as a secondary storage device?

____

____

17. Why is a hard disk sealed in an air-tight container? _______________

____

____

18. Where is a hard disk usually located (in terms of the computer)?

____

19. For each of the following, circle the secondary storage device which has the larger storage capacity.

    a. 360 K floppy disk

       1.2 MB floppy disk

    b. 10 MB hard drive

       720 K floppy disk

    c. 20 MB hard disk

       10 MB hard disk

    d. 20 MB hard disk

       40 MB magnetic tape

    e. 700 K floppy disk

       1.4 MB floppy disk

20. What is the most common use of magnetic tape?

____

21. List the type of secondary storage devices used most often in the medical office. What function is served by each?

____

____

____

CRITICAL LITERACY

Secondary Storage Device Assignment:

1. Observe the jacket of a floppy disk and identify the openings and notches listed below. Place a check mark in the space provided after you have correctly identified it.

   ________ 1. hub

   ________ 2. data access area

   ________ 3. index hole

   ________ 4. write-protect notch

2. Locate the manufacturer's label on a 5.25-inch floppy disk and answer the following questions:

   a. What company manufactured this disk? ________________

   b. What is the recording density indicated on the label (e.g., double-sided/double-density)?

   ____

3. Cut open the jacket of a 5.25-inch floppy disk that can no longer be used. Observe the contents and answer the following questions:

   a. What is the color of the floppy disk? ________________

   b. What is the shape of the floppy disk? ________________

   c. What color is the felt-liner? ________________

   d. Where is the felt liner located in relation to the disk?

   ____

4. Listed below are examples of data transmission using a secondary storage device. In the space provided, indicate if each is an example of reading (R) or writing (W).

   ________ a. Loading WordPerfect into RAM from a floppy disk.

   ________ b. Saving a term paper on a data disk.

   ________ c. Saving a form letter on a hard disk.

   ________ d. Loading a medical software program from a hard disk into RAM.

BASIC COMPUTER PROCEDURES

The previous sections have presented the theory necessary to work effectively with a computer system. This section presents procedures which are basic to the operation of a computer. Having mastered these procedures, it will be much easier for you to operate a medical office computer system as well as a home computer system. The computer procedures outlined in this section include the following:

1. Insertion of a floppy disk into a disk drive.

2. Loading an application program.

3. Booting the system.

4. Formatting a floppy disk.

5. Making a backup copy.

6. Shutting down the computer.

While the theory for these procedures is the same, the steps for performing the tasks vary based upon the computer system. Because most medical offices and educational institutions use IBM (or IBM compatible) computers, the procedures presented are for this type of computer system.

Insertion of a Floppy Disk into a Disk Drive

A floppy disk must be correctly inserted into the disk drive to ensure proper loading of the disk and to prevent damage to its magnetic surface. The procedure for inserting 5.25-inch and 3.5-inch floppy disks into the disk drive is presented below.

Insertion of a 5.25-inch disk

1. **Procedural Step**: Remove the floppy disk from its protective envelope. The disk should be held label-side up with the right thumb placed on top of the label and two fingers supporting the underside of the disk directly below the label. Do not touch any part of the exposed disk.
   Principle: Floppy disks are vulnerable to wear and must be handled properly. Touching the exposed part of the disk may result in flaking of the magnetic particles on the disk and loss of data.

2. **Procedural Step**: Open the door or latch of the disk drive.
   Principle: Some 5.25-inch disk drives have a door that must be lifted up while other disk drives have a latch that is turned to one side. Opening the door prepares the disk drive to receive the disk.

3. **Procedural Step**: Insert the disk into the disk drive with the label facing up, the write-protect notch on the right, and the data-access area inserted first. Slowly and firmly slide the disk (label-side up) all the way into the slot opening until you feel a small "click". Do not force the disk into the disk drive. If the disk will not slide in smoothly, take it out and try again.
   Principle: If the disk is inserted the wrong way, damage to the disk may occur. Forcing a disk into the disk drive may bend or scratch it causing a flaking of the magnetic material and loss of data. Forcing a disk can also damage the disk drive.

4. **Procedural Step**: Gently close the door or latch of the disk drive. Having to use force to close it is an indication that the disk is not properly positioned. Improperly positioned disks should be taken out and reinserted.
   Principle: The disk drive is unable to operate unless the door or latch is closed. Closing the door clamps the hub of the disk over the spindle of the disk drive and brings the read/write head in proper position above the disk. Improperly positioned disks will not allow proper alignment of the read/write head on the surface of the disk and, as a result, the disk drive is unable to read or write information.

Insertion of a 3.5-inch Disk

1. **Procedural Step**: Hold the disk with the label-side up with the right thumb placed over the label and two fingers supporting the underside of the disk, directly below the label.

2. **Procedural Step**: Slide the disk into the slot of the drive, metal end first and label-side up. An arrow in the upper left-hand corner of the disk assists in indicating the proper insertion of the disk.

3. **Procedural Step**: Press gently on the outer edge of the disk until it "clicks" and drops into place. When the disk is most of the way in, the drive's internal mechanism automatically pulls the disk into place. Once inserted, the metal covering of the disk slides to one side to allow the read/write head to access information on the disk.

Loading an Application Program

Before an application program can be used, a copy of it must be *loaded* or transferred into the computer's memory from a secondary storage device such as a hard disk or a floppy disk.

Hard Disk

Loading an application program from a hard disk is usually a matter of turning on the computer and selecting the desired program from a menu displayed on the screen of the monitor (Fig. 1-29). These menu options constitute all of the programs and data that have been previously transferred to the hard disk.

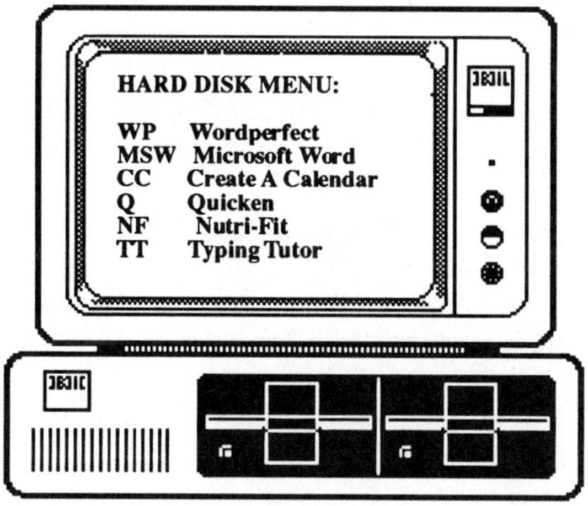

FIGURE 1 - 29. Hard disk menu indicating the programs stored on the hard disk.

Floppy Disk

Loading an application program stored on a floppy disk into the computer memory involves the following steps: The program disk is first inserted into the disk drive, and the drive is activated. Activation of the disk drive is accomplished by either a cold start or a warm start procedure. The *cold start method* is used when the computer has not been previously turned on, whereas the *warm start method* is used when the computer is currently in use. During activation, a copy of the program is retrieved from the disk and loaded into the computer's memory. The computer is then able to perform the functions specified by the application program.

Because the tracks on a disk are very narrow, the read/write head must be correctly positioned to read the magnetic particles of information within each track. If the head is not properly aligned with the tracks, an unpleasant grinding sound is heard from the disk drive as the drive attempts to correct the alignment error. If not possible, a system error message is displayed on the monitor and the disk drive ceases its operation (i.e., the indicator light goes off). To resolve the error, open the door of the disk drive, slide the disk part way out, and reinsert it. Gently close the door and reactivate the disk drive.

The procedure for loading an application program into computer memory is outlined on the following page. It is assumed that a copy of the operating system is already on the program disk, and therefore, loading the program also loads the operating system into the computer's memory. (Remember, a program cannot be loaded into computer memory without the operating system being available to tell the hardware how to run the software.)

Cold Start Method of Loading a Program

1. **Procedural Step**: Turn the printer on. The on/off switch is usually located on the back or side of the printer.

2. **Procedural Step**: Turn on the computer monitor. The on/off switch is usually located on the front or side of the monitor.

3. **Procedural Step**: Insert the program disk into drive A.

4. **Procedural Step**: Turn on the computer. The on/off switch is usually located in the back of the main unit of the computer. It may also be located on the front or side of the main unit.

5. **Procedural Step**: The initial start-up procedures take place as follows:

   a. The computer fan comes on.
   b. The computer performs a power-on self test in which it checks itself to determine if the system is functioning correctly. The length of the pause varies, but usually takes about 45 seconds.
   c. If the computer is functioning properly, an electronic beep occurs.
   d. The printer indicates readiness by making a zip and a clinking sound as the print head moves into position.

6. **Procedural Step**: Disk drive A is activated which is evidenced by a whirring sound coming from the drive and the indicator light coming on. Do not remove the disk from the drive while the light is on. (*Note*: If the indicator light stays on, but the program is not loading, you should *turn off* the computer, reinsert the disk in the disk drive, and begin again—starting with Step 3. To prevent damaging the disk, it should never be removed from a disk drive unless the indicator light is off.)

7. **Procedural Step**: Both DOS and the application program are loaded into the computer's memory during activation of disk drive A. When the indicator light goes out, the process is completed and the title screen of the program appears on the monitor.

8. **Procedural Step**: Since the computer is already on, the warm start method can now be used to load a different program. The warm start procedure is outlined on page 73.

Warm Start Method for Loading a Program

A warm start is accomplished by pressing a series of keys simultaneously. The keys that are pressed depend on the type of computer being used. For example, with an IBM PC, the following keys are pressed simultaneously: the Control key, the Alternate key and the Delete key (Ctrl-Alt-Del).

1. **Procedural Step**: Remove the program disk currently in drive A and insert another program disk into drive A.

2. **Procedural Step**: Press the appropriate series of keys for your computer system. Information on the specific keys to be pressed is found in the computer operating manual.

3. **Procedural Step**: Observe the computer monitor. The display screen goes blank momentarily, followed by activation of the disk drive. At this point, a copy of the program loads into the computer's memory. When the indicator light goes out, the process is complete and the title of the program is displayed on the screen.

Shutting Down the Computer

The following procedure is used to shut down the computer system after use.

1. Remove all disks from the disk drives. Immediately place all 5.25-inch disks in their protective envelopes.

2. Turn off the computer using the on/off switch.

3. Turn off the monitor.

4. Turn off the printer.

Booting the System

The process of loading a copy of DOS from the system disk into computer memory is known as *booting the system* or, more specifically, *booting DOS.* The procedure for booting DOS from a floppy disk is presented below.

Booting DOS From the System Disk

1. With your computer turned off, place the DOS disk in drive A.

2. Close the drive door and turn on the computer.

3. For a few seconds, your computer may appear to be doing nothing. Actually, a series of checks is being run to make sure that all is well inside the computer. You will hear some whirring and a short electronic beep and the indicator light on the disk drive will come on. The indicator light means that drive A has turned on and that DOS is being loaded into computer memory.

4. Prompts asking you to enter the current date and time are next displayed on the screen.

5. Once a valid date and time have been entered, DOS displays the system prompt (A>) followed by a blinking cursor. The system prompt is the official starting point. It confirms that the operating system is ready to respond to your command.

DOS is a command-driven operating system. This means the user must issue commands instructing DOS to do something. DOS commands are in the form of an abbreviation or a short word. For example, "format b:" tells DOS that you want to format a disk in drive B. While you can enter commands in uppercase or lowercase letters (or a combination of upper and lowercase), it is important to enter the command exactly as indicated in the DOS manual. Failure to enter the exact command may result in the following error message on the screen: *bad command or file name.* If this occurs, check your spelling and reenter the command.

Formatting a Floppy Disk

When you purchase a floppy disk, it is as nearly complete as the manufacturer can make it. Although it is divided into tracks and sectors, they are not yet marked. The manufacturer is unable to do this because the specific markings placed on the disk depend on the computer system in use. For example, an IBM computer uses a different marking system than does an Apple computer. Therefore, before a brand new floppy disk can be used, it must first have magnetic reference marks recorded on it by the computer system being used. Some disk suppliers sell preformatted disks at an extra cost; if you buy these, make sure they are formatted for the computer system you are using (e.g., IBM, Apple, Macintosh and so on).

Formatting (also called *initializing*) is the term for the process of marking the tracks and sectors of a disk. Once a disk has been formatted, it can be used to store and retrieve information. Previously used disks can be reformatted for storage of new information because formatting erases all existing information stored on the disk. A word of caution: a program disk should never be formatted because the entire program would be erased and the disk would be useless.

A disk formatted for one computer system can be reformatted for use with a different system. You can format and use the data disk with the IBM system and then reformat and use the same disk with the Apple system. Of course, you lose any information you have deposited on the IBM data disk during the reformatting process. If you try to use the IBM formatted disk in the Apple computer, the following error message appears on the screen: "Unformatted disk". This is the computer's way of telling you that the IBM formatted disk is not compatible with the Apple computer. The same error message appears when you try to use a brand new floppy disk in a computer system without having first formatted it.

It is the responsibility of the user to perform the formatting procedure. Disks are formatted with the operating system by following the instructions outlined in the operating system manual. In general, the user is required to boot the system which loads the operating system into the computer's memory. A formatting command (found in the manual) is then entered into the computer. As an example, the procedure for formatting a floppy disk using DOS is presented below.

In addition to marking the track and sector numbers, the operating system also performs two additional functions during the formatting process. It analyzes the disk for defects and determines any areas that are not acceptable for storing data. Detection of a defect causes a message to appear on the screen indicating that a portion of the disk is damaged. It is best to retire such a disk to avoid problems later on. The operating system also creates a directory area on the disk during the formatting process. A *directory* is a special area on the disk, similar to a table-of-contents, where the name and location of items (e.g., programs and data) are stored. The computer uses the directory to locate the items stored on the disk.

Formatting a Floppy Disk with DOS

The following procedure is used to format a floppy disk with DOS using an IBM computer with two floppy disk drives (and no hard drive).

1. Complete a label for the floppy disk and attach it to the disk jacket (e.g., WordPerfect Data Disk). If you are going to use an old disk, make sure that it does not contain any data you might need later on since all existing data on the disk will be erased.

2. Load DOS and wait for the date and time prompts to appear on the screen.

3. Respond to the date and time prompts and press the Enter key.

4. Wait for the system prompt (A>) to appear on the screen.

5. Enter the following FORMAT command at the system prompt:
   (A>) **format b:**
   (By entering this command, you are telling DOS to format the disk in drive B).

6. Press the Enter key to indicate that you want DOS to accept the command and carry it out.

7. The following message is displayed on the screen:
Insert new diskette for drive B:
and strike any key when ready

8. Insert the floppy disk drive B.

9. Strike any key.

10. The indicator light of the disk drive comes on and the following message is displayed:
Formatting. . . .
(This indicates the formatting process is taking place. Formatting a floppy disk takes approximately one minute).

11. When the formatting process is complete, the indicator light goes out and the following message appears:
Format complete.
Format another (Y/N)?

12. Press "N" or "n" (for "No") and press the Enter key to terminate the FORMAT command. (Note: To format another disk, you would press "Y" or "y" for "yes").

13. The system prompt (A>) appears on the screen indicating DOS is waiting for its next command.

14. Remove the disks from the disk drives. The formatted disk can now be used to store data with an application program. Once you begin using a data disk with an application program, it can be used only with that program. For example, a WordPerfect data disk can only be used with the WordPerfect application program. If you try to store data on it with another program (e.g., WordStar), an error message is displayed on the screen.

Backup Copy

A *backup copy* is a duplicate of a program or data kept for reference in case the original is damaged, lost, or destroyed. When working with a microcomputer, backup copies of important programs and data should always be made and stored in a safe place that is physically remote from the computer system.

Magnetic tape is frequently used to make a backup copy of the entire contents of a hard disk, as it is often impractical to use floppy disks for this task. Floppy disks are used to make backup copies of a) program disks, data disks and operating system disks and b) hard disks when only selected items need to be backed up (e.g., a term paper, a resume).

Once a backup copy has been made on a magnetic tape or floppy disk, the computer conducts a verifying process. During the verifying process, the computer reads back the data that was copied onto the backup medium to make sure it was copied correctly. This process is very important because, if the backup cannot be read, it will be useless if you ever need to recover data lost from the original. Should the verifying process fail, the backup procedure must be repeated from the beginning using a new backup medium.

Hard Disk Backup

The process of copying the data stored on your hard disk to another medium is known as *backing-up the disk.* Failure to backup the disk can spell disaster. Imagine, for example, the following: Your office has a computer system with an 80 MB hard disk. Included on the disk are 5,000 patient records, thousands of diagnosis and procedure codes, and a wealth of data on patient appointments and transactions. An electrician is rewiring your office building and a nail is accidentally driven through your main power cable, causing the entire computer system to go down. A computer repairman is called in and discovers that the electric failure has caused irreparable damage to the hard drive. Unfortunately, the office manager is not computer literate and has not been backing-up the hard disk. The result is that *all data* previously stored on the disk must be re-entered from written records (if even available). In computer terminology, this is known as a *computer nightmare*!

In the medical office, magnetic tape is commonly used to make a complete back-up of the contents of a hard disk. A backup copy of the hard disk should be made at the end of each working day. The magnetic tape should be labeled with a description of its contents and the date it was recorded. If more than one tape is used in making the backup, each should be numbered to indicate the sequence along with the total number in that set (e.g., 1 of 2; 2 of 2). It is important to document that the back-up is performed each day through the use of a log-book which is dated and initialed by the staff member completing the back-up procedure. In this way, if a problem arises with your computer, you will know exactly when the last backup was performed. In the event that the hard disk is damaged or destroyed, the backup copy can be re-loaded onto a new hard drive.

Backup copies should always be stored in a cool, dry place, away from electromagnetic fields. Most offices accomplish this by having the physician or a medical staff member take the magnetic tape home. It is not recommended that the tape be placed in a fire-proof safe in the office as the heat from a fire could irreparably damage the magnetic tape.

Floppy Disk Backup Copy

Because the magnetic material on a floppy disk is extremely vulnerable to damage and wear, backup copies should always be made of program disks, data disks, and operating system disks. The backup copy provides protection should something happen to the original disk. Most manufacturers of application programs permit the user to make a backup copy of the program disk. It is recommended that this be done as soon as the program is obtained. The original should be kept in a safe place and the backup used as the "working copy" for everyday operations. This saves the original to make more backup copies as they are needed.

Backup copies of data disks should be made as an ongoing process to include the latest data that has been stored on the disk. The loss of or damage to a data disk is especially critical since the data would all need to be re-entered from written records, if still available.

The original disk should always be write-protected before a backup copy is made. *Write-protect* is a procedure for preventing a disk from being written to. Once performed, the computer cannot a) make changes to information on the disk; b) erase any information on the disk; or c) write new information on the disk. The computer can, however, read information from a write-protected disk. Write protection protects the original from being accidentally erased should the user inadvertently insert it into the incorrect disk drive during the copying process.

To write-protect a 5.25-inch floppy disk, the write-protect notch is covered with a rectangular shaped piece of aluminum-like foil with an adhesive backing (Fig. 1-30). This piece of foil is known as a write-protect tab and is supplied with the disk. When you no longer wish to protect the contents of the disk, simply remove the tab, which then allows the disk to be written to. If you have a disk without a notch, this means that the disk is already write-protected and you cannot write information on it.

The write-protect tab is "built-in" on a 3.5-inch floppy disk and is located in the upper right corner of the disk. It consists of a small, sliding plastic square piece that is usually black in color. Write-protection is accomplished by sliding the plastic tab toward the edge of the disk, to expose the small square "window" beneath it. To remove the write-protection, slide the tab away from the edge of the disk to close the window (Fig. 1-31).

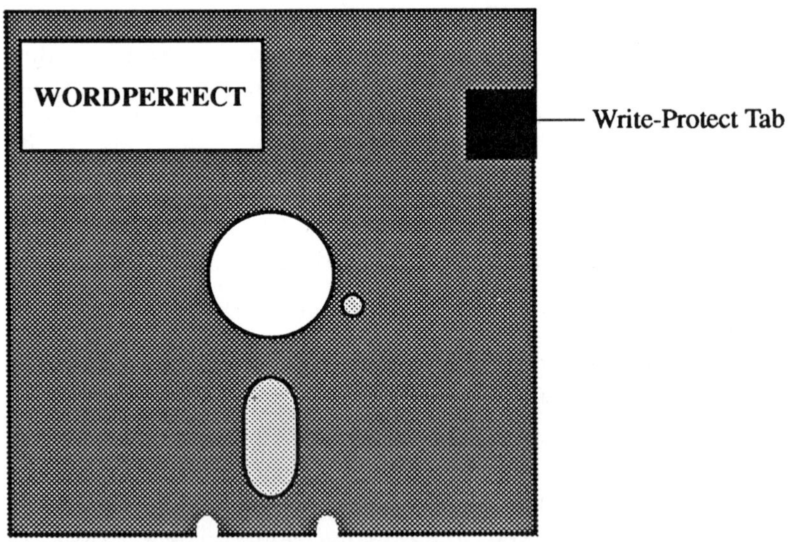

FIGURE 1 - 30. A 5.25-inch floppy disk is write-protected by covering the notch with a write-protect tab.

FIGURE 1 - 31. With a 3.5-inch disk, write-protection is accomplished by sliding the plastic tab toward the edge of the disk to expose the small square opening beneath it. To remove the write-protection, slide the tab away from the edge of the disk to cover the opening.

Backup copies are made using the operating system and following the instructions outlined in the accompanying operating system manual. Most operating systems also automatically format the disk (if needed) during the copying process. The backup copy should be properly labeled with the date and its contents to identify the information on the disk. In addition, the word "Backup" should be indicated on the label.

It is important to store duplicate copies of disks at a site remote from the location of the computer system. In the event of a major catastrophe, such as a fire or flood, this valuable information would still be available on the duplicate copy.

CHECKPOINT

1. Why is it important to properly insert a floppy disk into the disk drive?

   ____

2. How should a 5.25-inch disk be held and why? ______________________________

   ____

3. Why should a disk never be forced into the disk drive?

   ____

4. Why must the door of the disk drive be closed after insertion of the disk?

   ____

5. When is the cold start method used to activate the disk drive?

6. What occurs if the read/write head is not properly aligned with the tracks on a floppy disk? What should be done?

7. Why does the computer perform a power-on self test when it is turned on?

8. What is the purpose of formatting a disk?

9. What happens to any information already on a disk when it is formatted?

10. What would have to be done to use an IBM formatted disk in an Apple computer?

11. Where should you look to find operating system commands?

12. What is a backup copy?

13. What is the purpose of making a backup copy?

14. List three functions served by write-protection.

15. How is a 5.25-inch floppy disk write-protected?

16. How is a 3.5-inch floppy disk write-protected?______________________________

____

____

17. Where should backup copies be stored and why? ___________________________

____

____

CRITICAL LITERACY

Basic Computer Procedures Assignment: Listed below are basic computer procedures. Complete as many of these as possible. Place a check mark next to each one you complete.

________ 1. Insert a 5.25-inch disk into a disk drive.

________ 2. Insert a 3.5-inch disk into a disk drive.

________ 3. Load an application program using a warm start.

________ 4. Load an application program using a cold start.

________ 5. Boot the operating system.

________ 6. Format a floppy disk.

________ 7. Write-protect a 5.25-inch floppy disk.

________ 8. Write-protect a 3.5-inch floppy disk.

________ 9. Make a backup copy of a program disk or a data disk.

2 WORD PROCESSING

CHAPTER OUTLINE

LEARNING OBJECTIVES

After completing this chapter, you should be able to:

1. Define the terms listed in the vocabulary.
2. State the principal advantages of word processing.
3. Identify the hardware and software requirements for word processing.
4. List the four functions performed by all word processing programs.
5. Explain the purpose of the cursor.
6. Describe the following word processing features used to enter text: keystroking, word wrap, cursor movement, caps lock key.
7. Explain the advantages of the text editing function.
8. Describe the function of each of the following editing commands: deletion, insertion, centering, scrolling, block movement, search and replace and spelling checker.
9. Describe the filing functions included in a word processing program.
10. State the purpose of the filename.
11. Define text formatting and explain how documents can be formatted a number of different ways with a word processing program.
12. Describe the following text formatting features: line spacing, margins, justification, automatic pagination, boldface, superscript and subscript.

COMPUTER TERMINOLOGY

block—A group of characters such as a sentence or paragraph.
cursor—A position marker that indicates where the next character entered will be displayed on the screen.
document—Any single piece of writing that you work on, such as a letter, memo, or report. Another name for a document is a file.
edit—To revise the text in a document.
filename—The name you give a document when you create it.
saving (a document)—The process of transferring a copy of the text that has been entered into the computer to a secondary storage device.
text—The words, numbers, and punctuation that make up a word processing document.
text formatting—The arrangement or layout of text on paper.
word processing—The manipulation of words using an electronic device such as a computer.

Introduction

The term *word processing* refers to the process of manipulating words using an electronic device such as a computer. This application is the most common use for microcomputers in both the business and home. Word processing is used in the creation, modification and printing of letters, memos, reports, and other documents. In many respects word processing is similar to typing with a conventional typewriter, however, many functions are available with word processing that are beyond the capability of the typewriter.

The principle advantages of word processing are the rapid and accurate correction of errors and the specialized editing functions not possible with a typewriter (e. g., moving a block of text to another location in the document). Word processing eliminates having to retype the entire document due to errors or having to make carbon copies of a document when an identical form is required.

The hardware required for word processing includes a CPU, monitor, keyboard, and printer. The software requirement is a word processing application program. Examples of commercially available word processing programs include WordPerfect, Microsoft Word and WordStar. Since no two word processing programs are identical, it is important that the user carefully and thoroughly review the program user manual to become completely familiar with its capabilities. In general, all word processing programs perform four basic functions: a) entering text, b) editing text, c) filing text and d) formatting text. Each of these activities is discussed in detail below.

Entering Text

Text consists of the words, numbers, and punctuation that make up a word processing document. Text is entered into the computer using a keyboard. Word processing programs include an *enter mode* which provides the user with a blank screen which serves as a "workspace" for entering text. As the text is typed, it appears on, and begins to fill up the display screen. A position marker, known as a *cursor*, indicates where the

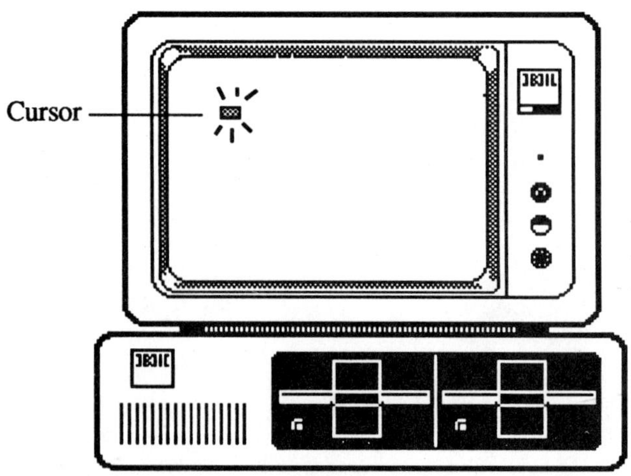

FIGURE 2 - 1. A cursor consists of a blinking rectangle or dash which automatically moves along the line of type as text is entered.

next character entered will be displayed on the screen. The cursor is a blinking rectangle or dash (approximately the width of one character) which automatically moves along the line of type as text is entered (Fig. 2-1).

The procedure for entering text is similar to typing using a standard typewriter. The keyboard of the computer functions almost like the keyboard of the typewriter. There are some variations, however, which are listed and described below.

Keystroking

The touch of the computer keyboard is much softer and smoother than that of an electric typewriter. As a result, less finger pressure is required to depress the keys which generally results in increased typing speed.

Word Wrap

Word wrap is a feature which automatically moves a word to the beginning of the next line if it goes past the right margin. Therefore, if the user is in the middle of a word when the right margin is reached, the entire word along with the cursor will automatically drop down to the beginning of the next line. Word wrap increases typing speed because it eliminates having to press a carriage return at the end of each line as is required with a typewriter.

Cursor Movement

The cursor can be moved to any location on the display screen without erasing or writing over the text. By using cursor movement keys (also called the *arrow keys*), the cursor can be moved one line up or down, and one character left or right with the depression of the appropriate arrow key (Fig. 2-2). For example, depressing the right arrow key moves the cursor one space to the right. If the computer system is equipped with a mouse, it can be used to move the cursor quickly around the screen. Cursor movement facilitates the text editing process, especially the insertion of new text and the correction of errors.

Caps Lock Key

The caps lock key is used to place all of the alphabetic keys into an uppercase position. This key is very similar to a shift-lock key on a typewriter, but with one major difference. The caps lock key affects only the alphabetic keys on the computer keyboard. In order to type a dollar sign or an asterisk, the shift key still must be depressed.

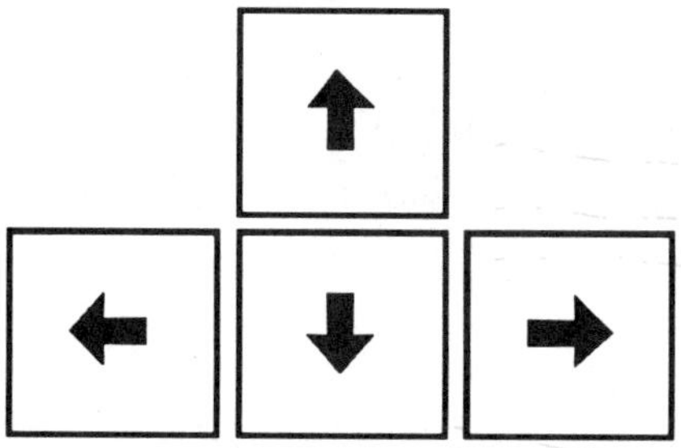

FIGURE 2 - 2. The cursor can be moved to any location on the display screen without erasing or writing over the text using the cursor movement keys, also called the arrow keys.

Editing Text

One of the more valuable functions of word processing is text editing. *Editing* refers to the changing or modifying of text in a document (the insertion or deletion of a word, for example), and in word processing it is accomplished through a series of commands. Although learning the editing commands of a word processing program takes time and effort, it provides a distinct advantage over the conventional method of editing with a typewriter. Specifically, the text can be edited without having to use correction paper or fluid because the corrections are made directly on the display screen rather than on paper. In addition, changes need only be made to that portion of the text requiring them. Therefore, the entire document does not have to be retyped as may be required with typewriter editing, and only that portion of the document that has been changed requires proof-reading because the remainder of the text remains untouched. These features greatly increase the speed and efficiency of text production.

Editing commands, in combination with cursor movement, are used to perform the editing operations of word processing. Cursor movement is used to move the cursor to the proper location on the display screen. The editing command is then activated by depressing a function key which is a special key on the computer keyboard. An example of an editing command would be the deletion of a character from a misspelled word on the display screen. The cursor is first moved to the location of the character to be deleted. The next step involves the depression of the proper function key (usually the Delete key). Depressing this key will result in the deletion of the character from the word and the movement of the remaining characters to the left to fill in the gap caused by the deleted character. The most commonly used editing operations are listed and described below.

Deletion

This is a feature in which a character, word, sentence, paragraph or larger block of text may be removed from the existing text.

Insertion

This is a feature in which a character, word, sentence, paragraph or larger block of text is added to the existing text paragraph. In insert mode, characters that are entered at the cursor location push existing text to the right.

Replacement

With this feature, characters that are entered at the cursor location replace or type over the existing character.

Centering

This is a feature which consists of a command that automatically centers a word or phrase between the margins as it is being entered. This feature eliminates the necessity of having to backspace from the center of a document.

Scrolling

Scrolling refers to the automatic movement of text up or down on the computer screen. Most documents created are too large to be seen in their entirety on the screen of the monitor. At the most, the screen can accommodate 24 to 25 lines of text. Once there is enough text to fill up a screen, the screen then acts as a "window" for viewing a portion

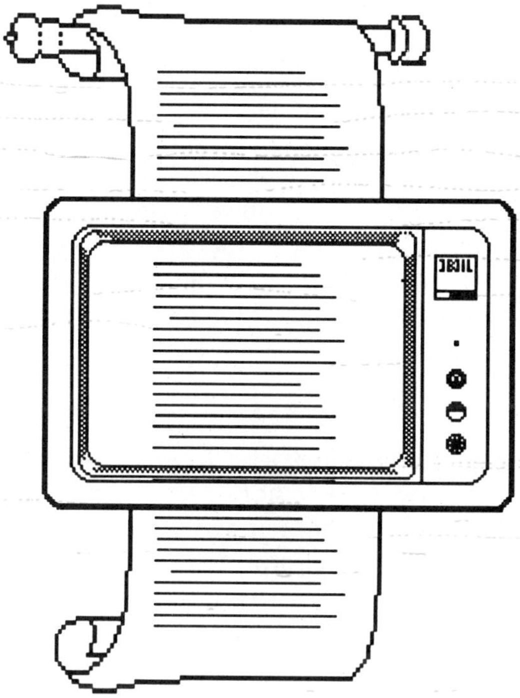

FIGURE 2 - 3. Scrolling is the automatic movement of text up or down on the computer screen. Once there is enough text to fill up a screen, the screen then acts as a "window" for viewing a portion of the document.

of the document (Fig. 2-3). Scrolling provides the mechanism to move the window up or down to view different parts of a document that is too large to fit entirely on the screen. Scrolling the document up moves the text forward toward the beginning of the document, while scrolling the document down moves the text backwards toward the end of the document. The term scrolling is used because this function is similar to that of "rolling out a scroll". Scrolling is used to move through the document at a rapid rate when performing text editing functions to different portions of the document.

Block Action

A *block* is a group of characters such as a sentence or paragraph. Block action is a feature which allows the user to select a block of text and then perform a specific operation on the entire block. Commonly performed block actions include moving a block of text, copying a block of text, saving a block of text, and deleting a block of text from a document. With this feature, for example, a block of text can be copied and moved to a different location in the document or to an entirely different document.

Search and Replace

A feature which allows the user to locate a designated word or short phrase throughout an entire document and automatically change it if desired. This feature is useful when a word used frequently in a document is misspelled, when it is necessary to change a frequently used word to another word, or when a word has been used too often.

Spelling Checker

A spelling checker is used to detect possible spelling mistakes in a document by comparing each word in the document with the list of words in its dictionary. When a word is found that does not match any of the words in the dictionary, the word is highlighted. The user then decides whether or not to change the word. Most spelling checkers are able to display a list of possible suggestions to assist in locating the correct word. One disadvantage of spelling checkers is that they are unable to spot words that are used incorrectly in context. For example, if you type the word *patent* for *patient*, the spelling checker will not detect the error since *patent* is spelled correctly. In addition, a spelling checker does not include proper names in its dictionary.

Filing Text

Filing forms the basis of many of the unique features of word processing programs. Without this capability, it would not be possible to edit text or format text for printing. Filing functions include the storage and retrieval of documents from a secondary storage device such as a floppy disk or a hard disk. The specific procedures for saving, retrieving, and revising a document are outlined in the program user manual.

Storing or *saving* a document is the process of transferring a copy of the text that has been entered into the computer to a secondary storage device. Saving a document can be compared to placing that document in a file folder and storing it in a filing cabinet.

As previously discussed in Chapter 1, text entered into the computer is placed into the computer's memory (RAM) for temporary storage. Therefore, it is important to save a document before turning off the computer because the removal of power will result in the loss of the document. When working on a large document, it is recommended that the text be saved periodically (e.g., every 15 minutes) to prevent the loss of the entire document in the event of a power failure.

Before a document can be saved, it must be assigned a *filename*. The filename is used for later retrieval of the document from the disk. The filename should be short, but descriptive of the document that is being saved. The maximum number of characters that can be used for a filename generally ranges between eight and fifteen based on the application program being used. Each document must be assigned its own unique name. A filename that has previously been assigned to another document stored on the disk cannot be used because the computer would have difficulty in properly retrieving the documents. Therefore, if you want to store several versions of the same document, you will have to save each with a different filename. An ongoing, updated catalog of the filenames is stored along with the documents on the disk. The application program permits the display of this catalog, consisting of the list of filenames, to assist the user in retrieving a stored document.

Stored documents can later be retrieved for text editing functions and/or printing the document. When an edited document is saved again under the same filename, the revised document replaces the one previously stored on the disk.

Formatting Text

Text formatting is the arrangement or layout of the text on paper; in other words, how it will appear as printed text. Text entering and printing are two separate functions in word processing. This is in contrast to the typewriter in which these functions occur simultaneously, and the format is integrated as the document is being typed. Because of this separation in word processing, a document can be formatted a number of different ways by simply changing the formatting instructions. For example, if a document has been printed using single spacing, and the user desires the same document in a double-spaced format, the line spacing value can be changed from single- to double-spacing without having to retype the document. Formatting options included in most word processing programs are listed and described on the following page.

Line Spacing

Line spacing refers to the amount of empty space between printed lines. Word processing programs can produce single-spaced, double-spaced, and triple-spaced documents.

Margins

This feature allows you to select how much of a margin you want between your text and the edge of the paper.

Justification

This is a feature for making lines of text even at the left and right margins. Justification provides margin columns of even width like those of textbook print, rather than a "ragged" right edge.

Automatic Pagination

This is a feature which automatically numbers the pages of the printed document. Most word processing programs also allow the user to select the position of the number on the page (e.g., top, bottom).

Boldface

Boldface is a type in which the main strokes of the letter are thicker than normal.

Superscript

This is a feature which allows a character to be printed half a line above the usual text baseline.

Subscript

This is a feature which allows a character to be printed half a line below the usual text baseline.

Home Work 92-93

CHECKPOINT

1. Define word processing. ______________________________

____

____

2. List two advantages of word processing. ______________________________

____

____

3. What is the term given to the words, numbers and punctuation making up a word processing document?

____

4. What is the purpose of the enter mode? ______________________________

____

____

5. What is the term given to the screen position marker?

____

6. How does keystroking on a computer keyboard compare with that of a typewriter?

____

____

7. How does word wrap increase typing speed? ______________________________

____

____

8. Which key would you use to perform the following?

   a. Move the cursor one space to the right: ______________________________

   b. Move the cursor one space to the left: ______________________________

   c. Move the cursor one line up: ______________________________

   d. Move the cursor one line down: ______________________________

9. What are two advantages of editing text with a word processing program?

____

____

10. What is the term used to describe the automatic movement of text up or down on the computer screen?

____

11. List two operations that can be performed on a block of text.

____

____

12. What is the purpose of the search and replace option? ________________

____

____

13. List two disadvantages of a spelling checker. ________________

____

____

14. Why is it important to save a document before turning off the computer?

____

____

15. What is the purpose of the filename? ________________

____

____

16. How do you save several versions of the same document?

____

____

17. What is the purpose of the catalog of filenames? ________________

____

____

18. What is the term used to describe the arrangement or layout of text on paper?

____

19. What is the name of the formatting feature which makes lines even at the right and left margins?

____

20. Which option would you use to change a document from single- to double-spacing?

____

CRITICAL LITERACY

Word Processing Assignment: You have just entered a five page patient instruction manual into your computer system using a word processing program. You now want to perform the tasks listed below. From the list of word processing options, select the one which will accomplish each task and place the corresponding letter in the space provided.

Word Processing Options:

A. Word Wrap
B. Cursor Movement
C. Deletion
D. Insertion
E. Scrolling
F. Block Action
G. Search and Replace
H. Spelling Checker
I. Save
J. Retrieve
K. Line Spacing
L. Margins
M. Justification
N. Automatic Pagination
O. Boldface

Tasks:

__________ 1. Store the document on a data disk.

__________ 2. Number the pages of the document.

__________ 3. Check for misspelled words.

__________ 4. Remove a sentence from the last paragraph.

__________ 5. Look for the word *doctor* and change it to *physician* throughout the entire document.

__________ 6. Move a paragraph from the beginning to the end of the document.

__________ 7. Add a sentence to the first paragraph.

__________ 8. Place the title of the document in dark letters.

__________ 9. Change the spacing of the document from double-spacing to single-spacing.

__________ 10. Move quickly from the first page of the document to the second page.

__________ 11. Give the right margin of the document an even edge, rather than a "ragged" edge.

3 MEDICAL OFFICE MANAGEMENT APPLICATIONS

CHAPTER OUTLINE

LEARNING OBJECTIVES

After completing this chapter, you should be able to:

1. Define the terms listed in Computer Terminology.
2. State the prerequisite knowledge necessary to perform administrative procedures on a computer.
3. List and explain the advantages and disadvantages of front office computerization.
4. Explain the purpose of a medical office management software program.
5. Identify the criteria to take into consideration in the selection of a medical office management application program.
6. Explain the purpose of the program user manual.
7. Explain what task is performed by each of the following medical office management systems: patient registration, posting transactions, appointments, patient billing, insurance billing, reports, and file maintenance.
8. Describe a multiuser computer system and explain the advantages of such a system.
9. Explain the function of the following applications: word processing, spreadsheets, communications, database management.
10. Define a database.
11. List and describe the advantages of a database.
12. Identify the information included in a medical practice database.
13. Explain the difference between a field, record, and file.
14. Explain what is meant by a menu-driven software program.
15. Explain the difference between a main menu and a submenu.
16. Explain the purpose of a menu screen and a data entry screen.
17. List the guidelines to follow when entering data into the computer.

COMPUTER TERMINOLOGY

alpha-numeric field—A field which allows the entry of both letters and numbers including special characters.

data entry—The input of data into the computer.

data entry screen—A screen used to enter data into the computer.

data field (field)—A single item of information (example: Name). A field consists of a title followed by a space for entering the data.

database—A large collection of data organized in a manner which allows for retrieval and use of that data.

database management—The task of storing data in a database and retrieving information from that data.

documentation—A written set of instructions accompanying an application program, designed to assist the user in understanding how to operate the program. Examples include the user manual, help screens and reference cards.

file—A complete collection of records (example: patient registration file).

main menu—A menu which lists the primary functions performed by an application program.

medical office management software program—A program which provides instructions to the computer for performing medical office management procedures. (Also termed medical management program).

menu—A list of the tasks or functions which can be performed by an application program. The user selects the function desired from this list of choices.

menu screen—A type of screen which displays a menu. Menu screens are used to move from one part of an application program to another.

multiuser computer system—A computer system consisting of one CPU that is shared by two or more terminals. In a multiuser system, one or more terminals can be used at the same time and these terminals can be doing different tasks simultaneously.

numeric field—A field which only allows the entry of digits and special characters associated with digits.

record—A set of fields pertaining to the same thing (example: patient registration record).

screen—Information displayed on the computer monitor.

source document—An original document from which data is extracted for input into the computer.

submenu—A menu which further defines a function listed in the main menu. A submenu lists the specific tasks that can be performed within each main menu option.

terminal—An input-output device consisting of a monitor and a keyboard.

user manual (program)—A manual that describes how to use an application program.

Introduction

Medical office management applications is the process of using computer knowledge to perform medical office administrative procedures on the computer. With the advent of the microcomputer, most medical offices now use a computer to perform administrative procedures which were previously performed manually. This in turn has increased the demand for qualified individuals trained in medical office management applications, not only to perform the administrative tasks on the computer but also to instruct other staff members in computer operation.

This chapter is designed as an introduction to medical office computer applications and is divided into three sections:

Computerizing the Front Office
Computer Applications
Medical Office Management Application Procedures

Each of these sections builds upon the next to provide you with the information necessary to work confidently with a medical management program as well as to complete the simulated medical office management program presented in Chapters 4 through 10.

COMPUTERIZING THE FRONT OFFICE

Computerizing the front office often leads to significant changes in the way administrative procedures are performed in the medical office. When the physician and staff first begin to consider taking this step, questions often arise regarding both the use of the computer and the tasks it can perform. Among the questions most frequently asked are:

1. What prerequisite knowledge is required to perform medical office management procedures on a computer?

2. What are the advantages and disadvantages of computerizing the front office?

3. What is a medical office management software program?

4. What tasks are performed by medical office management software programs?

5. What is a multiuser computer system?

This section addresses these questions, providing both explanations and examples. After acquiring this information, you will have a good understanding of what is required to computerize the front office including the implications of taking this step.

Prerequisite Knowledge for Computer Operation

Before beginning to work with a computer and medical management program, it is important to first acquire a thorough knowledge of computer concepts. Just as medical terminology is a necessary prerequisite to clinical procedure courses, a knowledge of computer concepts is necessary to effectively operate a computer system in the front office. The benefits include increased confidence and ease when working on the computer, and the ability to understand the computer terminology presented in the program user manual. Furthermore, a computer concepts base helps you to communicate better with computer software specialists such as the technical support staff for your medical management program. Working with technical support is often necessary when first learning the medical management program or when a problem is encountered with the program.

To acquire this base, Chapter 1 of this text provides a complete presentation of computer concepts. Make sure you thoroughly understand this information before proceeding with the remaining chapters.

Advantages and Disadvantages

Computers are often promoted as being the solution to all medical office management problems. While there are distinct advantages to using a computer, it should be realized that there are also some disadvantages which can lead to difficulties. It is important to be aware of these problem areas, so that steps can be taken to either prevent them altogether or to be better prepared for them if they occur. Adequate preparation will result in the least amount of disruption to the efficient running of the front office during the computerization process. The following discussion outlines both advantages and disadvantages of computerizing the front office.

Advantages of Computerization

The advantages of computerizing the front office include the following:

Speed and Productivity: One of the principal advantages of a computer is that it can process a large amount of information quickly. For example: if your physician asks you to compile a list of all the patients in the practice who have diabetes mellitus, accomplishing this task by hand would require considerable time and effort. However, with a computer an inquiry search can be performed in which the computer searches all the patient files and automatically generates a list of patients with diabetes in a fraction of the time.

Billing and health insurance requirements have placed a tremendous burden on the medical office of today. In addition, the completion of insurance claims becomes ever more complicated. Thus, a large portion of front office responsibility is often devoted to preparing and submitting patient statements and insurance claims. Because they are able to prepare and process these items in a short period of time through the use of cross-referencing, computers provide much assistance in this area. In addition, faster computer processing of these items usually leads to better collections for the medical office.

Efficiency: Computers are particularly beneficial in performing repetitive tasks in which information is used over and over again but in a different format. For example, once a patient's name and address has been entered into the computer, it can be used on a number of different forms without having to re-enter it. The computer automatically

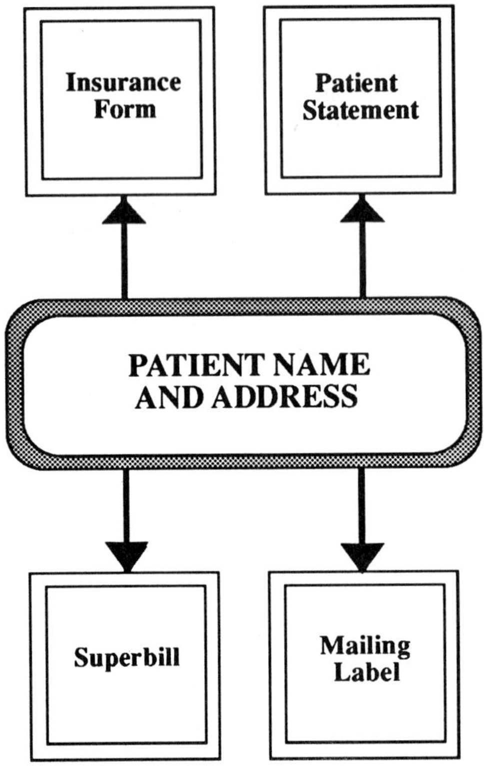

FIGURE 3 - 1. Computers are efficient. Once a patient's name and address has been entered into the computer, it can be used on a number of different forms. The computer automatically transfers the name and address where needed.

transfers this information where needed, based upon the task being performed. The patient's name and address can be automatically transferred by the computer to an insurance form, patient statement, superbill and mailing label depending upon the task being performed (Figure 3-1). Medical management programs also keep track of the status of functions that have been executed in the office, such as submission of insurance claims or delay in payment of a claim.

Accessibility: Once information has been entered into the computer system, it is much easier to retrieve when needed. For example, once patient registration information has been entered, it is quite simple to request registration information on a patient and have it instantly displayed on the screen of the monitor. This avoids having to perform the much more time-consuming task of manually hunting through a filing system to locate this information.

Reduced Costs: After the initial cost of purchasing the hardware and software, computerization of the front office helps to decrease operating costs by reducing the amount of time required to perform front office procedures.

Disadvantages of Computerization

The disadvantages of computerizing the front office include the following:

Initial Cost: An initial investment is required for the purchase of hardware and software. The cost of a medical management program varies considerably from vendor to vendor, while the hardware expense depends upon the complexity of the software, number of terminals, and type and number of printers. The combined expense of these items can easily fall into the thousands of dollars. This is why it is so important to first determine the computer requirements of the medical office before purchasing a computer system. Acquiring a system that does not meet the needs of the office can be a very costly mistake.

Time Investment: Because medical management programs perform highly sophisticated tasks, it takes considerable time to learn a program and use it with ease. Most software vendors provide on-site training of staff as well as technical support when problems are encountered. Even with all of this assistance, however, the orientation period can easily last a month or more and the complete conversion process can last as long as 6 months to a year. During this time the medical assistant may experience much frustration when difficulty is encountered in executing a task. However, once the initial training period is completed, most individuals agree the time and patience expended are justified by the outcome.

Start-Up Tasks: Certain tasks must be performed before the program becomes operational, or in other words, before it can be used to perform medical office management procedures. Examples of start-up tasks include: a) A list of the procedural and diagnostic codes most frequently used in the office must be entered into the computer system and b) Patient registration records must be set up which includes entering demographic and insurance data on each patient. All start-up tasks must be performed before the program can be used to operate the front office. Because of this, there is a transition period during which front office procedures are still being performed manually, while at the same time the start-up tasks are also being performed. This period is generally hectic as the start-up tasks may add to an already overburdened schedule. However, the start-up data only needs to be entered once. Later on, when the computer system is operational, additional information can be added as needed, although the length of input time is greatly diminished.

Computer System Malfunctions: Even the best hardware and software systems can and will occasionally fail, and one or more of the front office procedures will come to an abrupt halt. Some problems have no explanations, while others are directly related to a specific event, such as operator error, a software "bug", or a hardware malfunction.

Preventative Measures

The disadvantages of computerizing the front office can for the most part be overcome by implementing the preventative measures outlined below.

1. ***Selection of Hardware and Software:*** The hardware and software should be selected from experienced and established vendors. Some medical offices use a consultant to assist with this process. There are some important guidelines that should be followed in the selection of a computer system; a summary of these is presented in Table 3-1.

2. ***Qualified Personnel:*** Individuals working on the computer should be well-trained in computer concepts and applications. This can be accomplished by employing office staff who have graduated from a formal educational program or by having the front office staff attend computer workshops and seminars. Untrained staff can adversely affect and extend the transition period.

3. ***Proper Care and Maintenance of the Computer System:*** There is no doubt that proper care and maintenance of the computer system is directly related to reliable operation of the system. Chapter 1 presents the proper care and maintenance for each component in the computer system. Make sure you thoroughly review this information before working with a computer system. In addition to providing many years of reliable service, a well-cared for system is much less likely to malfunction.

TABLE 3 - 1. Guidelines for the Selection of Hardware and Software

1. Prepare a needs analysis to determine the functions you want the computer to perform in the front office. Choose the computer system based on the capabilities and requirements of the software and not the brand name of the hardware. The software should be selected *first* followed by the selection of the hardware that is able to run that software.

2. Choose reliable and experienced software and hardware companies. Check on the longevity of the company; a company without a strong financial base that has been in business for only a short period of time may go out of business leaving you without hardware or software support.

3. Visit other practice sites that have successfully installed and used the system for at least two years. Because of the complexity of program writing and development, almost all software programs contain "bugs" which are small errors that occur during the developmental process. Systems that have been running for several years are more likely to have successfully overcome these annoying and time-consuming errors. Talk to office personnel to get their candid opinion of the system's strengths and weaknesses.

4. Determine the type of site preparation required to install the system. You may need to hire an electrician to add the appropriate circuits and outlets for the CPU, terminals, and printer. Cables also need to be installed to run from the CPU to the terminals and printer(s).

5. Be sure the software vendor provides on-site training of the staff.

6. Make sure the hardware and software vendors have rapid and reliable local technical support available. The support staff should be helpful, friendly and knowledgeable.

7. Review the program user manual to make sure it is clear and easy to understand. The manual should include illustrations and tables. An index should be included for ease in locating information contained in the manual. On-line help screens should be available to assist new users in learning the program.

8. Make sure the computer system has the capacity for future upgrading and expansion. This avoids being left with an outdated software program and hardware when new advances are being made.

9. Review hardware and software manufacturer warranties thoroughly before purchasing the computer system.

10. Ask the computer vendor about the availability and cost of maintenance contracts. Most computer vendors offer a maintenance contract in which they guarantee that they will respond to a call within a few hours and that any problem will be corrected immediately. Customers with a maintenance contract are given repair priority over customers without such an agreement.

11. Be sure the system can generate insurance claim forms acceptable to the major third-party payers.

12. The accuracy of the computer system should be checked before making the complete conversion. This is accomplished by maintaining records manually as well as on the computer for a three-month period to see if the records compare well. (The concurrent use of the manual and automated methods is known as *running in parallel*.) If inconsistencies are detected while running in parallel, the problem can be corrected before the final conversion takes place.

Medical Office Management Software Programs

Medical office management software programs provide instructions to the computer for performing front office procedures. Just as a construction foreman provides instructions to his workers for erecting a building, medical management programs provide instructions to the computer for running a medical front office. In addition, just as there are different areas of construction specialization (brick mason, electrician, plumber), medical management programs consist of a number of areas of specialization. Each area of specialization is known as a *system,* and each system performs procedures related to its particular area of specialization. Examples of systems included in medical management programs are: patient registration system, posting transactions system, appointment system, patient billing system, insurance billing system, reports system, and file maintenance system (Fig. 3-2).

Each medical management program has specific capabilities which refers to both the systems included in the program and the tasks performed by those systems. Most medical offices use programs that are commercially available through local or regional computer software vendors. Therefore, when selecting a medical management program, it is important to assess the capabilities of each program under consideration. Let's say that (among other things) you want to use the computer to schedule patient appointments. If the program acquired for your office does not have this system, you will be unable to perform this task on the computer.

Areas of Specialization in a Medical Management Program:

1. Patient Registration System
2. Posting Transactions System
3. Appointment System
4. Patient Billing System
5. Insurance Billing System
6. Reports System
7. File Maintenance System

FIGURE 3 - 2. Each area of specialization in a medical management program is known as a system. Each system performs procedures related to its particular area of specialization.

As a general rule, most medical management programs include the same basic systems, but differ more in the features or *options* offered within each system. For example, the appointment system of one program may permit the user to indicate the reason for the patient visit in the printout of the appointment log while another program may not. Or, one program may be able to generate a superbill at the time of the patient visit, while another program may not have this feature. Therefore, it is important to have a knowledge of options available for medical management programs. This information will help you assist your physician in selecting the best program for your medical office.

The medical management program always includes documentation. *Documentation* is a written set of instructions designed to assist the user in understanding how to operate the program. Clear, concise, and easy-to-understand documentation makes it much easier to learn and use the program. Documentation includes the following: a) The program user manual which contains complete instructions for learning and using the program b) On-line help screens displayed on the computer monitor c) Reference cards containing frequently needed details for quick reference.

The selection of medical software should always be based on the specific requirements of your office, or in other words, the specific tasks that need to be performed in the front office. Before purchasing a medical management program, it is important to analyze these requirements and then identify a program which performs these tasks easily and efficiently. Listed below are the systems available for medical management programs and the tasks performed by each.

Patient Registration System

The patient registration system is used to set up a registration record for each patient in the medical practice. The patient registration record includes demographic and insurance information such as the patient's name and address, telephone number, sex, date of birth, social security number, the patient's insurance carrier, policy number, and group number. This system is also used to review and update information on existing registration records. For example, if the patient's address changes, this system is used to delete the old address and enter the new address. Information entered into the patient registration file is used for a number of procedures such as preparing a new patient's chart, posting transactions, and processing patient statements and insurance claims.

Posting Transactions System

When a patient has been seen by the physician, the medical assistant must post the charges of the office visit and any payments made by the patient. The posting transactions system is responsible for performing this task. This system lets you enter charges for all the services and procedures performed for a patient. In addition, it also permits you to post payments made by the patient or a third-party payer. In most programs, this system lets you print out a "walk-away" hardcopy for the patient of one or more of the following: superbill, patient statement, or insurance claim.

Appointment System

The appointment system handles all procedures related to appointment scheduling. These include making an appointment, canceling an appointment, finding an appointment, printing an appointment log, and printing a patient reminder card. Currently, many medical offices prefer to use an appointment book for patient scheduling rather than the computer. Even though the computer is faster, the medical office staff usually prefer to have a written record of appointments available rather than storing this information in the computer system.

Patient Billing System

One of the most important tasks required for the effective functioning of a medical office is to ensure prompt payment of patient bills. The function of the patient billing system is to prepare bills and print billing statements. When patient charges and payments are posted, this information is stored in the computer and is available when needed by the patient billing system. This system is responsible for searching the medical practice database to obtain the information necessary to generate bills for patients with outstanding balances.

Insurance Billing System

The function of the insurance billing system is to prepare and generate insurance claims. As procedures and diagnoses are entered into the computer during posting transactions, they are stored in the medical practice database. Later on, this information is available when needed to prepare insurance claims. From the information stored in the database, the computer is able to automatically fill out every major portion of the claim form.

Reports System

The function of the reports system is to generate a variety of reports for the medical practice. The information contained in the reports is accessed by the computer from the medical practice database. These reports allow the physician to review and analyze many business and practice activities.

File Maintenance System

Before a medical office management program becomes operational, or in other words, before you can start performing front office procedures on the computer, a number of start-up tasks must be performed in the file maintenance system. These tasks are required in order to customize the program to meet the specific requirements of your medical office and include entering practice information, assigning user passwords, entering provider information, entering diagnosis and procedure codes, entering insurance carriers, entering place of service information, and entering referring physicians into the computer system.

Multiuser Computer System

Frequently more than one person needs to perform a task on the computer at the same time. This would not be possible if the computer system consisted of only one CPU, one monitor and one keyboard. To alleviate this problem at the lowest possible cost, most medical offices purchase a multiuser computer system. A multiuser system consists of a computer with a large memory capacity and a hard disk. Attached to the CPU by cables are two or more terminals. Each terminal consists of a monitor and keyboard and communicates directly with the CPU (Fig. 3-3). Thus, with a multiuser computer system, more than one terminal can be used at the same time and each of these terminals can be doing different tasks. For example, one person can look up patient data at one terminal, while another is processing insurance claims at a second terminal, and still another can be transcribing at a third terminal. All of these tasks are processed by the same CPU sharing the same program.

The number of terminals depends on the size of the practice, the physical lay-out of the medical office, and the type of procedures performed on the computer. For example, as many as four or more terminals may be required in a clinic performing all of its front

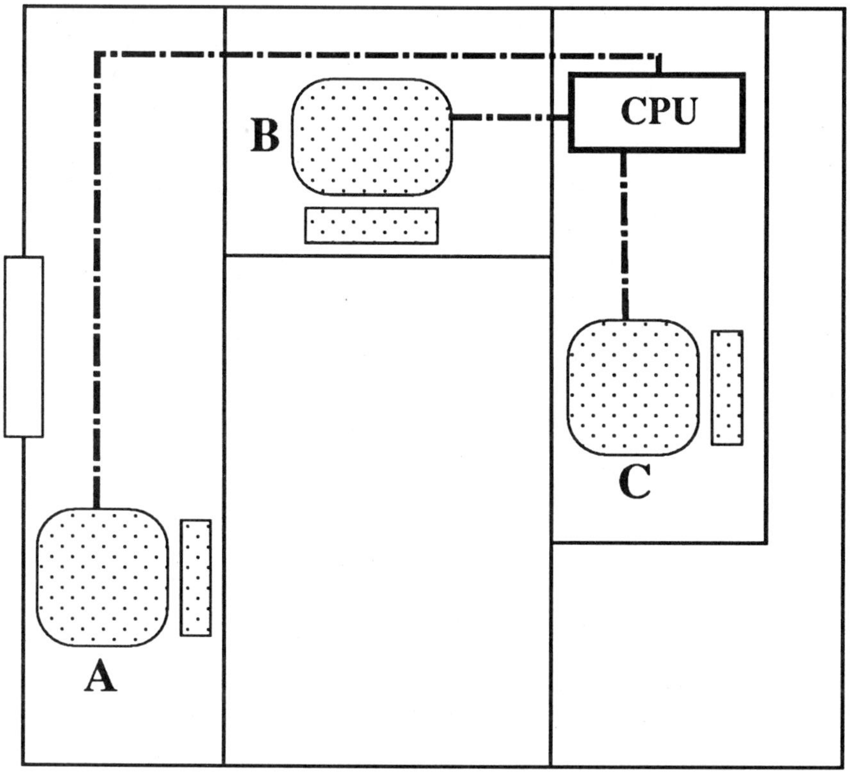

Use of the Terminals:

Terminal A: New patient registration, appointment scheduling, posting patient charges and payments.

Terminal B: Word processing and generating reports.

Terminal C: Posting payments received in the mail, processing patient statements, processing insurance claims.

FIGURE 3 - 3. Multiuser Computer System. With a multiuser computer system, more than one terminal can be used at the same time to perform different tasks as shown in the above example.

office procedures on the computer. On the other hand, two terminals may easily serve the needs of a single-physician office using the computer to perform only patient transaction, billing and word processing functions.

The terminals should be located so as to correspond with the major functions for which they are used. Some of these functions may be combined in one work area (e.g., processing insurance claims) or spread among several (e.g., looking up patient data). Refer again to Fig. 3-3 for an illustration of a multiuser system. In this example, one terminal is conveniently located in the receptionist's area. This terminal is used for new patient registration, making appointments and posting patient charges and payments. Another terminal is located in the back of the front office and is used for word processing and generating reports for the medical practice. A third terminal is located in a room adjacent to the front office and is used for posting payments received in the mail and processing patient statements and insurance claims.

The location of the CPU is not as crucial as the location of the terminals. Except when turning the computer on and off and doing backups, you do not need to have access to the CPU itself. Hence, the CPU can be placed in an out-of-the-way location. The only limitations in the placement of the CPU are cable length to the terminals, environmental factors such as temperature and humidity and adequate electric service.

The number of printers used with a multiuser computer system depends on the type and volume of printed output. Because of the time involved in loading and aligning paper in a printer, it is not practical to change forms throughout the day. Therefore if you regularly want to use two different forms during the day (e.g., superbills and insurance claims), your computer system should have more than one printer. For efficiency, it is best to locate the printer near the user (Fig. 3-4). In addition enough space should be made available around the printer for storing the paper and for changing paper and forms.

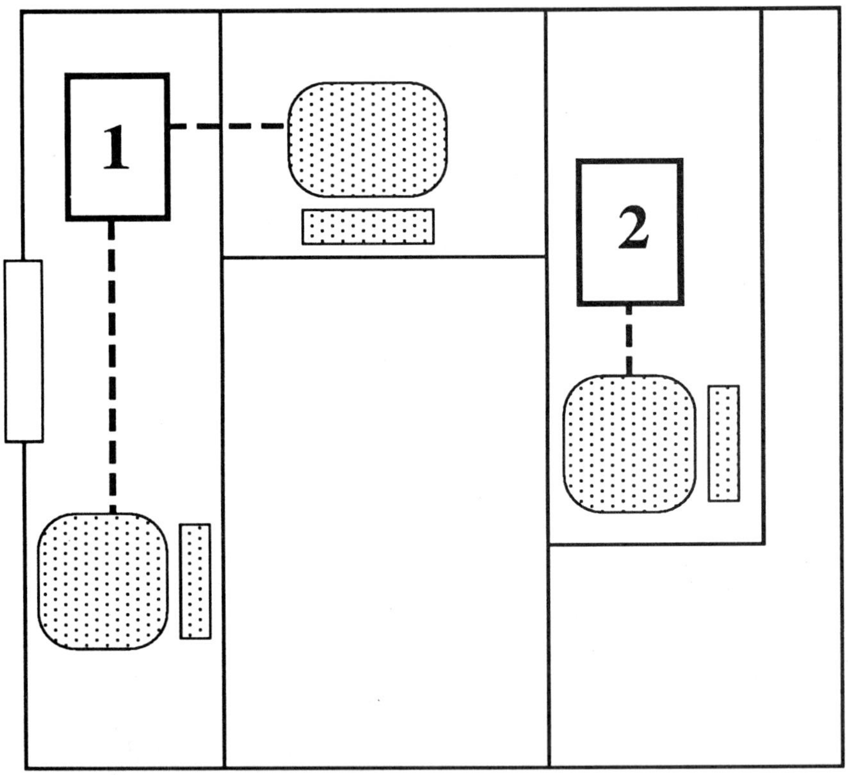

Use of the Printers:

Printer 1: Appointment log, medical histories, reports.

Printer 2: Patient statements and insurance claims.

FIGURE 3 - 4. The number of printers used with a multiuser computer system depends on the type and volume of printed output.

CHECKPOINT

1. List three important reasons for acquiring a computer concepts base before working with a computer system.

2. What are two advantages of computerization of the front medical office?

3. What are two disadvantages of computerization of the front medical office?

4. What is the purpose of the program user manual?

5. What functions are performed by the patient registration system?

6. What functions are performed by the posting transactions system?

7. What functions are performed by the patient billing system?

8. What functions are performed by the insurance billing system?

9. What functions are performed by the reports system?

10. What functions are performed by the file maintenance system?

11. What is a multiuser computer system?

12. Where should the terminals be located with a multiuser computer system?

13. List two instances of when you need access to the CPU in a multiuser system.

14. Where should the printer(s) be located in the office?

CRITICAL LITERACY

Computerizing the Front Office Assignment: You are employed in a clinic which has just acquired a multiuser computer system. You have been given the responsibility of facilitating the computerization of the front office. Complete the following:

1. Your physician asks you to suggest some ideas for making the transition period less hectic. List your ideas below.

2. Computer Phobia, one of the administrative staff members, is extremely nervous and hesitant to use the computer system and would rather "stick-to-the-old-way" of doing things. Provide some suggestions below which might help her in adjusting to working with a computer.

___

___

___

___

3. During the conversion process, the following situations occur. Using the computer knowledge you acquired in Chapter 1, respond to each according to how you would handle the situation. Explain the rationale for each response.

   a. Computer Phobia indicates that the printer won't work. The last task she performed was to advance the paper using the form-feed control.

   ___

   ___

   ___

   b. A pharmaceutical salesman, eager to see your new computer system, accidentally spills some coffee on the keyboard of one of the terminals.

   ___

   ___

   ___

   c. Computer Phobia would like to place her terminal near a window to obtain brighter lighting.

   ___

   ___

   ___

   d. You notice that someone has placed the cassette tape backup on top of the computer monitor.

   ___

   ___

   ___

   ___

COMPUTER APPLICATIONS

Types of Applications

In the previous section specific systems or areas of specialization included in medical management programs (patient registration, posting transactions, patient billing, and so on) were discussed. These systems rely on four important computer applications which are built into medical software programs and which form the foundation on which the programs work. These applications are word processing, spreadsheets, communications, and database management. Each is listed and described below.

Word Processing

Word processing involves the use of the computer to enter, edit, file and format text. Refer to Chapter 2 for a detailed presentation of word processing. A medical management program uses the word processing application to produce mailing lists, letters, medical histories and reports.

Spreadsheets

A spreadsheet is an electronic ledger designed to perform repetitive calculations quickly. Spreadsheets are used to produce financial reports and to analyze and process statistics. Medical management programs rely on spreadsheets to generate financial reports for the office such as the daily report and the aged accounts receivable report. In addition, spreadsheets are used in the medical office for practice analysis including, for example, printouts of the revenue generated by each physician in the practice or a list of the procedures performed during a specified time period and the total revenue generated by each procedure. By analyzing practice statistics, a physician can identify specific areas needing improvement.

Communications

Communications applications provide the means for one computer to "talk" with another over telephone lines. Electronic communication between computers greatly reduces the time it takes to send information. Medical management programs rely on this application for the electronic submission of insurance claims (Fig. 3-5). In addition, some offices use the communications application to send letters and messages electronically.

Database Management

Database management is the storing and retrieving of data in and from a database. Database management allows the user to store large amounts of data that can be easily retrieved and manipulated. Medical management programs rely heavily on a database to perform the majority of the administrative procedures in the medical office. Database management increases efficiency in record-keeping and eliminates numerous time-consuming repetitive tasks. Because of the importance of database management to a medical management program, the remainder of this section presents a thorough study of the functions served by a database.

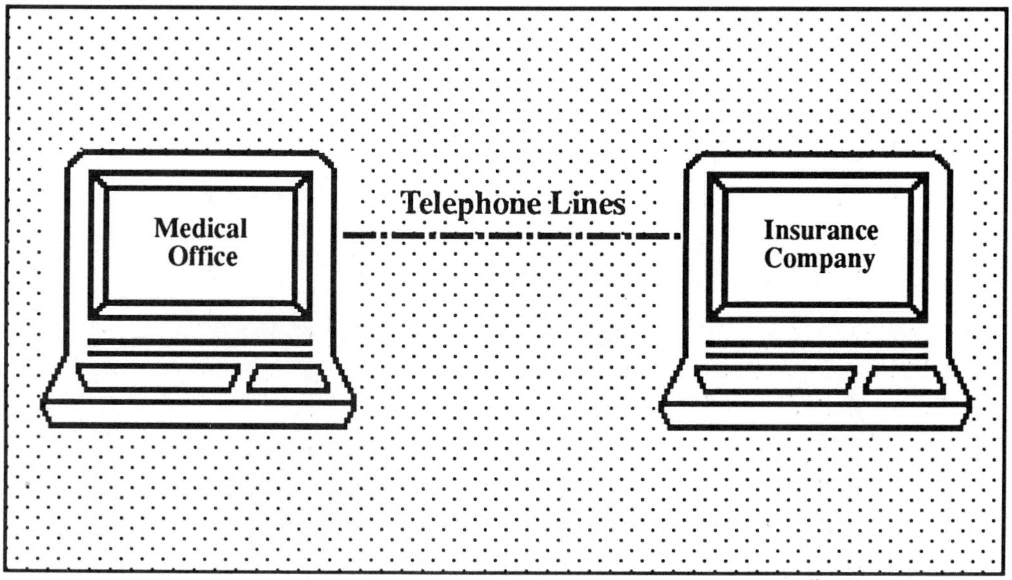

FIGURE 3 - 5. Medical management programs use the communications applications for the electronic submission of insurance claims.

Database

A database is a collection of related data organized in a manner which allows for retrieval and use of that data by anyone needing it. The advantages of using a computer to perform database management tasks are numerous and are described as follows. The computer can do lengthy, often tedious, work much more quickly and accurately than if done by hand. Once information is stored in the computer, it becomes easier for other individuals to retrieve and share the data. Data entered into a database is also easier to keep track of, eliminating the need to locate various notes, folders, memos, and so on. Finally, the computer helps to eliminate the redundancy of maintaining the same information in different types of records stored in different ways, and provides a system of safeguards to guarantee both data integrity and security.

To help you understand why a database is so important to a medical management program, the following comparison is given: Let's say that you are employed by a physician who is just opening a medical practice. When you first begin, your filing cabinets are empty. As the physician builds up the practice, you will be filling these cabinets with file folders of information (patient records) which are organized in a manner to allow for their later retrieval as needed. Comparing this to computer operation, the patient records entered into the computer make up "computerized filing cabinets" (known as a *database* in computer terminology).

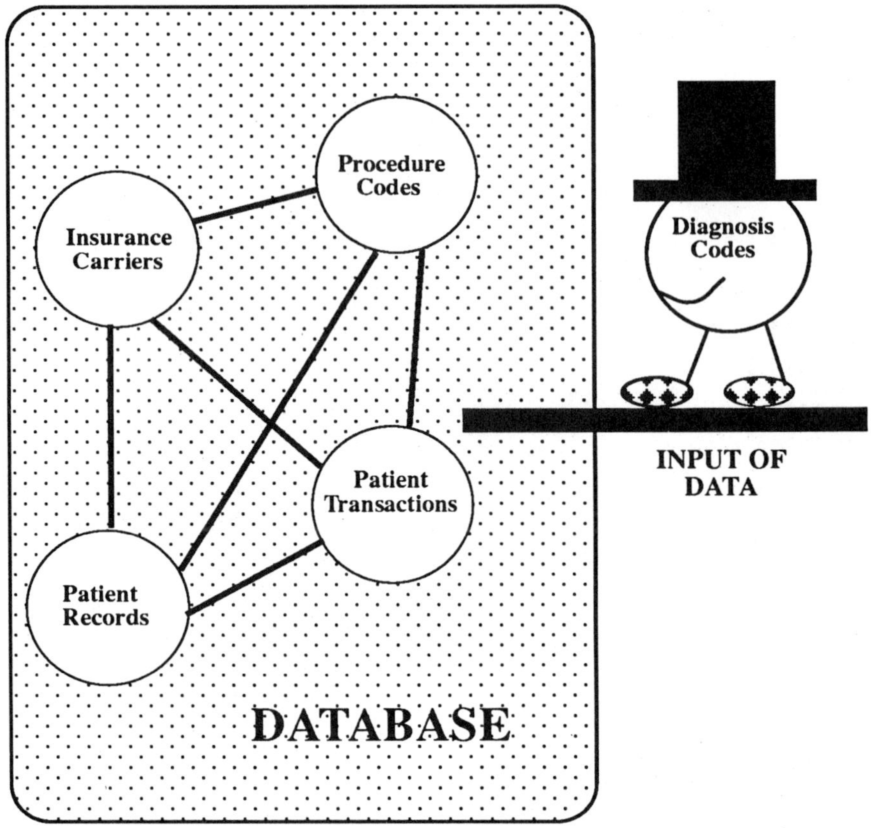

FIGURE 3 - 6. All of the data entered into the computer becomes part of the database. A database is a large "pool" of information that can be accessed in a multitude of ways according to the task being performed.

The main difference between a manual and computerized office, however, is that *all* the data that you enter into your computer becomes part of the database, not just the patient records. In other words, the database for a medical practice consists of patient records, patient transactions, diagnosis codes, procedure codes, insurance carriers, and so on (refer to Fig. 3-6). This information is stored on a hard disk for later retrieval and use as needed. A database also provides the ability to add new information, to modify existing information, and to delete unneeded information. When you need to look up something that has been stored in the database, it is displayed on the same screen that was used for entering the data. In addition, this information can be printed out, as needed, in hardcopy form.

The most significant aspect of a database is that the computer can cross-reference all of the information stored in its database. For example, information can be obtained from a patient registration record and be combined with transaction and insurance carrier information for the batch processing of insurance claims. You should think of your medical practice database as a large pool of information that can be accessed in a multitude of ways according to the task being performed. As you would imagine, a database saves much time and effort in performing medical office management tasks.

Organization of a Database: Fields, Records, and Files

Just as the patient records in a filing cabinet must be organized in such a manner so as to allow for ease in retrieving them when needed (e.g., alphabetically, color-coded), so must a database have a method of organization. If information were haphazardly arranged in a database, it would be very difficult and time-consuming for the computer to locate it when needed. The means of organization used by a computer to arrange data include *fields*, *records* and *files* (Fig. 3-7). These are computer terms often used in the program user manual. They are described in detail in the following paragraphs, starting with the lowest level of data organization (field) and proceeding to the highest level (file).

A *data field*, usually referred to as simply a field, is defined as a single item of information. A field consists of a title followed by a space for entering the data. Refer to Fig. 3-8 which is an illustration of a patient registration data entry screen. As you will note, there are a number of items of information that must be entered into this data entry screen. Each separate item of information makes up one field. Thus, there are seventeen fields on this data entry screen. The first field consists of the Name (title) followed by a space for entering the information.

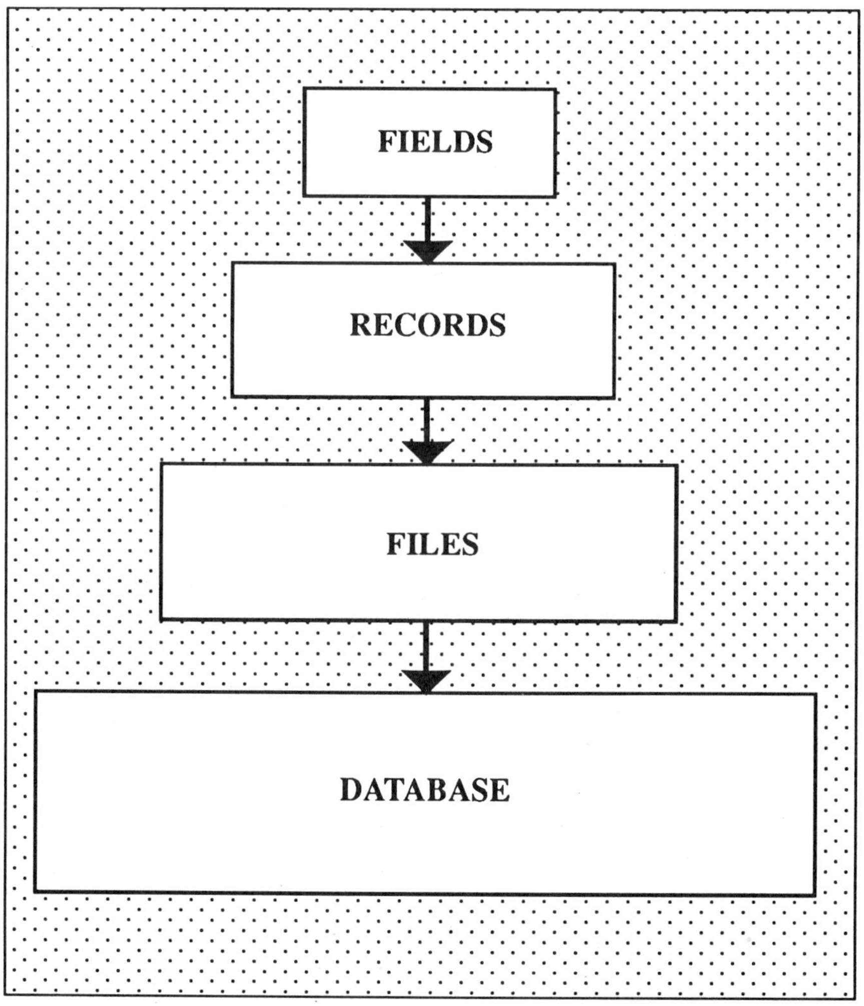

FIGURE 3 - 7. The means of organization used by a computer to arrange data includes fields, records and files.

The next highest level of organization of a database is a record. (Refer to Fig. 3-8 of the patient registration data entry screen.) You are required to complete a patient registration data entry screen for each patient coming to your medical office. Each of these patient registration "forms" is known as a record and consists of the same seventeen fields. Thus, a *record* is defined as a set of related fields pertaining to a general area of information. Let's say that your physician has a client base of 4,000 patients. Once you have completed the task of entering all of the patient registration information, you would have 4,000 patient registration *records* stored in the medical practice database.

The highest level of organization of a database is a file. A *file* is defined as a complete collection of related records. Referring to the above example, the 4,000 patient registration records collectively are known as the *patient registration file*. Additional examples of files which are included in a medical office database are as follows: procedure code file, diagnosis code file, insurance carrier file, and the provider file. As just explained, each of these files consists of records, and each record consists of fields.

Advantages of a Medical Practice Database

In the medical office, database management serves many valuable functions. Because the information in a database can be used for more than one purpose, much time and effort is saved that can be devoted to more demanding responsibilities. Specific examples of the benefits of a medical practice database are discussed below.

The principle advantage of a database is that the computer has the ability to cross-reference all of the information in the database. For example, the information in the patient information file can be used by any part of the medical management program. Let's say that your physician wants you to send a form letter to all his/her patients informing them of a change in location of the office. To type the name and address of each patient on the letter and envelope would require a considerable amount of time. However, with a computer the name and address of each patient is stored in its database, specifically in the patient registration file. The computer accesses the patient registration file and selects the first three fields from each patient registration record (name; address; city, state, and zip code). This information is then transferred to the letters and mailing labels in a much shorter time period. The primary use of cross-referencing is in the batch processing of patient statements and insurance forms and in the generation of status reports.

Another advantage of a database is the ease it offers in updating files. For example, let's say that one of your patients gets married and changes her last name. Using the manual system, a number of records would have to be changed such as the patient's chart, the patient's ledger, and insurance claim information. With database management, the last name would only have to be changed once (in the patient registration file). This not only saves as great deal of time, but also eliminates the possibility of overlooking a place where the change should occur.

With database management, the computer can quickly and easily access any information stored in its database. This avoids having to hunt through written documents to locate necessary information. For example, if you need to look up a patient's social security number, you can quickly access this information from the database without having to pull the patient's chart from the filing cabinet.

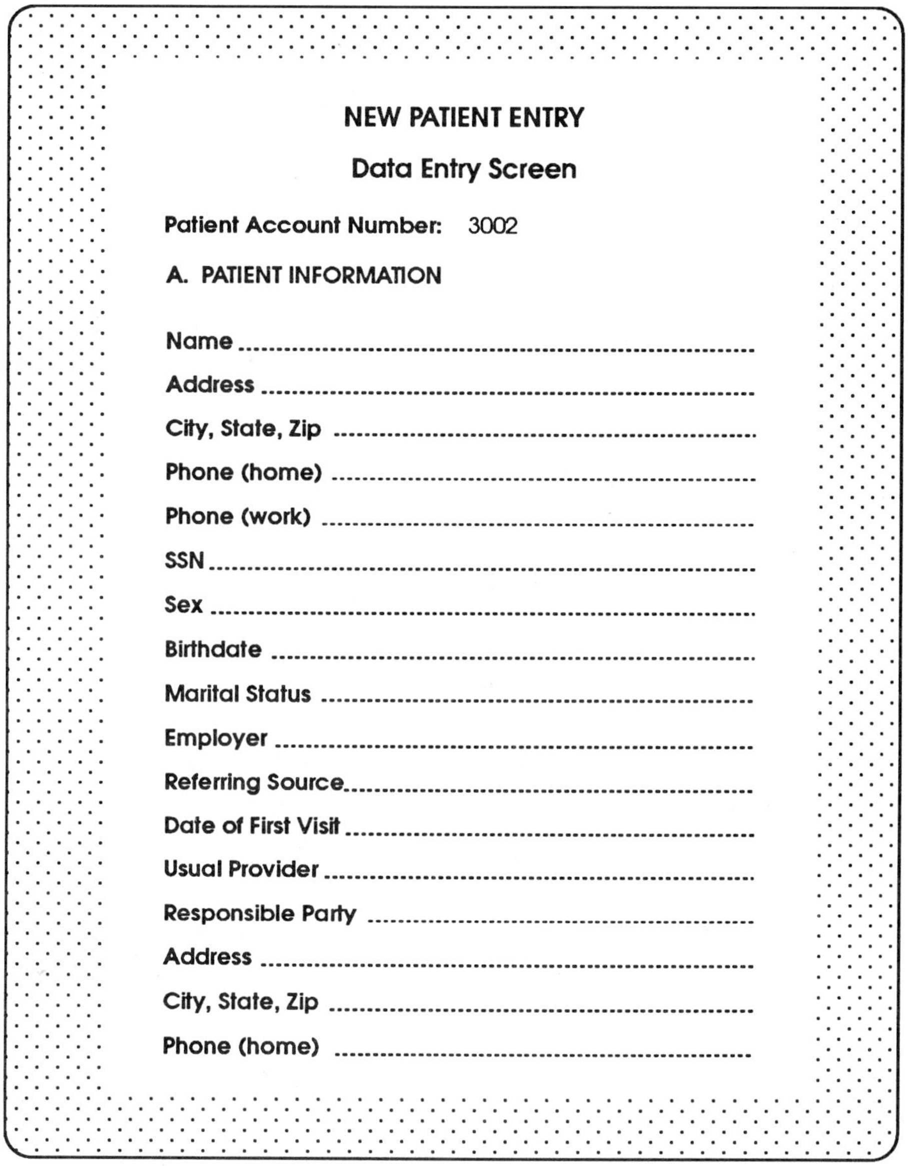

NEW PATIENT ENTRY

Data Entry Screen

Patient Account Number: 3002

A. PATIENT INFORMATION

Name ....

Address ....

City, State, Zip ....

Phone (home) ....

Phone (work) ....

SSN ....

Sex ....

Birthdate ....

Marital Status ....

Employer ....

Referring Source ....

Date of First Visit ....

Usual Provider ....

Responsible Party ....

Address ....

City, State, Zip ....

Phone (home) ....

FIGURE 3 - 8. Patient Registration data entry screen. Each separate item of information (e.g., Name) makes up one data field. Each of these patient registration "forms" is known as a record.

CHECKPOINT

1. List and describe the four applications that form the foundation of medical management programs.

____

____

____

____

2. What is a database? ______________________________

____

____

3. What functions can be performed on the information in a database?

____

____

4. What is the most significant aspect of a database? ______________________________

____

____

5. What is a field? ______________________________

____

6. What is a record? ______________________________

____

7. What is a file? ______________________________

____

CRITICAL LITERACY

Medical Office Management Applications Assignment: Listed below are functions performed by medical management programs. Determine which of the following applications is being used to perform each task and indicate this information in the space provided: word processing, spreadsheets, communications, database management.

1. Typing a patient referral letter.

   ____

2. Finding the next available time for scheduling a patient appointment.

   ____

3. Generating an aged accounts receivable report.

   ____

4. Typing a medical history.

   ____

5. Looking up the CPT code for an ear irrigation.

   ____

6. Submitting insurance claims electronically across the phone lines.

   ____

7. Looking up the address of Paul Gleason.

   ____

8. Generating a report which indicates the revenue generated by each physician in the practice.

   ____

9. Sending an ECG across the telephone lines for means of interpretation.

   ____

MEDICAL OFFICE MANAGEMENT APPLICATION PROCEDURES

Before working with a medical management program, it is important to have knowledge of the following: a) the mechanism used to move from one part of the program to another, b) the completion of a data entry screen and c) guidelines for entering data. This section presents a thorough discussion of these areas and also provides examples and illustrations to facilitate your understanding of each area. Once you have completed this section, you are ready to begin working on the *Medical Practice Manager Simulated Program* presented in Chapters 4 through 10.

Menu Selection

A medical management program must have a mechanism by which the user can move from one part of the program to another, in other words from one system to another. For example, let's say that you need to enter charges for a patient who has just been seen by the physician, and then make a return appointment for that patient. In this case, you would first go to the posting transactions system to post the charges, and from there you would go to the appointment system to schedule the return visit. Most programs use a menu as the means of moving from one system to another. Using computer terminology, such a program is described as being *menu-driven*.

A *menu* is a list of the tasks or functions which can be performed by the program. The user selects the function he/she wants to execute from the list of available alternatives. In simpler terms, a menu is a list from which you select what to do next. Menus assist the user in moving from one function to another without having to memorize a lot of commands. By looking at the menu, all of the selections available can be seen.

Refer to Fig. 3-9 for an illustration of a menu. As you will note, this menu lists the specific tasks that can be performed. In order to perform a particular task, it must first be selected from the menu. Making a menu selection can be accomplished in a number of ways. First, a selection can be made by typing the number or letter that corresponds to the function to be performed. For example, in Fig. 3-9, to select the patient registration function by number, you would type in the number "1" in the space entitled "Enter Selection". To select this same function by letter, you would type in the letter "P" in the "Enter Selection" space. A third selection method is to position the cursor over the selection desired and highlight it. Once a selection has been identified, the Enter key must be pressed to tell the computer you are ready to move to that part of the program. The menu screen then disappears from the monitor, and the screen of the option selected is displayed.

Types of Menus

Menus are classified into the following categories: main menus and submenus. A *main menu* (also termed a master menu) lists the primary functions performed by the software program while a *submenu* further defines these functions. Once a selection has been made from the main menu screen, the submenu appears on the monitor indicating the specific tasks that can be performed.

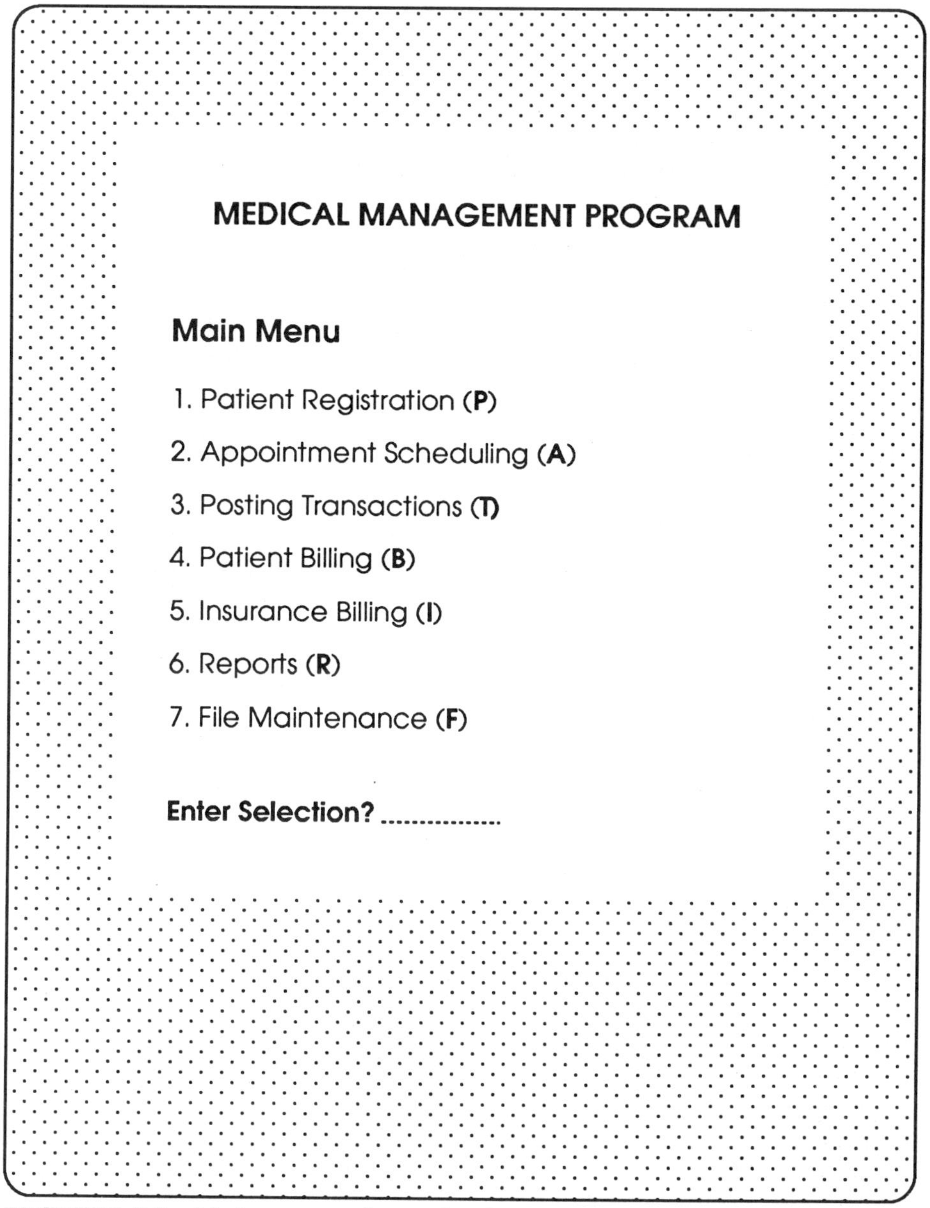

FIGURE 3-9. Main menu of a medical management program.

To be more specific, the main menu of a medical management program lists the systems included in the program, while the submenu lists the specific tasks that can be performed within each system. Refer again to Fig. 3-9 which is an example of a main menu. This menu includes the following systems: Patient Registration, Appointment Scheduling, Posting Transactions, Patient Billing, Insurance Billing, Reports, and File Maintenance. Each of the systems in the main menu is further classified into a submenu; for example, Fig. 3-10 is an illustration of the submenu for the Patient Registration System. As you should note, this submenu lists the specific tasks that can be performed within the Patient Registration System.

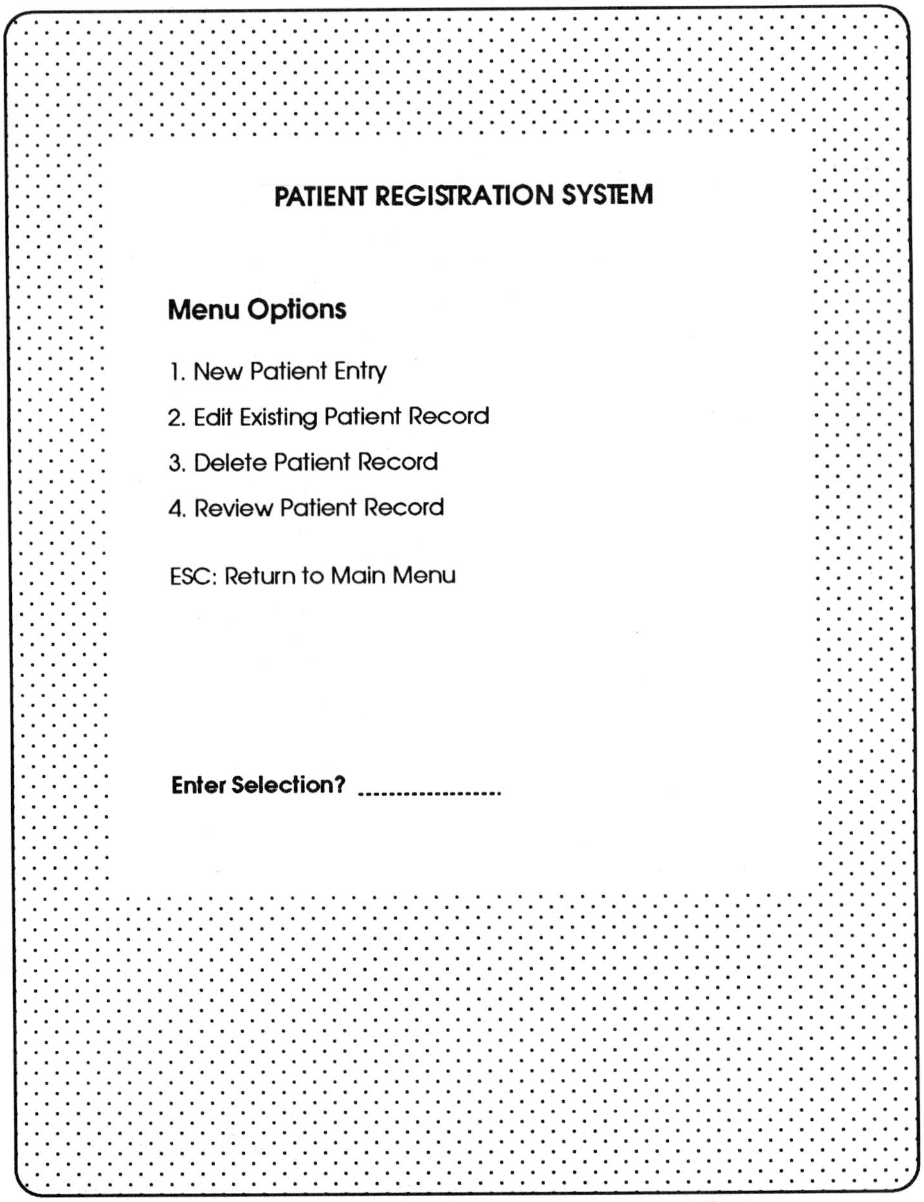

FIGURE 3 - 10. Submenu for the Patient Registration System.

Completion of a Data Entry Screen

A *screen* is defined as the information displayed at any one time on your computer monitor. You are looking at a screen when you turn on your computer and observe a visual display. Screens are further classified according to the type of information displayed on them. The screens used most often with a medical management program are menu screens and data entry screens. A *menu screen* is used to move from one part of the software program to another (see Menu Selection, page 120). On the other hand, a *data entry screen* is used to enter information or data into the computer. The data entry screen displayed depends on the task being performed. For example, if you are entering diagnosis codes, you will be working with the diagnosis code data entry screen; if you are entering insurance carriers, you will be working with the insurance carrier data entry screen and so on.

Refer to Fig. 3-11 for the example of a data entry screen used to enter patient registration information. You should note that this screen resembles the same type of

NEW PATIENT ENTRY

Data Entry Screen

Patient Account Number: 3002

A. PATIENT INFORMATION

Name ....

Address ....

City, State, Zip ....

Phone (home) ....

Phone (work) ....

SSN ....

Sex ....

Birthdate ....

Marital Status ....

Employer ....

Referring Source ....

Date of First Visit ....

Usual Provider ....

Responsible Party ....

Address ....

City, State, Zip ....

Phone (home) ....

FIGURE 3 - 11. Patient Registration data entry screen.

"fill-in-the-blank" form used to obtain patient registration information if this procedure were being completed manually. Hence, data entry is very similar to filling out a preprinted form except that the information is typed into an on-screen form instead of a paper form.

The information on a data entry "form" is arranged to provide a logical grouping of related data within the form. Referring to Fig. 3-11, for example, the patient registration information is entered in the order of name, address, city, state, telephone number and so on. Once you have completed a data entry form, it is stored in the medical practice database where it is available for immediate retrieval. A number of functions can be performed on data entry forms. Any information on the form can be changed, such as when a patient has a change of address. The form can be displayed on the monitor if reference information on that patient is required, such as looking up a patient's social security number. The form can be printed out if a hardcopy is needed. And finally, the form can be deleted altogether as when the patient relocates and transfers his/her records to a new physician.

Data Entry Guidelines

In order to complete a data entry screen, you must have a knowledge of some basic guidelines. The information presented below provides general data entry guidelines. Specific guidelines are presented in your program user manual.

Screen Title

The title of each screen is usually displayed at the top of the screen. The screen title lets you know where you are in the program at any time. Examples of screen titles include the following:

Main Menu *(Refer to Fig. 3-9)*
Patient Registration System *(Refer to Fig. 3-10)*
Procedure Codes Data Entry Screen *(Refer to Fig. 3-12)*

Source Document

Many times you will enter data into the computer from a source document. A *source document* is an original document which usually has been completed by hand and from which data is copied for input into the computer. Examples include patient information sheets and encounter forms.

Field Type

The field type refers to the type of data that can be entered into each field on a data entry screen. The three field types most commonly used are alpha-numeric, numeric, and dates. An *alpha-numeric field* allows for the entry of either letters or both letters and numbers into the field. Refer to Fig. 3-12 which is a completed data entry screen for procedure codes. The office code field and description field are alpha-numeric fields. As you can see, letters have been entered into the office code field and the description field. A *numeric field* allows only the entry of digits and special characters associated with digits (e.g., dollar sign, decimal, percent, and hyphen) into the field. Referring to Fig. 3-12, the CPT code field and the standard charge field are both numeric fields. If you try to enter letters into a numeric field, the computer will not accept them and an error message will appear on the screen. A *date only field* allows for the entry of a valid date which must be entered using the following format: MMDDYY (i.e., month, day and year). For example, March 5, 1992 is entered as follows: 030592. If an invalid date is entered, such as June 33, 1992 (entered as 063392), the computer will not accept it and an error message will appear on the screen.

Field Length

Each field on a data entry screen allows the entry of only so many characters, after which it will no longer accept input. This is known as the field length. For example, a last name field may have a field length of up to 18 characters. The field length is made known to the user by either a series of dots, an underline or a highlighted rectangular box located to the right of the field title. Each time you enter a character, a dot, underline or highlighted space is replaced by the character you type. The field type and length are indicated in the program user manual. Examples of how this information is presented in the manual is as follows:

Carrier Name: 20 A/N *(This field accepts up to 20 alpha and / or numeric characters.)*
Phone: 10 N *(This field accepts up to 12 numeric digits.)*
Enter Another Carrier (y/n)?: 1 A y/n *(This field accepts one alpha character and the character is restricted to a "y" or an "n".)*

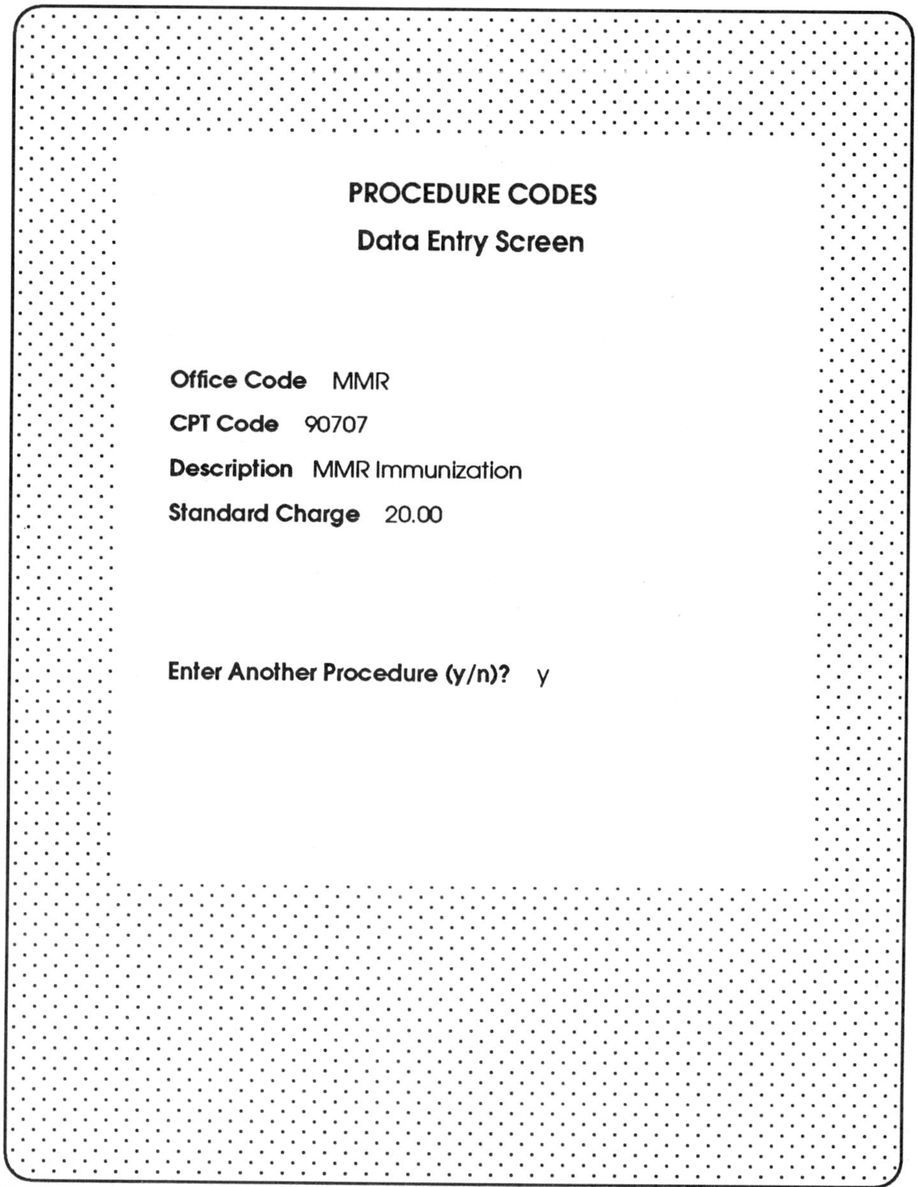

FIGURE 3 - 12. Procedure Codes data entry screen.

Prompt

A prompt is a message displayed by the computer to indicate that it is ready to accept keyboard input. A prompt tells you what information should be entered or asks some question pertaining to the system as a whole. The title of each data field in a record is a good example of a prompt. In order to respond to a prompt, the cursor must be positioned to the right of the prompt. Examples of prompts are as follows:

Patient Name
Enter Selection?
Format Another (y/n)?
Enter Another Payment (y/n)?
Print Bills (y/n)?

Special Function Keys

Some of the special function keys routinely used when entering data into the computer system are described as follows. The Enter key (or Return key) must be pressed after entering data into each data field to tell the system you are finished with that field. When the Enter key is depressed, the computer accepts the data and moves on to the next data field. The four arrow keys can be used to move the cursor around the data entry screen as may be required when entering data. The cursor moves in the direction of the arrow key that is depressed (i.e., up, down, right or left).

Message

At times, the computer displays a message on the screen to which no response is needed. The purpose of these messages is to tell you that the system is in the process of performing a requested task, or the task has been completed or denied. Examples of messages are as follows:

Formatting. . . .
Formatting Complete
Saving Text. . . . .
File Saved
Transfer Complete

Error Message

An error message is a warning notice displayed on the screen indicating the computer has detected a mistake or malfunction. If you enter incorrect commands or data, an error message appears on the screen. In addition, an electronic beep may sound when the message is displayed. The error message usually indicates what is wrong with your entry and what should be done to correct the problem. Examples of data entry error messages are as follows:

1. If you enter a patient number that cannot be found, the following error message appears: "Invalid patient number. Re-enter valid number".
2. If you try to add an insurance carrier that has already been entered, the following message will appear: "Insurance carrier already on file. Re-enter another carrier".
3. If you enter an invalid CPT code, the following message will appear: "Procedure code not on file".

Default Field

A default field is a value that has previously been assigned by the user or system and is presented as the usual response for a particular field. If the user wants to use the value presented, he/she simply presses the Enter key, thus saving key strokes and speeding the data entry process by not having to enter data into the field. If the user does not want to use the default value, he/she can override it by simply entering the information desired into the field. Examples of how default fields appear on a data entry screen are as follows:

Prepare Bills (y/n)? y (*"y" is the default value*)
Place of Service O (*"O" is the default value*)

Help Function

Many computer programs provide a handy on-screen reference that a user can turn to when questions arise. For example, if you have forgotten the format for entering a date into the system (i.e., MMDDYY), you can consult a Help screen to refresh your memory. The method you use to access the Help screen is indicated in the program user manual.

CHECKPOINT

1. What is a menu?

2. What is meant by menu-driven software?

3. List three ways to make a selection from a menu.

4. What is a main menu?

5. What is a submenu?

6. What is a screen?

7. What is the difference between a menu screen and a data entry screen?

8. What functions can be performed on a data entry form?

9. What is the purpose of the screen title?

10. What is a source document? List two examples of source documents.

11. What type of data can be entered into an alpha-numeric field?

12. What type of data can be entered into a numeric field?

____

13. How would you enter the following dates into the computer?

    a. August 10, 1992 _______________

    b. January 9, 1993 _______________

    c. April 28, 1993 _______________

    d. November 26, 1993 _______________

    e. May 3, 1993 _______________

14. What happens when the field length has been exceeded?

____

15. What is a prompt? _______________

____

16. Why must the Enter key be pressed after entering data into a data field?

____

____

17. What is the purpose of a message? _______________

____

18. What is an error message? _______________

____

19. What advantage is offered by a default field? _______________

____

20. What is the purpose of a help screen? _______________

____

INSURANCE CARRIERS

Data Entry Screen

Carrier Code ....

Carrier Name ....

Address..

City, State, Zip ....

Phone..

Contact Person ....

Electronic Claims (y/n)? ....

Signature on File (y/n)? ......y..................................

Enter Another Carrier (y/n)? ....

CRITICAL LITERACY

Data Entry Assignment: You are entering insurance carrier information into the computer system using the screen illustrated above. Respond to the following questions:

1. What type of screen is being displayed (menu screen or data entry screen)?

____

2. What is the name of the screen title?

____

3. How many data fields are included on this screen?

____

4. Indicate whether the following is an example of an alpha-numeric field (A/N) or a numeric field (N).

   a. Carrier Name __________

   b. Address __________

   c. Phone __________

   d. Contact Person __________

   e. Electronic Claims (y/n)? __________

5. Which field is an example of a default field?

   ____

6. What key should be depressed after entering data into each field?

   ____

7. You have just entered data into the Carrier Code field and an electronic beep sounds along with the display of the following statement: "Carrier code already on file. Re-enter another code".

   a. What is the name of the statement displayed on the screen?

   ____

   b. What should you do next? __________

   ____

8. You have just completed the Phone field but want to go back to change data entered into the Address field. Which special function key would you use to accomplish this? (Be specific.)

   ____

   ____

4 INTRODUCTION TO THE MEDICAL PRACTICE MANAGER

LEARNING OBJECTIVES

After completing this chapter, you should be able to:

1. Identify the six systems included in the *Medical Practice Manager.*
2. State the function of the Patient Registration System.
3. State the function of the Posting Transactions System.
4. State the function of the Patient Billing System.
5. State the function of the Insurance Billing System.
6. State the function of the Reports System.
7. State the function of the File Maintenance System.

Guidelines for Completing the *Medical Practice Manager*

The remaining chapters in this text (Chapters 4 through 10) present a simulated medical management program entitled the *Medical Practice Manager*. On-paper you will have the opportunity to work through a medical management program similar to programs used in medical offices and clinics. Both menu screens and data entry screens from actual medical management programs are illustrated in the *Medical Practice Manager*. In this way, you should be able to easily transfer this knowledge and skill to operating a medical office management computer system.

The *Medical Practice Manager* includes the following systems: Patient Registration, Posting Transactions, Patient Billing, Insurance Billing, Reports, and File Maintenance. Each remaining chapter covers a different system in the *Medical Practice Manager* and each chapter builds upon the next one. Therefore, if you complete a chapter and do not understand it, repeat that chapter before proceeding to the next.

The chapter organization is designed to facilitate learning the Medical *Practice Manager* and is arranged in the categories listed below.

Objectives

Presented at the beginning of each chapter are statements of competency and learning objectives. The competencies delineate the task or skills to be mastered in the chapter, while the learning objectives address the theory or knowledge required to perform the skill.

Introduction

The chapter introduction describes and explains the purpose of the system including the options included in the system and the task performed by each option. In addition, any special terminology relating to the system is thoroughly explained.

Checkpoint

This section presents questions covering the information in the introductory material. In this way the student can assess his/her knowledge of the theory underlying each system in the *Medical Practice Manager*.

Menu Screens and Data Entry Screens

Illustrations of menu screens and data entry screens are provided for each competency. These screens are identical to those in medical management programs used in medical offices and clinics. Worksheets (described below) provide instructions on completing the screens.

Worksheets

Each chapter includes accompanying worksheets which focus on the completion of a specific task in the *Medical Practice Manager*. Each worksheet includes the following categories:

1. ***Competency***: The competency identifies the task to be completed in the *Medical Practice Manager*.
2. ***Guidelines***: The guidelines further define the task and provide any additional theory needed to accomplish the task.

3. ***Documentation:*** Documentation is included for those competencies in which a data entry screen must be completed. The documentation is analogous to the program user manual and explains the information to be entered into the data entry screen.

Learning Activities

The learning activities provide step-by-step guidelines for completing each competency in the *Medical Practice Manager* at the level of skill required in the medical office.

Begin the Simulated Program

You are now ready to begin working on the *Medical Practice Manager Simulated Program*. The first competency is to become familiar with the capabilities of the *Medical Practice Manager*. Turn the page to begin completion of this competency.

MEDICAL PRACTICE MANAGER

Main Menu

1. Patient Registration
2. Posting Transactions
3. Patient Billing
4. Insurance Billing
5. Reports
6. File Maintenance

Enter Selection? ....

Worksheet 1: Main Menu

COMPETENCY

Identify the name and function of each system in the Main Menu of the *Medical Practice Manager*.

GUIDELINES

Your medical office (Riverside Family Practice Clinic) has just brought in a computer system. The software consists of a medical management program entitled the *Medical Practice Manager*. Your hardware consists of an IBM computer with 4 MB of memory (RAM) and an 80 MB hard disk. You are responsible for helping to set up and operate this new computer system. The first task is that of becoming familiar with the capabilities of the *Medical Practice Manager*. Refer the Main Menu screen illustrated on the opposite page and complete the Learning Activities presented below.

LEARNING ACTIVITIES

1. How many systems are included in the Main Menu? ____________________

2. Is this an example of a menu screen or a data entry screen?

   ____

3. Refer to pages 105 to 106 and state the function of each of the following systems:

   a. Patient Registration ____________________

   ____

   b. Posting Transactions ____________________

   ____

   c. Patient Billing ____________________

   ____

   d. Insurance Billing ____________________

   ____

   e. Reports ____________________

   ____

   f. File Maintenance ____________________

   ____

4. You are now ready to begin the *Medical Practice Manager Simulated Program*. Turn the page to begin the program.

5 FILE MAINTENANCE SYSTEM: START-UP TASKS

COMPETENCIES

After completing this chapter, you should be able to perform the following:

1. Enter practice information into the computer system.
2. Enter user passwords into the computer system.
3. Enter provider information into the computer system.
4. Enter diagnosis codes into the computer system.
5. Enter procedure codes into the computer system.
6. Enter insurance carriers into the computer system.
7. Enter place of services into the computer system.
8. Enter referring physicians into the computer system.

LEARNING OBJECTIVES

After completing this chapter, you should be able to:

1. Explain the general purpose of start-up tasks.
2. Explain the specific purpose for performing the following start-up tasks: practice information, user passwords, provider information, diagnosis codes, procedure codes, insurance carriers, place of service, referring physicians.
3. Identify the system in the *Medical Practice Manager* used to perform start-up tasks.
4. Define and state the purpose of the federal tax identification number.
5. Define the following terms: provider and insurance carrier.
6. List three functions served by the ICD-9-CM and CPT-4 coding systems.
7. Explain the purpose of diagnosis code modifiers.
8. Explain the purpose of the diagnosis and procedure "in house" office codes.
9. Define and explain the purpose of a signature on file form.

Introduction

Before a medical management program becomes operational, or in other words, before you can start performing front office procedures on the computer, a number of start-up tasks must be performed. These tasks are required in order to customize the program to meet the specific requirements of your medical office. For example, in order to prepare insurance claims, you must first enter all of the insurance carriers with which your patients are affiliated.

Types of Start-Up Tasks

Start-up tasks require the entering of data that is used on a daily basis into your computer . This data then becomes part of the medical practice database and is organized in a manner which allows for later retrieval and use. The specific start-up tasks that must be performed to make the computer system operational are listed and briefly described below.

Practice Information: This start-up task customizes your computer system with the name, address, phone number and federal tax identification number of your medical practice.

User Passwords: This start-up task provides security to your computer system by assigning a password to each individual using the computer. This password must be typed in by the user before he/she can work on the computer.

Providers: This start-up task allows you to enter and store information regarding the physicians in your medical practice. As a result, anytime this information is needed on a document or form (e.g., insurance claim form) the computer system will transfer this information from the provider file and place it on the form.

Diagnosis Codes: This start-up task lets you compile and store a list of diagnoses along with their corresponding ICD-9-CM codes. This information can then be transferred to any document requiring it such as superbills and insurance claim forms.

Procedure Codes: This start-up task allows you to compile and store a list of medical services and procedures performed in your medical office along with the CPT-4 code and standard office charge for each procedure. This information can then be transferred to any document requiring it.

Insurance Carriers: An *insurance carrier* is a company that provides an insurance policy. Other names for an insurance carrier include: insurer, third-party carrier and third-party payor. This start-up task allows you to enter and store information regarding the insurance carriers used by patients in the practice which is needed for processing insurance claims.

Place of Service: This start-up task allows you to compile and store information on the facilities where the physician performs medical services and procedures.

Referring Physicians: This start-up task lets you compile and store information about physicians who refer patients to your medical office.

Start-Up Tasks: The Medical Practice Manager

Start-up tasks are performed in the File Maintenance System of the *Medical Practice Manager*. The File Maintenance System permits you to compile and store tables of information in the medical practice database (e.g., Diagnosis Codes Table, Insurance Carrier Table). In the course of daily operations, these tables are constantly referenced for information. In addition, you can add, change, delete or print information in these tables as needed. The information in these tables is accessed through "in-house" office codes assigned during the data entry process, as is described in detail in this chapter. Using codes to access this information saves you much time and effort in not having to manually retype information you use repeatedly.

You are now ready to begin working on the *Medical Practice Manager Simulated Program*. Turn to the next page to move to the Main Menu of the *Medical Practice Manager*.

CHECKPOINT

1. Explain the purpose of each of the following start-up tasks.

   a. Practice Information ______________________________

   ____

   b. User Passwords ______________________________

   ____

   c. Providers ______________________________

   ____

   d. Diagnosis Codes ______________________________

   ____

   e. Procedure Codes ______________________________

   ____

   f. Insurance Carriers ______________________________

   ____

MEDICAL PRACTICE MANAGER

Main Menu

1. Patient Registration
2. Posting Transactions
3. Patient Billing
4. Insurance Billing
5. Reports
6. File Maintenance

Enter Selection? ....

Worksheet 1: File Maintenance System

COMPETENCY

Access the File Maintenance System.

GUIDELINES

You are responsible for performing the start-up tasks required to make your computer system operational. In order to perform the tasks, you must first access the File Maintenance System from the Main Menu on the opposite page. The Learning Activities provide you with the information necessary to attain this competency. Once you have completed these activities, you will be directed to turn to the next page. This will illustrate the screen you have moved to as well as the next competency to be attained.

LEARNING ACTIVITIES

1. What is the function of the File Maintenance System? ______________________

   ____

2. What number should you select to move to this system?

   ____

3. a. Make this selection on the Main Menu screen in the space entitled *Enter Selection*.

   b. Turn the page to move to the next screen.

FILE MAINTENANCE SYSTEM

Menu Options

1. Practice Information
2. User Passwords
3. Provider Information
4. Diagnosis Codes
5. Procedure Codes
6. Insurance Carriers
7. Place of Service
8. Referring Physicians

ESC: Return to Main Menu

Enter Selection? ....

Worksheet 2: File Maintenance System

COMPETENCY

Identify the name and function of each option in the File Maintenance System.

GUIDELINES

You are now in the File Maintenance System. Refer to the opposite page for an illustration of the menu screen listing the options available within this system. You should first become familiar with these options by completing the Learning Activities presented below.

LEARNING ACTIVITIES

1. Is the File Maintenance menu an example of a main menu or a submenu?

   ____

2. What option (by name and number) would you select to perform the following tasks?

   a. Enter ICD-9-CM codes into the system ____________

   b. Enter referring physicians into the system ____________

   c. Enter CPT-4 codes into the system ____________

   d. Assign a user password ____________

   e. Enter insurance carriers into the system ____________

   f. Enter providers into the system ____________

3. You are now ready to begin the start-up tasks. The first task is that of entering medical practice information. In order to complete this task, you must first access the Practice Information data entry screen. Turn to the next page to begin this competency.

FILE MAINTENANCE SYSTEM

Menu Options

1. Practice Information
2. User Passwords
3. Provider Information
4. Diagnosis Codes
5. Procedure Codes
6. Insurance Carriers
7. Place of Service
8. Referring Physicians

ESC: Return to Main Menu

Enter Selection? ....

Worksheet 3: Practice Information

COMPETENCY

Access the Practice Information data entry screen.

GUIDELINES

You are still in the File Maintenance menu from which you must access Practice Information. The purpose of the Practice Information option is to customize your computer system with the name, address, and phone number of your medical office. This information becomes part of the medical practice database and is stored in the Practice Information file. It can then be automatically transferred to patient statements, insurance claims, patient reminders and any other document requiring the practice name and address.

LEARNING ACTIVITIES

1. What is the function of the Practice Information option? ____________________

   ____

2. Which number should you select to move to this option?

   ____

3. a. Make this selection on the screen in the space entitled *Enter Selection.*

   b. Turn the page to move to the next screen.

PRACTICE INFORMATION

Data Entry Screen

Office Name Riverside Family Practice Clinic

Address 400 Broad Street

City Norman

State OK

Zip Code 73070

Phone 4053607444

Federal Tax ID Number 32-6025986

ESC: Return to File Maintenance Menu

Worksheet 4: Practice Information

COMPETENCY

Enter practice information into the computer system.

GUIDELINES

Opposite is a data entry screen that has been completed with practice information. As you should note, this screen resembles a pre-printed, fill-in-the-blank form. You are responsible for entering information regarding your medical office into your computer system. Each data field is described under documentation to identify the information to be entered into the field.

DOCUMENTATION

Office Name: Enter the business name of the practice.

Address: Enter the street address of the medical office.

City: Enter the city of the medical office.

State: Enter the two-letter state abbreviation of the medical office.

Zip Code: Enter the zip code of the medical office.

Phone: This is the phone number of the office's main telephone which is used by patients for scheduling appointments or asking questions concerning health. Phone numbers are entered much like any other field except that you do not need to add any formatting guides: [( ) and –] to separate the area code, prefix and number. The system will automatically add the proper formatting. For example, to enter the phone number (313) 871-7889, you would enter 3138717889. When this information is redisplayed, the system automatically adds the formatting commands.

Federal Tax ID Number: This is a number assigned to the medical office by the federal government. It is used for medical office tax purposes. *Note:* The federal tax identification number is also referred to as the employer identification number or simply the tax identification number.

LEARNING ACTIVITIES

1. How many data fields are included in the Practice Information data entry screen?

___

2. Why is it unnecessary to add formatting guides when entering the phone number of the medical practice?

___

___

3. Who assigns the federal tax identification number? What is its purpose?

___

___

4. What are two other names for the federal tax identification number?

___

___

5. Complete the Practice Information data entry screen using the following information:

   Riverside Family Practice Clinic
   400 Broad Street
   Norman, Oklahoma 73070
   Phone: (405) 360-7444
   Federal Tax ID Number: 32-6025986

6. a. After completing the Practice Name data entry screen, return to the File Maintenance menu. Which key should you press to return to this menu?

   ___

   b. Turn the page to move to the File Maintenance menu.

PRACTICE INFORMATION

Data Entry Screen

Office Name ....

Address ....

City ....

State ....

Zip Code ....

Phone ....

Federal Tax ID Number ....

ESC: Return to File Maintenance Menu

FILE MAINTENANCE SYSTEM

Menu Options

1. Practice Information
2. User Passwords
3. Provider Information
4. Diagnosis Codes
5. Procedure Codes
6. Insurance Carriers
7. Place of Service
8. Referring Physicians

ESC: Return to Main Menu

Enter Selection? ....

Worksheet 5: User Passwords

COMPETENCY

Access the User Passwords data entry screen.

GUIDELINES

You are now back in the File Maintenance menu. The next start-up task which must be performed is that of assigning user passwords. The User Passwords option is used to assign a password to each person who will be using the program. The Medical Practice Manager requires that each individual have a password to gain access to the system. This provides front office security to prevent anyone from obtaining information from the computer without authorization. In addition, when you establish passwords, every transaction is marked with an operator code to indicate who entered that transaction. In the event of a problem or question, the individual entering the transaction can be identified.

LEARNING ACTIVITIES

1. What is the function of the User Passwords option? ______________________

   ____

2. Which number should you select to move to this option?

   ____

3. a. Make this selection on the screen in the space entitled *Enter Selection.*

   b. Turn the page to move to the next screen.

USER PASSWORDS

Data Entry Screen

User Name Berry, Barbara A

User Initials BAB

User Password CANDY

Enter Another User (y/n)? y

Worksheet 6: User Passwords

COMPETENCY

Enter user passwords into the computer system.

GUIDELINES

Opposite is a data entry screen that has been completed for user passwords. You are responsible for entering a password for yourself into the computer system. You should keep your password a secret by not telling it to anyone or writing it down anywhere. From this point forward, in order to gain access to the Medical Practice Manager, your password must first be entered. (Note: After the User Password file has been set up, you are required to enter your password in order to work on the computer. Once entered, the system will take you into the Main Menu so that you can begin working on the computer. To prevent someone from reading over your shoulder when you type in your password, the symbol # will be displayed on the screen for each character of your password. For example, if your password is CANDY, the following will appear on the screen when you type in the word "candy": #####).

DOCUMENTATION

User Name: Enter the name of the user with the last name first, followed by a comma, and the first name and middle initial.

User Initials: Enter the initials of the user.

User Password: Enter a six-character or less password for the user.

Enter Another User (y/n)?: A "y" response takes you to a new data entry screen for entering another user into the system, while an "n" response returns you to the File Maintenance menu.

LEARNING ACTIVITIES

1. What symbol is displayed on the screen for each character in your password? What is the reason for the system displaying a symbol instead of characters?

    ____

    ____

2. What happens after you correctly enter your password?

    ____

3. What is the purpose of marking transaction entries with the operator code?

    ____

    ____

4. Complete the User Password data entry screen on the opposite page using your name and initials. Decide upon a password of six-characters or less that you would like to use for yourself and enter it in the appropriate field.

5. a. Return to the File Maintenance menu to perform the next start-up task.

    b. What keystroke must be made to return to the File Maintenance Menu?

    ____

    c. Enter this keystroke on the screen.

    d. Turn the page to move to the File Maintenance menu.

USER PASSWORDS

Data Entry Screen

User Name ....

User Initials ....

User Password ....

Enter Another User (y/n)? ....

FILE MAINTENANCE SYSTEM

Menu Options

1. Practice Information
2. User Passwords
3. Provider Information
4. Diagnosis Codes
5. Procedure Codes
6. Insurance Carriers
7. Place of Service
8. Referring Physicians

ESC: Return to Main Menu

Enter Selection? ....

Worksheet 7: Provider Information

COMPETENCY

Access the Provider Information data entry screen.

GUIDELINES

The Provider Information option is used to enter information regarding all the providers in the medical practice. A provider is defined as a person who provides medical care to a patient (i.e., a physician). Once the information for each provider has been entered into the system, it can be printed on anything that requires it without having to re-enter it. Examples include patient statements, superbills, insurance claims, and status reports. Each provider is assigned a unique code which is used when entering a transaction for a patient account. Because the computer system can use codes to rapidly locate or refer to information, it is then possible to see at a glance which physician in the practice provided which services to any patient in the system. The use of provider codes also allows the system to keep track of what each physician staff member is contributing to the medical practice as a whole.

LEARNING ACTIVITIES

1. What is the function of the Provider Information option? ____________________

   ____

2. Which number should you select to move to this option?

   ____

3. a. Make this selection on the screen in the space entitled *Enter Selection*.

   b. Turn the page to move to the next screen.

PROVIDER INFORMATION

Data Entry Screen

Provider Code KH

Provider Name Howe, Keith M

Degree MD

Specialty Family Practice

Social Security Number 801292598

Federal Tax ID Number 32-6025986

Enter Another Provider (y/n)? y

Worksheet 8: Provider Information

COMPETENCY

Enter providers into the computer system.

GUIDELINES

Opposite is a data entry screen that has been completed for provider information. There are two physicians in the medical practice: Dr. Howe and Dr. Westmoreland. As illustrated on the opposite page, Dr. Howe has just been entered into the computer system. It is your responsibility to enter Dr. Westmoreland into the system.

DOCUMENTATION

Provider Code: Enter a short meaningful code to identify the provider. In a small practice, the first letter of the doctor's last name is often used. In a larger practice, two or three initials may be necessary.

Provider Name: Enter the name of the provider with the last name first followed by a comma, and the first name and middle initial.

Degree: Enter the professional degree of the physician (e.g., MD, DO).

Specialty: Identifies the physician's specialty (e.g., Family Practice, Peds, OB/GYN, Cardiology)

Social Security Number: Enter the provider's social security number in this field. Social security numbers are entered much like any other field except that they contain formatting guides (-). The system will automatically add the proper formatting, therefore you do not need to do this. For example, to enter the social security number 304-89-7731, you would enter 304897731.

Federal Tax ID Number: This is a number assigned to the medical office by the federal government. It is used in processing government insurance claims (e.g., Medicare, Medicaid) and for medical office tax purposes.

Enter Another Provider (y/n)?: A "y" response takes you to a new Provider Information data entry screen to enable you to enter another provider. An "n" response returns you to the File Maintenance menu.

LEARNING ACTIVITIES

1. What is the definition of a provider? ____________________

   ____

   ____

2. List three examples of documents on which provider information is printed.

   ____

   ____

3. What is the advantage of using "in-house" office codes to enter information into the computer?

   ____

   ____

4. Why is it unnecessary to add formatting guides when entering the physician's social security number?

   ____

5. Complete the Provider Information data entry screen on the opposite page with the information below:

   James A. Westmoreland, M.D.
   400 Broad Street
   Norman Oklahoma 73070
   Social Security Number: 301-44-8906
   Federal Tax ID Number: 32-6025986
   Provider Code: JW
   Specialty: Family Practice

6. a. After completing the Provider Information data entry screens, return to the File Maintenance menu.

   b. Turn the page to move to the File Maintenance menu.

PROVIDER INFORMATION

Data Entry Screen

Provider Code ....

Provider Name ....

Degree ....

Specialty ....

Social Security Number ....

Federal Tax ID Number ....

Enter Another Provider (y/n)? ....

FILE MAINTENANCE SYSTEM

Menu Options

1. Practice Information
2. User Passwords
3. Provider Information
4. Diagnosis Codes
5. Procedure Codes
6. Insurance Carriers
7. Place of Service
8. Referring Physicians

ESC: Return to Main Menu

Enter Selection? ....

Worksheet 9: Diagnosis Codes

COMPETENCY

Access the Diagnosis Codes data entry screen.

GUIDELINES

The Diagnosis Code option is used to compile and store a list of ICD-9-CM codes and related descriptions for all diagnoses pertinent to the medical practice. The abbreviation, ICD-9-CM stands for International Classification of Diseases, Ninth Revision, Clinical Modification which is a system of diagnostic coding consisting of three bound volumes as follows:

Volume 1: Diseases: Tabular List
Volume 2: Diseases: Alphabetic List
Volume 3: Procedures: Tabular List and Alphabetic Index

The ICD-9-CM system assigns a code to each disease entity. The ICD-9 code consists of three digits that may be followed by a decimal point and one or two additional digits. The extra digits are termed modifiers and are used to further define the disease category. One of the most important functions served by the ICD-9 coding system is to facilitate faster processing of insurance claims by insurance carriers. Diagnosis codes are also used to identify the physician's reason and/or justification for performing certain procedures and to characterize diseases of the patients as a means for tracking disease processes throughout the country. All government insurance programs and most private insurance companies now require claim forms be submitted using ICD-9-CM codes to identify the patient's diagnosis. In order to set up the diagnostic code file, you must enter the diagnosis description and ICD-9 code for the diagnoses appropriate to your medical practice. Once entered, this information can be transferred, using an "in-house" office code to any document requiring it (e.g., superbills, insurance claims, patient statements), thus saving you much time and effort by not having to retype it for each separate document.

LEARNING ACTIVITIES

1. What is the function of the Diagnosis Codes option? ____________________

2. What number should you select to move to this option? ____________________

3. a. Make this selection in the space entitled *Enter Selection*.

   b. Turn the page to move to the next screen.

DIAGNOSIS CODES
Data Entry Screen

Office Code CHF

ICD - 9 Code 428.0

Description Congestive Heart Failure

Enter Another Diagnosis (y/n)? y

Worksheet 10: Diagnosis Codes

COMPETENCY

Enter diagnosis codes into the computer system.

GUIDELINES

Initially you should enter the diagnoses most frequently treated in your medical office. These will vary based upon the type of practice. For example, the diagnoses used most in a general practice office will be different than those used in a specialty office such as cardiology. Your office may already have a pre-printed form such as a superbill, encounter form or other type of reference sheet with the diagnosis descriptions and codes listed from which you can work. Thereafter, once your computer system is operational, diagnosis information can be added or deleted as needed. Refer to the completed diagnosis code data entry screen on the opposite page. As you will note, this screen consists of three data fields consisting of an office code, ICD-9 code and the diagnosis description. The office code is an "in-house" code which provides a short-cut for accessing information in the diagnosis code file. For example, the office code for congestive heart failure is CHF. By entering this easy-to-remember code for patient transactions, both the diagnosis description (Congestive Heart Failure) and the ICD-9 code (428.0) will be transferred to the required document. This eliminates having to enter the lengthier and more difficult to remember ICD-9 code during daily transactions thus saving you time and effort.

DOCUMENTATION

Office Code: Enter a short, meaningful code to be used as a short-cut for accessing information in the diagnosis code file.

ICD-9 Code: Enter the ICD-9-CM code in this data field. If the code includes a decimal point, it should be typed in as presented in the code. Each ICD-9 code may only be used once. If you try to add a code that has already been entered, an error message will appear on the screen as follows: ERROR: ICD-9 code already on file. Re-enter another code.

Description: Enter the diagnosis description. This is the description which will be printed on insurance claims, patient statements, and superbills.

Enter Another Diagnosis (y/n)?: A "y" response takes you to a new Diagnosis Codes data entry screen while an "n" response returns you to the File Maintenance menu.

LEARNING ACTIVITIES

1. Complete the diagnosis data entry screens on the following pages using the diagnoses listed below. Use the Diagnosis Codes reference sheet below as the source document to obtain the information necessary to complete this task.

   a. Anemia, Iron Deficiency
   b. Hypertension
   c. Low Back Pain
   d. Otitis Media
   e. Upper Respiratory Infection
   f. Urinary Tract Infection

2. a. After completing the last data entry screen, return to the File Maintenance menu.

   b. Turn to page 170 to move to the File Maintenance menu.

DIAGNOSIS CODES

Office Code	Description	ICD-9 Code
AP	Abdominal Pain	789.0
AR	Allergic Rhinitis	477.0
AN	Anemia, Iron Deficiency	280
ANG	Angina Pectoris	413.9
ARTH	Arthritis	715.9
BRON	Bronchitis	466.0
CHF	Congestive Heart Failure	428.0
EMP	Emphysema	492.8
HT	Hypertension	401
FLU	Influenza	487.1
LBP	Low Back Pain	724.2
OM	Otitis Media	382.9
STREP	Strep Throat	034
URI	Upper Respiratory Infection	465.9
UTI	Urinary Tract Infection	599.0

DIAGNOSIS CODES

Data Entry Screen

Office Code ....

ICD - 9 Code ....

Description ....

Enter Another Diagnosis (y/n)? ....

DIAGNOSIS CODES

Data Entry Screen

Office Code ....

ICD - 9 Code ....

Description ....

Enter Another Diagnosis (y/n)? ....

DIAGNOSIS CODES

Data Entry Screen

Office Code ....

ICD - 9 Code ....

Description ....

Enter Another Diagnosis (y/n)? ....

DIAGNOSIS CODES

Data Entry Screen

Office Code ....

ICD - 9 Code ....

Description ....

Enter Another Diagnosis (y/n)? ....

DIAGNOSIS CODES

Data Entry Screen

Office Code ....

ICD - 9 Code ....

Description ....

Enter Another Diagnosis (y/n)? ....

DIAGNOSIS CODES

Data Entry Screen

Office Code ....

ICD - 9 Code ....

Description ....

Enter Another Diagnosis (y/n)? ....

FILE MAINTENANCE SYSTEM

Menu Options

1. Practice Information
2. User Passwords
3. Provider Information
4. Diagnosis Codes
5. Procedure Codes
6. Insurance Carriers
7. Place of Service
8. Referring Physicians

ESC: Return to Main Menu

Enter Selection? ....

Worksheet 11: Procedure Codes

COMPETENCY

Access the Procedure Codes data entry screen.

GUIDELINES

The Procedure Code option is used to compile and store a list of CPT-4 codes for the medical services and procedures (along with their corresponding descriptions) performed in your medical office. This file also includes the standard office charge for each procedure. The abbreviation, CPT-4, stands for Current Procedural Terminology, 4th edition. CPT-4 is a coding system developed by the American Medical Association to provide a uniform language among physicians for reporting medical, surgical and diagnostic services. As with the ICD-9-CM coding system, government insurance programs and most private insurance companies require claim forms be submitted using CPT codes to identify the procedures performed on each patient. The CPT system consists of one bound volume organized into five sections: Medical, Anesthesiology, Surgery, Radiology, and Pathology and Laboratory. The CPT system assigns a 5 digit code to each procedure. A two-digit code known as a modifier may be attached to the procedure code to provide a more defined and accurate description of the procedure performed (e.g., 90020-30 where "30" is the modifier code for the procedure 90020). In order to set up the procedure code file, you must enter the procedure description, CPT code and standard charge for the procedures performed in your medical office. Once entered, this information can be transferred using an "in-house" procedure code to any document requiring it such as superbills, insurance claims, and patient statements.

LEARNING ACTIVITIES

1. What is the function of the Procedures Codes option? ______________________

   ____

2. What number should you select to move to the Procedure Codes option?

   ____

3. a. Make this selection in the space entitled *Enter Selection*.

   b. Turn the page to move to the next screen.

PROCEDURE CODES

Data Entry Screen

Office Code MMR

CPT Code 90707

Description MMR Immunization

Standard Charge 20.00

Enter Another Procedure (y/n)? y

Worksheet 12: Procedure Codes

COMPETENCY

Enter procedure codes into the computer system.

GUIDELINES

Opposite is a completed data entry screen for procedure codes. Initially you should enter the medical services and procedures most often performed in your medical office. As with the diagnosis code file, these will vary based upon the type of medical practice. Your office may already have a pre-printed form with the procedures and codes listed from which you can begin. Thereafter, once your computer system is operational, information can be added or deleted in this file as needed.

DOCUMENTATION

Office Code: Enter a short, meaningful code to be used as a short-cut for accessing the information in the diagnosis code file.

CPT Code: Enter the CPT-4 code in this data field. Each CPT code may only be used once. If you try to add a code that has already been entered, an error message will appear on the screen as follows: ERROR: CPT code already on file. Re-enter another code.

Description: Enter the procedure description. This is the description which will be printed on insurance claims, patient statements, superbills, and so on.

Standard Charge: This is the usual fee your office charges for the procedure. Enter the amount of the charge for the procedure using digits and a decimal point. The system assumes that any charges entered will be dollar figures, therefore a dollar sign ($) is not required (e.g., enter $20.00 as 20.00).

Enter Another Procedure (y/n)?: A "y" response takes you to a new Procedure Code data entry screen, while an "n" response returns you to the File Maintenance menu.

LEARNING ACTIVITIES

1. Complete the procedure code data entry screens on the following pages using the procedures listed below. Use the Procedure Codes reference sheet below to obtain the information necessary to complete this task.

   a. New Patient, Level II
   b. Established Patient, Level III
   c. ECG and Interpretation
   d. Oral Polio Vaccine Immunization
   e. CBC with Differential
   f. Urinalysis

2. a. After completing the last data entry screen, return to the File Maintenance menu.

   b. Turn to page 178 to move to the File Maintenance menu.

PROCEDURE CODES

Office Code	Description	CPT Code	Charge
NP1	New Patient, Level I	99201	15.00
NP2	New Patient, Level II	99202	20.00
NP3	New Patient, Level III	99203	25.00
NP4	New Patient, Level IV	99204	40.00
NP5	New Patient, Level V	99205	60.00
EP1	Established Patient, Level I	99211	10.00
EP2	Established Patient, Level II	99212	15.00
EP3	Established Patient, Level III	99213	20.00
EP4	Established Patient, Level IV	99214	25.00
EP5	Established Patient, Level V	99215	35.00
IRR	Ear Irrigation	69210	10.00
ECG	ECG and Interpretation	93000	50.00
PEL	Pelvic Exam	58999	20.00
SIG	Sigmoidoscopy	45330	40.00
SUT/R	Suture Removal	90699	10.00
DPT	DPT Immunization	90701	15.00
MMR	MMR Immunization	90707	20.00
OPV	Oral Polio Vaccine Immunization	90712	10.00
CBC/D	CBC with Differential	85031	15.00
GLU	Glucose	82947	10.00
HCT	Hematocrit	85014	10.00
UA	Urinalysis	81000	10.00
TC	Throat Culture	87060	10.00

PROCEDURE CODES

Data Entry Screen

Office Code ....

CPT Code ....

Description ....

Standard Charge ....

Enter Another Procedure (y/n)? ....

PROCEDURE CODES

Data Entry Screen

Office Code ....

CPT Code ....

Description ....

Standard Charge ....

Enter Another Procedure (y/n)? ....

PROCEDURE CODES

Data Entry Screen

Office Code ....

CPT Code ....

Description ....

Standard Charge ....

Enter Another Procedure (y/n)? ....

PROCEDURE CODES

Data Entry Screen

Office Code ....

CPT Code ....

Description ....

Standard Charge ....

Enter Another Procedure (y/n)? ....

PROCEDURE CODES

Data Entry Screen

Office Code ....

CPT Code ....

Description ....

Standard Charge ....

Enter Another Procedure (y/n)? ....

PROCEDURE CODES

Data Entry Screen

Office Code ....

CPT Code ....

Description ....

Standard Charge ....

Enter Another Procedure (y/n)? ....

FILE MAINTENANCE SYSTEM

Menu Options

1. Practice Information
2. User Passwords
3. Provider Information
4. Diagnosis Codes
5. Procedure Codes
6. Insurance Carriers
7. Place of Service
8. Referring Physicians

ESC: Return to Main Menu

Enter Selection? ....

Worksheet 13: Insurance Carriers

COMPETENCY

Access the Insurance Carriers data entry screen.

GUIDELINES

The Insurance Carriers option is used to compile and store information on all the insurance carriers used by patients in the practice. Once this data is entered, the computer automatically fills in insurance company information required on claim forms from the data stored in this file. This information is also used in preparing accounting reports and practice analysis reports.

LEARNING ACTIVITIES

1. What is the function of the Insurance Carriers option? ____________________

   ____

2. What number should you select to move to this option?

   ____

3. a. Make this selection in the space entitled *Enter Selection.*

   b. Turn the page to move to the next screen.

INSURANCE CARRIERS
Data Entry Screen

Carrier Code MC

Carrier Name Medicare

Address 1205 Henderson Road

City, State, Zip Norman, OK, 73070

Phone 4052328806

Contact Person Karen Cochran

Electronic Claims (y/n)? n

Signature on File (y/n)? y

Enter Another Carrier (y/n)? y

Worksheet 14: Insurance Carriers

COMPETENCY

Enter insurance carriers into the computer system.

GUIDELINES

Opposite is a completed data entry screen for insurance carriers. You are responsible for entering insurance carrier information into your computer system. This information is then accessed by using the carrier code.

DOCUMENTATION

Carrier Code: Enter a short, meaningful code to be used as a short-cut for accessing information in this file. The code can be the initials or the first three characters of the plan name (e.g., AET for Aetna or MNY for Mutual of New York).

Carrier Name: Enter the name of the insurance company as you wish it to appear on claim forms.
Address: Enter the street address of the insurance carrier.
City, State, Zip: Enter the city, state, and zip code of the carrier.
Phone: Enter the telephone number of the insurance carrier.
Contact Person: Enter the name of the individual at the insurance company to contact for authorization purposes or questions pertaining to insurance claims.

Electronic Claims (y/n)?: A number of insurance companies allow the transmission of insurance claim information from the medical office over the phone lines. If this question is answered "y", no paper claims will be printed and the information will instead be filed in your computer until transmitted to the insurance company. An "n" response means that paper claims will be printed.

Signature on File (y/n)?: A signature on file form is a signed patient release used in an office to eliminate the need for the patient's signature on each insurance claim. This field is used to indicate if the insurance company accepts a signature on file or if the patient must actually sign each claim sent to the company. Most insurance companies do not require that patients sign the release on each individual insurance claim, especially if the claim is produced by a computer. If this question is answered "y", this means that the medical office has a signed statement from patients using this company permitting the release of information to the insurance company for claims evaluation. The following text prints out on the insurance claim: "Signature on File". An "n" answer means that this insurance carrier requires the patient's signature on all insurance claim forms submitted.

Enter Another Carrier (y/n)?: A "y" response takes you to a new Insurance Carrier data entry screen, while an "n" response returns you to the File Maintenance menu.

LEARNING ACTIVITIES

1. List three examples of documents on which insurance carrier information is printed.

   ____

2. How are electronic claims transmitted? ______________________________

   ____

3. What is a signature on file form? What advantage is served by an insurance carrier accepting a signature on file?

   ____

   ____

4. Complete the insurance carrier data entry screens on the following pages using the information below.

   Blue Cross
   101 Dublin Road
   Norman, OK 73070
   Phone: (405) 840-1441
   Contact: Bill Henry
   Carrier Code: BC
   Electronic Claims: yes
   Signature on File: yes

   Aetna Insurance Company
   2450 Broad Street
   Norman, OK 73070
   Phone: (405) 947-0707
   Contact: Donna Wamsley
   Carrier Code: AET
   Electronic Claims: no
   Signature on File: yes

   Metropolitan Insurance Company
   2120 Court Street
   Norman, OK 73070
   Phone: (405) 840-2122
   Contact: Martha Skeeles
   Carrier Code: MET
   Electronic Claims: no
   Signature on File: yes

2. a. After completing the last data entry screen, return to the File Maintenance menu.
   b. Turn to page 186 to move to the File Maintenance menu.

INSURANCE CARRIERS

Data Entry Screen

Carrier Code ....

Carrier Name ....

Address ....

City, State, Zip ....

Phone ....

Contact Person ....

Electronic Claims (y/n)? ....

Signature on File (y/n)? ....

Enter Another Carrier (y/n)? ....

INSURANCE CARRIERS

Data Entry Screen

Carrier Code ....

Carrier Name ....

Address..

City, State, Zip ....

Phone..

Contact Person ....

Electronic Claims (y/n)? ....

Signature on File (y/n)? ....

Enter Another Carrier (y/n)? ....

INSURANCE CARRIERS

Data Entry Screen

Carrier Code ....

Carrier Name ....

Address..

City, State, Zip ....

Phone..

Contact Person ....

Electronic Claims (y/n)? ....

Signature on File (y/n)? ....

Enter Another Carrier (y/n)? ....

FILE MAINTENANCE SYSTEM

Menu Options

1. Practice Information
2. User Passwords
3. Provider Information
4. Diagnosis Codes
5. Procedure Codes
6. Insurance Carriers
7. Place of Service
8. Referring Physicians

ESC: Return to Main Menu

Enter Selection? ....

Worksheet 15: Place of Service

COMPETENCY

Access the Place of Service data entry screen.

GUIDELINES

The Place of Service option is used to compile and store information on the facilities where the physician performs medical services and procedures such as the physician's office, hospital, emergency room, extended care facilities, and the patient's home. This information is automatically printed when required on documents such as patient statements and insurance claims. It is also used in the generation of statistical information for practice analysis reports. In order to set up the Place of Service file, you must enter the necessary information for each facility. Once entered, all you have to do to identify a place of service is to specify the office code for that particular facility.

LEARNING ACTIVITIES

1. What is the function of the Place of Service option? ______________________

   ____

2. What number should you select to move to this screen?

   ____

3. a. Make this selection in the space entitled *Enter Selection*.

   b. Turn the page to move to the next screen.

PLACE OF SERVICE

Data Entry Screen

Facility Code O

Facility Name Riverside Family Practice Clinic

Address 400 Broad Street

City, State, Zip Norman, OK, 73070

Phone 4053607444

Federal Tax ID Number 32-6025986

Enter Another Facility (y/n)? y

Worksheet 16: Place of Service

COMPETENCY

Enter place of service into the computer system.

GUIDELINES

Opposite is a completed data entry screen for place of service. You are responsible for entering information into your computer system on the facilities in which your physicians perform medical services and procedures.

DOCUMENTATION

Facility Code: This code consists of a short, meaningful abbreviation to be used as a short-cut for accessing information in this file. The following codes should be used: O: Physician's Office; IH: Inpatient Hospital; OH: Outpatient Hospital; NH: Nursing Home; P: Patient's Home; SN: Skilled Nursing Facility; A: Ambulance.

Facility Name: Enter the name of the facility.

Address: Enter the street address of the facility.

City, State, Zip: Enter the facility's city, state and zip code.

Phone: Enter the phone number of the facility.

Federal Tax ID Number: Enter the federal tax identification number of the facility.

Enter Another Facility (y/n)?: A "y" response takes you to a new Place of Service data entry screen, while an "n" response returns you to the File Maintenance menu.

LEARNING ACTIVITIES

1. Complete the Place of Service data entry screens with the following information.

   Grant Hospital
   3066 Chestnut Street
   Norman, OK 7307
   Phone: (405) 232-3816
   Facility Code: OH
   Federal Tax ID No: 62-8093600

   Woodland Nursing Home
   312 Sunnyside Avenue
   Norman, OK 73070
   Phone: (405) 840-3927
   Facility Code: NH
   Federal Tax ID No: 46-3985526

2. a. After completing the last data entry screen, return to the File Maintenance menu.
   b. Turn the page to move to the File Maintenance menu.

PLACE OF SERVICE

Data Entry Screen

Facility Code ....

Facility Name ....

Address ....

City, State, Zip ....

Phone ....

Federal Tax ID Number ....

Enter Another Facility (y/n)? ....

PLACE OF SERVICE
Data Entry Screen

Facility Code ....

Facility Name ....

Address ....

City, State, Zip ....

Phone ....

Federal Tax ID Number ....

Enter Another Facility (y/n)? ....

FILE MAINTENANCE SYSTEM

Menu Options

1. Practice Information
2. User Passwords
3. Provider Information
4. Diagnosis Codes
5. Procedure Codes
6. Insurance Carriers
7. Place of Service
8. Referring Physicians

ESC: Return to Main Menu

Enter Selection? ....

Worksheet 17: Referring Physicians

COMPETENCY

Access the Referring Physicians data entry screen.

GUIDELINES

The Referring Physicians option is used to compile and store information on physicians who refer patients to your medical office. A referral code is assigned to each referring physician. Once identified, the system can monitor the number of referrals and the revenues generated by those referrals. In order to set up the Referring Physicians file, you must enter the necessary information for each physician. Once entered, all you have to do to identify a particular referring physician for an account is to specify the designated code for that physician.

LEARNING ACTIVITIES

1. What is the function of the Referring Physicians option? ____________________

   ____

2. What number should you select to move to this screen?

   ____

3. a. Make this selection in the space entitled *Enter Selection*.

   b. Turn the page to move to the next screen.

REFERRING PHYSICIANS

Data Entry Screen

Referral Code BN

Referral Name Benjamin Nelson, MD

Address 312 Longview Heights

City, State, Zip Norman, OK, 73070

Phone 4057553269

Enter Another Referral (y/n)? y

Worksheet 18: Referring Physicians

COMPETENCY

Enter referring physicians into the computer system.

GUIDELINES

Opposite is a completed data entry screen for referring physicians. You are responsible for entering referring physician information into you computer system.

DOCUMENTATION

Referral Code: A unique code for each referring physician that is used as a short-cut for accessing information in this file.

Referral Name: Enter the name of the referring physician and his/her professional degree.

Address: Enter the street address of the referring physician

City, State, Zip: Enter the referring physician's city, state and zip code.

Phone: Enter the phone number of the referring physician.

Enter Another Referral (y/n)?: A "y" response takes you to a new Referring Physicians data entry screen, while an "n" response returns you to the File Maintenance menu.

LEARNING ACTIVITIES

1. Once entered into the database, how is referring information useful to the medical practice?

____

____

1. Complete the Referring Physicians data entry screens on the following pages with the information below.

   Ryan O. Gassaway, MD
   3344 Holly Boulevard
   Norman, Oklahoma 73070
   Phone: (405) 232-6650
   Referral Code: RG

   Shirley A. Pearce, MD
   72 Hill Street
   Norman, Oklahoma 73070
   Phone: (405) 840-3991
   Referral Code: SP

2. After entering referring physicians into the system, proceed to Chapter 6.

REFERRING PHYSICIANS

Data Entry Screen

Referral Code ....

Referral Name ....

Address ....

City, State, Zip ....

Phone ....

Enter Another Referral (y/n)? ....

REFERRING PHYSICIANS

Data Entry Screen

Referral Code ....

Referral Name ....

Address ....

City, State, Zip ....

Phone ....

Enter Another Referral (y/n)? ....

6 PATIENT REGISTRATION

COMPETENCY

After completing this chapter, you should be able to perform the following:

Enter new patients into the computer system.

LEARNING OBJECTIVES

After completing this chapter, you should be able to:

1. List three medical office management functions that require the access of data from the Patient Registration file.
2. Explain the function of the New Patient Entry option.
3. Explain the function of the Edit Existing Patient Record option.
4. Explain the function of the Delete Patient Record option.
5. Explain the function of the Review Patient Record option.

Introduction

The Patient Registration System is used to set up a registration record for each patient in the practice. The patient registration record includes patient demographic and insurance information. Patient registration records are stored in the Patient Registration file which is a key element of the medical practice database. This file is continually accessed by virtually all the other systems in the *Medical Practice Manager* to obtain information necessary to perform such functions as posting transactions, scheduling appointments, and processing patient statements and insurance claims. In addition to setting up new patient registration records, this system is also used to review and update information on existing records and to delete patient registration records.

Patient Registration Options

The *Medical Practice Manager* includes four options within the Patient Registration System. Each of these options is used to perform specific functions which are listed and described below:

Enter New Patient: This option is selected when you want to enter new patients into the system. When first setting up the computer system, you will have to enter all the patients in the medical practice. Thereafter, only new patients need to be entered. To reduce data entry errors, most offices use a patient information sheet as a source document. The patient is given the information sheet to complete which includes spaces for filling in his/her demographic and insurance information. The data is then entered (from this sheet) into the computer. To speed the data entry process, the fill-in-the blank spaces on the information sheet (e.g., name, address, phone) should be sequenced the same as those on the "on-screen" patient registration form. To identify each patient's account, the *Medical Practice Manager* automatically assigns an account number to each patient registration record. Each account number is four digits in length, starting with 0001 and continuing in ascending order (i.e., 0002, 0003, 0004, and so on). This number can later be used to access that patient's account.

Edit Existing Patient Record: This option should be selected when you want to change or update information on a patient registration record. Examples of when this is necessary include a change in marital status, a change of last name, a change of address and/or phone number, a change in insurance company, and so on. The edit screen is identical to the New Patient Entry screen except that it is used to make changes rather than adding a new patient.

Delete Patient Record: The Delete Patient Record option is selected when you want to remove a patient registration record from your database. This option is used when a patient dies, moves away, or transfers to a new physician.

Review Patient Record: The Review Patient Record option provides a means for quickly locating information about a particular patient. This option is commonly used to look up the patient's address, phone number, social security number, and so on. Unlike the Edit Existing Record option, this option cannot be used to change or update information on the patient's registration record.

Once a patient has been entered into the system, the *Medical Practice Manager* allows you to access the record by the patient's account number, last name, or social security number. After entering the appropriate information, the system displays the patient registration record you requested on the screen of the computer monitor.

CHECKPOINT

1. What information is included on the patient registration record?

   ____

2. List four examples of functions performed by the computer that accesses information stored in the Patient Registration file?

   ____

   ____

3. What is generally used as a source document when entering new patients into the system?

   ____

4. What is used to identify each patient entered into the system?

   ____

5. What is the purpose of the Edit Existing Patient Record option?

   ____

   ____

6. What is the purpose of the Review Patient Record option?

   ____

   ____

7. What are the three ways to access patient records in the *Medical Practice Manager*?

   ____

   ____

   ____

MEDICAL PRACTICE MANAGER

Main Menu

1. Patient Registration
2. Posting Transactions
3. Patient Billing
4. Insurance Billing
5. Reports
6. File Maintenance

Enter Selection? ....

Worksheet 1: Patient Registration System

COMPETENCY

Access the Patient Registration System.

GUIDELINES

You are responsible for entering patient registration information into your computer system. The "labor-intensive" chore of entering all the patients coming to your medical office (in order to set up your computer system) has already been performed. The total number of patients entered thus far is three-thousand (3,000); however, your physicians saw several new patients today and it is your responsibility to enter them into the system.

LEARNING ACTIVITIES

1. What is the function of the Patient Registration System? ______________________

   ____

2. What number should you select to move to this system?

   ____

3. a. Make this selection on the screen in the space entitled *Enter Selection.*

   b. Turn the page to move to the next screen.

PATIENT REGISTRATION SYSTEM

Menu Options

1. New Patient Entry
2. Edit Existing Patient Record
3. Delete Patient Record
4. Review Patient Record

ESC: Return to Main Menu

Enter Selection? ....

Worksheet 2: New Patient Entry

COMPETENCY

Access the New Patient Entry data entry screen.

GUIDELINES

There are four options included in the Patient Registration System as illustrated on the menu screen on the opposite page. Make sure you are completely familiar with the function of each of these options by first reviewing the information on pages 200 to 201 followed by completion of the Learning Activities presented below.

LEARNING ACTIVITIES

1. What option (by name and number) would you select to perform the following tasks?

   a. To remove a patient record from the system of a patient who has moved away and changed physicians.

   ____

   b. To look up the address of a patient to send him some information on medication he is taking.

   ____

   c. To change the last name, address, and phone number of a newly married patient.

   ____

   d. To look up the work phone number of a patient to call him to change his appointment time.

   ____

   e. To enter a new patient account into the medical practice database.

   ____

2. You are now ready to enter new patients into the system. What number should you select to move to this option?

   ____

3. a. Make this selection on the screen in the space entitle *Enter Selection.*

   b. Turn the page to move to the next screen.

NEW PATIENT ENTRY

Data Entry Screen

Patient Account Number: 3001

A. PATIENT INFORMATION

Name Gribble, Betsy A

Address 6 North May Avenue

City, State, Zip Norman, OK, 73070

Phone (home) 4053604653

Phone (work)

SSN 278346721

Sex F

Birthdate 051278

Marital Status S

Employer Student

Referring Source RG

Date of First Visit 102191

Usual Provider JW

Responsible Party Gribble, Donald J

Address 6 North May Avenue

City, State, Zip Norman, OK, 73070

Phone (home) 4053604653

Worksheet 3: New Patient Entry

COMPETENCY

Enter new patients into the system.

GUIDELINES

The New Patient Entry data entry screen consists of two screens: Patient Information and Insurance Information. The Patient Information screen includes general demographic and personal patient data such as the patient's name, address, phone number, sex, birthdate and so on. The Insurance Information screen consists of information needed by the system in order to bill charges to an insurance carrier such as the name of the insured party, the carrier name, the policy and group number. Once this data has been entered, the computer can use it to generate insurance claims without the user having to re-enter it over and over again. As you should note from the data entry screen on the opposite page, a four digit patient account number is automatically assigned to the patient and is displayed at the top of the screen. Since 3,000 patients have already been entered into the system, the last patient number was 3000, making the number for this patient 3001.

DOCUMENTATION - PATIENT INFORMATION

Name: Enter the name of the patient with the last name first, followed by a comma and the first name and middle initial.
Address: Enter the patient's street address in this data field.
City, State, Zip: Enter the city name followed by a comma, the two-letter state abbreviation, and the zip code.
Phone Numbers: Enter the patient's home and work phone numbers, including the area code. You do not need to add the formatting guides [( ) and —] as the system will automatically do this for you.
SSN: Enter the patient's social security number. You do not need to add the formatting guides (-) as the system will automatically do this for you.
Sex: Enter M for male or F for female.
Birthdate: Enter the patient's birthdate using the following format: MMDDYY.
Marital Status: Enter M for married, S for single, D for divorced and W for widowed.
Employer: Enter the name of the patient's employer in this data field. If the patient is not employed, this field should be used to designate the patient's status (e.g., child, student, homemaker, retired).
Referring Source: Enter the referral code of the physician who referred the patient to the medical office. If the patient was referred by a source other than a physician, enter the name of that individual.
Date of First Visit: Enter the date the patient first visited the office using the following format: MMDDYY.
Usual Provider: Enter the provider code of the physician responsible for the patient or the physician with whom the patient normally schedules his/her visit.
Responsible Party: The responsible party (also known as the guarantor) is the person who is responsible for paying an account's bills. Enter the name of the responsible party with the last name first, followed by a comma and the first name and middle initial.
Address: Enter the address of the responsible party as you want it to appear on patient statements.
City, State, Zip: Enter the responsible party's city name followed by a comma, the two-letter state abbreviation, and the zip code.
Phone: Enter the home phone number of the responsible party.

DOCUMENTATION - INSURANCE INFORMATION

Subscriber Name: This is the name of the insured person. Enter this information with the last name first, followed by a comma and the first name and middle initial.

Address: Enter the street address of the subscriber in this field.

City, State, Zip: Enter the subscriber's city name followed by a comma, the two-letter state abbreviation, and the zip code.

Insurance Carrier: Enter the carrier code of the insurance company that insures this individual.

Subscriber ID Number: Enter the policy number of the patient's insurance plan.

Subscriber Group Number: Enter the group number of the patient's insurance plan.

Relationship: Enter the relationship of the patient to the subscriber (insured party) using one the following codes: SE for self; SP for spouse, CH for child; and O for other.

Accept Assignment (y/n)?: An "n" indicates that the physician does not accept assignment from the insurance company and wants payment from the patient. The office may still generate an insurance form as a courtesy for the patient. A "y" indicates that the office accepts the responsibility to receive the initial payment for a bill from the carrier and may generate the insurance claim to the carrier.

Enter Another Patient (y/n)?: A "y" response takes you to a new data entry screen, while an "n" response returns you to the File Maintenance menu.

NEW PATIENT ENTRY

Data Entry Screen

B. INSURANCE INFORMATION

Subscriber Name Gribble, Donald J

Address 6 North May Avenue

City, State, Zip Norman, OK, 73070

Insurance Carrier BC

Subscriber ID Number 322897766

Subscriber Group Number 332

Relationship CH

Accept Assignment (y/n)? n

Enter Another Patient (y/n)? y

LEARNING ACTIVITIES

1. What is the purpose of the Patient Information screen?

    ____

    ____

2. What is the purpose of the Insurance Information screen?

    ____

    ____

3. What is the responsibility of the guarantor? ______________________________

    ____

4. What information must be entered in the subscriber identification number field?

    ____

5. What does it mean when a physician accepts assignment?

    ____

    ____

6. Complete a New Patient Entry screen for two new patients using the Patient Information sheets on the following pages as your source documents. Use the following guidelines when completing the data entry screens:

    Date of First Visit: Use today's date for the date of the first visit.

    Accept Assignment (y/n)?: The physician does not accept assignment from the insurance company.

7. After entering new patients into the system, proceed to Chapter 7.

RIVERSIDE FAMILY PRACTICE CLINIC

Information Sheet

A. PATIENT INFORMATION

Name *Michael E. Boyd* Phone (home) *405-947-3310*

Address *42 Baltic Avenue* Phone (work) *405-755-8933*

Norman, Oklahoma 73070

Social Security Number *347-89-2901* Sex *M*

Birthdate *April 28, 1948*

Marital Status *X* Married ___ Single ___ Divorced ___ Widowed

Employer *General Motors*

Referred By *Shirley Pearce, MD*

Responsible Party *Michael E. Boyd* Phone (home) *405-947-3310*

Address *42 Baltic Avenue*

Norman, Oklahoma 73070

B. INSURANCE INFORMATION

Subscriber Name *Michael E. Boyd*

Address *42 Baltic Avenue*

Norman, Oklahoma 73070

Insurance Carrier *Aetna Insurance Company*

Subscriber ID Number *00347892901*

Subscriber Group Number *433*

Relationship *X* Self ___ Spouse ___ Child ___ Other

Provider *Keith Howe, MD*

NEW PATIENT ENTRY

Data Entry Screen

Patient Account Number: 3002

A. PATIENT INFORMATION

Name ....

Address ....

City, State, Zip ....

Phone (home) ....

Phone (work) ....

SSN ....

Sex ....

Birthdate ....

Marital Status ....

Employer ....

Referring Source ....

Date of First Visit ....

Usual Provider ....

Responsible Party ....

Address ....

City, State, Zip ....

Phone (home) ....

NEW PATIENT ENTRY

Data Entry Screen

B. INSURANCE INFORMATION

Subscriber Name ....

Address ....

City, State, Zip ....

Insurance Carrier ....

Subscriber ID Number ....

Subscriber Group Number ....

Relationship ....

Accept Assignment (y/n)? ....

Enter Another Patient (y/n)? ....

RIVERSIDE FAMILY PRACTICE CLINIC

Information Sheet

A. PATIENT INFORMATION

Name *Martha L. Wiley* Phone (home) *405-840-5428*

Address *313 Astor Road* Phone (work) *405-755-3668*

Norman, Oklahoma 73070

Social Security Number *291-33-4610* Sex *F*

Birthdate *August 8, 1961*

Marital Status *X* Married ___ Single ___ Divorced ___ Widowed

Employer *Mutual Finance Incorporated*

Referred By *Ryan Gassaway, MD*

Responsible Party *Thomas J. Wiley* Phone (home) *405-840-5428*

Address *313 Astor Road*

Norman, Oklahoma 73070

B. INSURANCE INFORMATION

Subscriber Name *Thomas J. Wiley*

Address *313 Astor Road*

Norman, Oklahoma 73070

Insurance Carrier *Metropolitan Insurance Company*

Subscriber ID Number *291334610*

Subscriber Group Number *755*

Relationship ___ Self *X* Spouse ___ Child ___ Other

Provider *James Westmoreland, MD*

NEW PATIENT ENTRY

Data Entry Screen

Patient Account Number: 3003

A. PATIENT INFORMATION

Name ....

Address ....

City, State, Zip ....

Phone (home) ....

Phone (work) ....

SSN ....

Sex ....

Birthdate ....

Marital Status ....

Employer ....

Referring Source..

Date of First Visit ....

Usual Provider ....

Responsible Party ....

Address ....

City, State, Zip ....

Phone (home) ....

NEW PATIENT ENTRY

Data Entry Screen

B. INSURANCE INFORMATION

Subscriber Name ....

Address ....

City, State, Zip ....

Insurance Carrier ....

Subscriber ID Number ....

Subscriber Group Number ....

Relationship ....

Accept Assignment (y/n)? ....

Enter Another Patient (y/n)? ....

7

POSTING TRANSACTIONS

COMPETENCIES

After completing this chapter, you should be able to perform the following.

1. Post patient charges.
2. Post patient payments.

LEARNING OBJECTIVES

After completing this chapter, you should be able to:

1. Explain the function of the Posting Charges option.
2. State the purpose of a route slip.
3. Describe batch entry.
4. Explain the function of the Posting Payments option.
5. Explain the function of the Accounts Adjustment option.
6. Explain the function of the Patient Account Summary option.

Introduction

One of the tasks performed most often on a day-to-day basis in a medical office is that of recording patient transactions. The Posting Transactions System in the *Medical Practice Manager* is used to perform this task. This system enables you to post all charges and payments received in the course of a day. The Posting Transactions System also allows you to adjust previously made entries that were made in error and to review a patient's complete transaction record. Additionally, the information entered into this file is stored in the medical practice database for later use in processing patient statements and insurance claims as will be discussed in Chapters 8 and 9. It is important to enter this information carefully and accurately. Entry errors are a common source of problems in medical office computer operations.

Posting Transactions Options

The *Medical Practice Manager* includes four options within the Posting Transactions System. Each of these options is used to perform specific functions which are listed and described below:

Posting Charges: When a patient is seen by the physician, you will want to enter the services and procedures performed for the patient and the fees charged for these services. The Posting Charges option is used to perform this task of entering bills into the system. This option is also used to post payments received from the patient at the *time of service* (TOS) and to generate an "on-the-spot" receipt for the patient. Most offices enter charges from a source document generically known as a *route slip*. This term is used because the slip is routed from the front office to the doctor and then back to the front office. Specific examples of route slips include encounter forms, charge slips, and superbills. Route slips can either be ordered from an office supply vendor or generated by the computer. Patient demographic information (name, address, phone) is included on the upper part of the route slip. The lower part of the form is customized to include a list of the most common procedures and diagnoses used in the medical office with spaces for entering those not preprinted on the form. The route slip is attached to the patient's chart and the physician checks off the diagnoses and procedures appropriate to the patient's visit. The medical assistant can then post charges from the route slip during patient departure or later on by "batching" all the route slips together and entering them all at one time; for example, at the end of office hours. *Batch entry* means that all the information requiring entry is grouped together and entered at one time.

Posting Payments: The Posting Payments option is used to enter various types of payments received after the time of service. These include payments from insurance carriers, the patient's guarantor (responsible party), and the patient. The type of payments that may be entered are personal checks from the patient, insurance carrier's checks, cash, and credit card payments. Most medical offices prefer to post payments using batch entry.

Make Account Adjustments: The Make Account Adjustments option is selected when you need to change data on a patient's bill that has previously been posted; in other words, to make adjustments to the charges and/or payments previously entered. This option is used when posted information is incomplete or inaccurate; examples include the posting of an incorrect procedure and posting a payment to the wrong account.

Patient Account Summary: The Patient Account Summary option is used to review the activity of an account including all charges, payments, and adjustments sequenced with the most current visit date appearing first. The account summary also includes the reason for the charge, the method of payment, and the outstanding account balance. One of the more frequent tasks you will perform with your computer will be to answer inquiries from patients about their accounts. This option provides a means for quickly looking up information regarding a patient's financial account when a patient calls with inquiries about charges or insurance payments. Patient's accounts are accessed by the patient's account number, last name, or social security number. After entering the appropriate information, the system displays the patient transaction record you requested on the screen of the monitor.

CHECKPOINT

1. What is the purpose of a route slip? ____________________

   ____

2. What information is included on a route slip? ____________________

   ____

   ____

3. What is the definition of batch entry? ____________________

   ____

   ____

4. Which option is used to post payments received after the time of service?

   ____

5. What information is included in a patient account summary?

   ____

   ____

MEDICAL PRACTICE MANAGER

Main Menu

1. Patient Registration
2. Posting Transactions
3. Patient Billing
4. Insurance Billing
5. Reports
6. File Maintenance

Enter Selection? ....

Worksheet 1: Posting Transactions System

COMPETENCY

Access the Posting Transactions System.

GUIDELINES

You are responsible for posting charges for the new patients just entered into the system. In order to do this, you must first access the Posting Transactions System.

LEARNING ACTIVITIES

1. What is the function of the Posting Transactions System?

   ____

2. What number should you select to move to this system?

   ____

3. a. Make this selection on the screen in the space entitled *Enter Selection.*

   b. Turn the page to move to the next screen.

POSTING TRANSACTIONS SYSTEM

Menu Options

1. Post Charges
2. Post Payments
3. Make Account Adjustments
4. Patient Account Summary

ESC: Return to Main Menu

Enter Selection? ....

Enter Patient Number, Name, or SSN ....

Worksheet 2: Posting Charges

COMPETENCY

Access the Post Charges data entry screen.

GUIDELINES

There are four options included in the Posting Transactions System as illustrated on the menu screen on the opposite page. Make sure you are familiar with the function of each of these options by first reviewing the information on pages 218 to 219 followed by completion of the Learning Activities presented below.

LEARNING ACTIVITIES

1. What option (by name and number) would you select to perform the following tasks?

   a. To post a payment received from Blue Cross for Kevin Dobbs

   ____

   b. To change the amount charged for a procedure for Karen Spencer

   ____

   c. To look up the date of the last payment made by Sue Long

   ____

2. a. You are now ready to post patient charges. What number should you select to move to this option?

   ____

   b. Make this selection on the screen in the space entitled *Enter Selection.*

   c. The first charges are to be posted to the account of Betsy Gribble (Account Number: 3001).

   d. Enter the proper identification for this patient in the space provided on the menu screen.

   e. Turn the page to move to the next screen.

POST CHARGES

Data Entry Screen

Account Number 3001

Betsy A. Gribble
6 North May Avenue
Norman, OK 73070

Date of Service 102192

Place of Service O

Provider JW

Diagnosis Code	**ICD-9 Code**	**Description**
STREP	*034*	*Strep Throat*

Procedure Code	**CPT Code**	**Description**	**Amount**
NP2	*99202*	*New Patient, Level II*	*$20.00*
TC	*87060*	*Throat Culture*	*$10.00*

Visit Payment F

TOS Payment Amount 30.00

TOS Payment Type CK

Print a Bill (y/n)? n

Post Charges for Another Patient (y/n)? y

Enter Patient Number, Name or SSN 2320

Worksheet 3: Posting Charges

COMPETENCY

Post patient charges.

GUIDELINES

The data entry screen on the opposite page is completed almost entirely through the use of codes that you previously set up during your start-up procedures. From the information stored in the medical practice database, these codes are then translated into the proper full length information required for billing.

DOCUMENTATION

Account Number: No entry is necessary. The system automatically displays the account number of the patient requested.

Patient's Name and Address: No entry is necessary. The system automatically displays the name and address of the patient requested.

Date of Service: Enter the date of the service in this field using the following format: MMDDYY.

Place of Service: This documents the place where the procedure occurred. Enter the code representing the place of service (i.e., O, IH, OH, NH).

Provider: Enter the provider code of the physician who performed the procedure.

Diagnosis Code: Enter the office code for this diagnosis. The ICD-9-CM code and the diagnosis description (shown in italics) are automatically generated by the system upon entry of the office code.

Procedure Code: Enter the office code for the medical services or procedures performed. The CPT-4 code, the procedure description, and the standard charge (shown in italics) are automatically generated by the system upon entry of the office code. *Note*: The system allows you to override the amount of the charge displayed by entering a dollar amount into this data field.

Visit Payment: Enter the visit payment using one of the following codes:

F (Fully paid patient)—The patient pays the bill in full at the time of service.

P (Partially paid patient)—The patient pays only a portion of the bill at the time of service.

C (Charge)—The patient is allowed to charge the service and will be billed later for the visit.

I (Insurance)—The insurance company is to be billed for the visit.

(Continued next page)

TOS Payment Amount: This field is used to indicate the amount of any payment made by the patient at the time of service. Enter the dollar amount received from the patient using digits and a decimal point. The system assumes that any amount entered will be dollar figures, therefore a dollar sign is not required.

TOS Payment Type: Enter the type of payment using the following codes CA for cash, CK for check, and CC for credit card.

Print a Bill (y/n)?: A "y" response results in the printout of a superbill for the patient which serves as a patient receipt. A superbill is a statement for an individual patient showing the services rendered, charges, and diagnosis. It contains all the information required for a patient to file a claim with his/her insurance company. To use this option however, the office must have a printer that is assigned solely to printing these "walk-away" bills.

Post Charges for Another Patient (y/n)?: A "y" response takes you to a new data entry screen for means of posting charges for another patient, while an "n" response returns you to the Posting Transactions menu.

Enter Patient Number, Name, or SSN: Enter appropriate identification information to request the patient desired. You have a choice of entering either the patient's account number, the patient's last name, or the patient's social security number.

LEARNING ACTIVITIES

1. What information is automatically generated by the system when the diagnosis code is entered?

 ____

2. What information is automatically generated by the system when the procedure code is entered?

 ____

3. What is a superbill? ______________________________

 ____

 ____

4. What information is included on a superbill? ______________________________

 ____

 ____

5. Post charges for two patients using the encounter forms on the following pages. Use the following guidelines when completing the data entry screens:

 Date of Service: Use today's date.

 Place of Service: All patient visits took place at the physician's office.

 Diagnosis Code/Procedure Code: Be sure to enter the office code for the diagnosis and procedure(s) rather than the ICDA or CPT code.

 Print a Bill (y/n)?: Answer "no" to this field.

 Enter Patient Number, Name, or SSN: Patient account numbers have already been entered for you into this field.

6. After you are finished posting charges, return to the Posting Transactions menu.

7. Turn to page 232 to move to the Posting Transactions menu.

RIVERSIDE FAMILY PRACTICE CLINIC
Encounter Form

Patient's Name *Paul Gleason*

Address *34 Cardiff Lane*

Norman, Oklahoma 73070

Account Number *2320* **Date of Service** ______

OFFICE PROCEDURES			DIAGNOSIS		
Visit - New Patient					
______	NP1	New Patient, Level I	______	AP	Abdominal Pain
______	NP2	New Patient, Level II	______	AR	Allergic Rhinitis
______	NP3	New Patient, Level III	______	AN	Anemia, Iron Deficiency
______	NP4	New Patient, Level IV	______	ANG	Angina Pectoris
______	NP5	New Patient, Level V	______	ARTH	Arthritis
Visit - Established Patient			______	BRON	Bronchitis
______	EP1	Established Patient, Level I	______	CHF	Congestive Heart Failure
______	EP2	Established Patient, Level II	______	CONJ	Conjunctivitis
______	EP3	Established Patient, Level III	______	EMP	Emphysema
X	EP4	Established Patient, Level IV	______	HT	Hypertension
______	EP5	Established Patient, Level V	______	FLU	Influenza
			______	LBP	Low Back Pain
			______	OM	Otitis Media
Immumizations/Injections			______	STREP	Strep Throat
			______	URI	Upper Respiratory Infection
______	DPT	Immunization-DPT	X	UTI	Urinary Tract Infection
______	MMR	Immunization-MMR	______	Other	______
______	OPV	Oral Polio Vaccine			
______	ALL	Allergy Injection	**Physician**	*Westmoreland*	
Miscellaneous Procedures					
______	IRR	Ear Irrigation	**Charges**	*$35.00*	
______	PEL	Pelvic Exam			
______	SIG	Sigmoidoscopy	**Payment**	*$35.00*	
______	US	Ultrasound			
Laboratory			X	**Cash**	
______	CBC/D	CBC with Diff	______	**Check**	
______	GLU	Glucose	______	**Credit Card**	
______	HCT	Hematocrit	______	**File Insurance**	
X	UA	Urinalysis			
______	TC	Throat Culture			

POST CHARGES

Data Entry Screen

Account Number 2320

Paul Gleason
34 Cardiff Lane
Norman, OK 73070

Date of Service ....

Place of Service ....

Provider ....

Diagnosis Code **ICD-9 Code** **Description**

Procedure Code **CPT Code** **Description** **Amount**

Visit Payment ....

TOS Payment Amount ....

TOS Payment Type ....

Print a Bill (y/n)? ....

Post Charges for Another Patient (y/n)? y

Enter Patient Number, Name or SSN 1538

RIVERSIDE FAMILY PRACTICE CLINIC
Encounter Form

Patient's Name *Leah Crock*

Address *264 Hooper Street*

Norman, Oklahoma 73070

Account Number *1538* **Date of Service** ______

OFFICE PROCEDURES	DIAGNOSIS
Visit - New Patient	
___ NP1 New Patient, Level I	___ AP Abdominal Pain
___ NP2 New Patient, Level II	___ AR Allergic Rhinitis
___ NP3 New Patient, Level III	_X_ AN Anemia, Iron Deficiency
___ NP4 New Patient, Level IV	___ ANG Angina Pectoris
___ NP5 New Patient, Level V	___ ARTH Arthritis
Visit - Established Patient	___ BRON Bronchitis
___ EP1 Established Patient, Level I	___ CHF Congestive Heart Failure
_X_ EP2 Established Patient, Level II	___ CONJ Conjunctivitis
___ EP3 Established Patient, Level III	___ EMP Emphysema
___ EP4 Established Patient, Level IV	___ HT Hypertension
___ EP5 Established Patient, Level V	___ FLU Influenza
	___ LBP Low Back Pain
	___ OM Otitis Media
Immumizations/Injections	___ STREP Strep Throat
___ DPT Immunization-DPT	___ URI Upper Respiratory Infection
___ MMR Immunization-MMR	___ UTI Urinary Tract Infection
___ OPV Oral Polio Vaccine	___ Other ______
___ ALL Allergy Injection	
Miscellaneous Procedures	**Physician** *Howe*
___ IRR Ear Irrigation	
___ PEL Pelvic Exam	**Charges** *$25.00*
___ SIG Sigmoidoscopy	
___ US Ultrasound	**Payment** *$25.00*
Laboratory	
___ CBC/D CBC with Diff	___ **Cash**
___ GLU Glucose	_X_ **Check**
_X_ HCT Hematocrit	___ **Credit Card**
___ UA Urinalysis	___ **File Insurance**
___ TC Throat Culture	

POST CHARGES

Data Entry Screen

Account Number 1538

Leah Crock
264 Hooper Street
Norman, OK 73070

Date of Service ....

Place of Service ....

Provider ....

Diagnosis Code	**ICD-9 Code**	**Description**

Procedure Code	**CPT Code**	**Description**	**Amount**

Visit Payment ....

TOS Payment Amount ....

TOS Payment Type ....

Print a Bill (y/n)? ....

Post Charges for Another Patient (y/n)? ....

POSTING TRANSACTIONS SYSTEM

Menu Options

1. Post Charges
2. Post Payments
3. Make Account Adjustments
4. Patient Account Summary

ESC: Return to Main Menu

Enter Selection? ....

Enter Patient Number, Name, or SSN ....

Worksheet 4: Posting Payments

COMPETENCY

Access the Post Payments data entry screen.

GUIDELINES

You are now back in the Posting Transactions menu. You are responsible for posting payments you have just received in the mail. In order to do this, you must first access the Post Payments option.

LEARNING ACTIVITIES

1. What is the function of the Posting Payments option? ______________________

   ____

2. What number should you select to move to this option?

   ____

3. a. Make this selection in the space entitled *Enter Selection.*

   b. The first patient for whom you will be posting a payment is John J. Smith (Account Number: 2500).

   c. Enter the proper identification for this patient in the space provided on the menu screen.

   d. Turn the page to move to the next screen.

POST PAYMENTS

Data Entry Screen

Account Number 2500

John J. Smith
10 Dearborn Street
Norman, OK 73070

Last STM Date 8/30/92
Balance $40.00
Last Payment $20.00
Last Payment Date 7/15/92

Payment Amount 40.00

Date of Payment 091592

Type of Payment CK

Source of Payment P

Enter Another Payment (y/n)? y

Enter Patient Number, Name or SSN 2110

Worksheet 5: Posting Payments

COMPETENCY

Post patient payments.

GUIDELINES

The Posting Payments option is used to post payments received after the time of service.

DOCUMENTATION

Account Number: No entry is necessary. The system automatically displays the account number of the patient requested.
Patient's Name and Address: No entry is necessary. The system automatically displays the name and address of the patient requested.

Last STM Date: No entry is necessary. This indicates the date the patient's last statement was printed and is automatically displayed by the computer system.
Balance: No entry is necessary. This indicates the patient's outstanding balance and is automatically displayed by the computer system.
Last Payment: No entry is necessary. This is the last payment amount received on this account and is automatically displayed by the computer system.
Last Payment Date: No entry is necessary. This is the date that the last payment was received and is automatically displayed by the computer system.

Payment Amount: Enter the total amount of the payment using digits and a decimal point. The system assumes that any amount entered will be a dollar figure, therefore a dollar sign is not required.

Date of Payment: Enter the date the payment was received in MMDDYY format.

Type of Payment: Enter the method of payment using the following codes: CA for cash, CK for check, and CC for credit card.

Source of Payment: Enter the source of payment using the following codes: P indicates the patient made the payment and an I indicates the insurance carrier made the payment.

Enter Another Payment (y/n)?: A "y" response takes you to a new data entry screen to post another payment while an "n" response returns you to the Posting Transactions menu.

Patient Number, Name, or SSN: Enter appropriate identification information to request the patient desired.

LEARNING ACTIVITIES

1. What information is automatically generated by the system and displayed on Post Payments data entry screen?

____

____

2. What information is indicated in each of the following fields?

   a. Last STM Date _______________________________

   b. Balance _______________________________

   c. Last Payment _______________________________

   d. Last Payment Date _______________________________

3. Post payments for the following two patients.

   Patient: Henry Clark
   Account Number: 2110
   Payment Amount: $85.00
   Type of Payment: Check
   Source of Payment: Insurance

   Patient: Saralyn Griggs
   Account Number: 850
   Payment Amount: $30.00
   Type of Payment: Check
   Source of Payment: Patient

4. Use the following guidelines when completing the data entry screens:

   Date of Payment: Use today's date.

   Enter Patient Number, Name or SSN: Patient numbers have already been entered for you into this field.

5. After entering payments into the system, proceed to Chapter 8.

POST PAYMENTS

Data Entry Screen

Account Number 2110

Henry Clark
151 Thomas Street
Norman, OK 73070

Last STM Date 5/22/93
Balance $85.00
Last Payment $30.00
Last Payment Date 6/21/92

Payment Amount ....

Date of Payment ....

Type of Payment ....

Source of Payment ....

Enter Another Payment (y/n)? ....

Enter Patient Number, Name or SSN 850

POST PAYMENTS

Data Entry Screen

Account Number 850

Saralyn Griggs
23 Court Street
Norman, OK 73070

Last STM Date 5/27/93
Balance $30.00
Last Payment $20.00
Last Payment Date 7/13/92

Payment Amount ....

Date of Payment ....

Type of Payment ....

Source of Payment ....

Enter Another Payment (y/n)? ....

8 PATIENT BILLING

COMPETENCY

After completing this chapter, you should be able to perform the following:

Process patient statements.

LEARNING OBJECTIVES

After completing this chapter, you should be able to:

1. Describe the patient billing routine.
2. List three sequences in which patient statements can be printed.
3. Identify the information included on patient statements in each of the following categories: general information, transaction information, and financial information.
4. Describe the following formats used to print patient statements: insert statements and mailer statements.
5. Define the following terms: current charges, previous balance, billing period, aging accounts, dunning message.
6. Explain the difference between monthly billing and cycle billing.
7. List the five categories used to age accounts.
8. Explain the function of each of the following patient billing options: Process Patient Statements, Print Billing Labels, Billing Summary Report.

Introduction

The Patient Billing System is one of the more important components of a medical management program. An inadequate billing system can adversely affect the amount of revenue generated by the medical office. Although many medical offices now request payment at the time of service, there are many instances when no payment is received from the patient, such as when the charges are to be billed to an insurance carrier or when the patient cannot pay his/her bill at the time of the visit. The function of the Patient Billing System is to prepare bills and print billing statements. As procedures and diagnoses are entered into the computer while posting transactions, they are stored in the medical practice database. Later on, this information is available when needed to prepare patient bills.

The Patient Billing Routine

To generate statements, the Patient Billing System follows a billing routine which occurs in two stages. The first stage is to prepare the bills following the specifications entered by the user as to who is to be billed, and when, and how it is to be done. In preparing the bills, the system first scans all the financial accounts in the medical practice database to access those with a balance due. If a finance charge is being added to overdue accounts, the system automatically calculates it and adds it to the balance due. If the accounts are being aged, the system performs this function and includes a designated dunning message on overdue accounts. While bills are being prepared by the computer, it will appear as if the computer is doing nothing because the computer does not display each bill as it is being prepared. In actuality, the computer is working extremely hard accessing information from the database and performing necessary mathematical calculations. The amount of time it takes to prepare the bills will vary depending upon the number of bills being prepared.

Once the bills have been prepared, the computer moves to the second stage of the billing routine which is the actual printing of the billing statements known as *patient statements*. Patient statements are printed on continuous "computer" paper which can either be preprinted forms or plain white paper depending on the office preference. Patient statements can be printed in various sequences based on the needs of the practice. Examples include: a) in numerical order by account number, b) in alphabetical order by guarantor's name, or c) by zip code. The zip code printing order is preferred by large clinics who send out numerous bills because they can receive a postage discount by presorting their mail according to zip code. Patient statements are printed in sequence—one right after another—until they have all been printed. The patient statement is always addressed to the guarantor, that is, the person responsible for paying the bill. For example, charges for a minor child would be sent to his/her parent or guardian.

Information Included on Patient Statements

Billing statements include a variety of information which is grouped into the following categories: a) general information, b) transaction information, and c) financial information.

The top of the statement includes the general information as follows:

Name, address, and phone number of the medical office
Patient name and account number
Statement date
Name and address of the guarantor

The main body of the statement includes the transaction information as follows:

Services and procedures performed
Provider of each service and procedure
Procedure and diagnosis code for each service
Charge for each service and procedure
Correspondence with insurance carriers (e.g., insurance claims submission)
Payments made by the patient and his/her insurance carrier
Date of each of the above transactions

The bottom of the statement includes financial information as follows:

Total of new charges
Total payments received
Balance due
Date of last payment
Outstanding balance (by aging categories)

Other miscellaneous information included on patient statements includes dunning messages for delinquent accounts, statement messages, special messages, and the patient's next appointment date.

Formats for Patient Statements

Patient statements can be printed in two different formats as follows: insert statements and mailer statements. *Insert statements*, as the name indicates, are inserted into an envelope for mailing to the patient. Most offices use window envelopes for insert statements. With this method, the statement is printed with a large white space around the guarantor's name and address which is then visible through the "window" of the envelope. If a standard plain envelope is being used, mailing labels for each guarantor must be printed and attached to the envelopes. *Mailer statements* (also known as *speed mailers* and *datamailers*) have the patient statement and a return envelope for payment already inserted in a mailing envelope as it comes off the printer in continuous form. Although mailer statements must be separated from each other at their perforations, much time is saved in not having to stuff envelopes.

Billing Terminology

Before you begin working on the Patient Billing System, it is important to have an understanding of the following terms:

Current (New) Charges: The amount on a patient's statement that represents new services provided during the present month.

Billing Period: A *billing period* refers to the period of time between patient billing, or in other words, how often the patient is billed. Most offices bill the patient once a month (every 30 days), however some offices may choose to bill a patient after each visit. The schedule for printing the bills may vary from one office to another based upon the size of the practice. Small practices usually print all the bills at one time (once a month) while larger practices may print bills twice a month or even on a weekly basis. The latter arrangement is known as *cycle billing* and is recommended for practices that send out a large volume of patient statements. With cycle billing, the patient accounts are divided into smaller, more manageable, groups and each group of patient statements is sent out intermittently during the month. Most offices using cycle billing subdivide the accounts into four groups alphabetically by last name and send one group out each week. For example, the first cycle of patient statements sent out the first week of the month are to patients whose last names begin with the letters A through E, the second cycle of patients statements are sent out the second week to patients whose last names begin with the letters F through L, the third week, M through R, and the fourth week, S through Z. The principle advantage of cycle billing is that it provides for a steady flow of funds throughout the month which helps in budget management of the office. This billing method also prevents an end-of-the-month crisis of trying to process all the bills at one time as often occurs when printing bills once a month.

Aging Accounts: *Aging accounts* is the term used to describe the process of categorizing each account with an outstanding balance by the length of time the amount has been owed. The accounts are aged into the following five categories as follows:

Current (0 to 30 days)
31-60 days
61-90 days
91-120 days
120 days and over

The date the statement is sent to a patient indicating current charges is day 1 or the day aging begins. If the charges billed to a patient have not been paid by the time the next statement is sent, the account is considered 30 days old because the patient has had 30 days in which to pay the bill. Each time statements are sent and the bill is not paid, the amount due ages by a 30 day time period.

Computer systems have the ability to automatically calculate and age the balance due on each overdue account to indicate how long the account has been overdue. As previously mentioned, accounts are aged during the first stage of the billing routine, and the age of the account is indicated on the patient statement when it is printed.

Dunning Message: A *dunning message* is a phrase printed on overdue patient statements to remind the patient the account is past due. The specific message indicated is based on the length of time the balance has been outstanding (e.g., Your account is 60 days past due. Please remit!)

Patient Billing Options

The *Medical Practice Manager* includes three options within the Patient Billing System. Each of these options is used to perform specific functions which are listed and described below.

Process Patient Statements: The Processing Patient Statements option is used to prepare and print patient statements for all accounts with a non-zero balance. This option provides you with a data entry screen for specifying who is to be billed, and when and how it is to be done.

Print Billing Labels: This option is used to print mailing labels for bills. It is used when the medical office prints patient statements that are inserted into plain standard envelopes. When this option is selected, mailing labels are printed for all bills included in the current billing run.

Billing Summary Report: This option is used to print a summary report of bills which is a list of all guarantors billed in this billing run. The Billing Summary report also includes the patient's name and account number and bill total along with a grand total of all the bills printed.

CHECKPOINT

1. List and describe the two stages included in the billing routine.

____

____

2. What is the difference between an insert statement and a mailer statement?

____

____

3. Describe cycle billing. ____

____

____

4. What is the definition of aging accounts? ____

____

____

5. What is a dunning message? ____

____

____

MEDICAL PRACTICE MANAGER

Main Menu

1. Patient Registration
2. Posting Transactions
3. Patient Billing
4. Insurance Billing
5. Reports
6. File Maintenance

Enter Selection? ....

Worksheet 1: Patient Billing System

COMPETENCY

Access the Patient Billing System

GUIDELINES

You are responsible for entering the necessary information to prepare and print bills for patients with outstanding balances. In order to do this, you must first access the Patient Billing System.

LEARNING ACTIVITIES

1. What is the function of the Patient Billing System? ______________________________

   ____

2. What number should you select to move to this system?

   ____

3. a. Make this selection on the screen in the space entitled *Enter Selection*.

   b. Turn the page to move to the next screen.

PATIENT BILLING SYSTEM

Menu Options

1. Process Patient Statements
2. Print Billing Labels
3. Billing Summary Report

ESC: Return to Main Menu

Enter Selection? ....

Worksheet 2: Patient Statements

COMPETENCY

Access the Process Patient Statements data entry screen.

GUIDELINES

There are three options included within the Patient Billing System as illustrated on the menu screen on the opposite page. Make sure you are familiar with the function of each of these options by first reviewing the information on page 243, then complete the Learning Activities presented below.

LEARNING ACTIVITIES

1. What option (by name and number) would you select to perform the following tasks?

   a. Print mailing labels for bills ______________________________

   b. Print a billing summary report ______________________________

2. You are now ready to process patient statements. What number should you select to move to this option?

   ____

3. a. Make this selection on the screen in the space entitled *Enter Selection.*

   b. Turn the page to move to the next screen.

PROCESS PATIENT STATEMENTS

Data Entry Screen

Statement Date ....

Finance Charge (y/n)? ....

Skip Insurance (y/n)? ....

Minimum Balance ....

Printing Sequence ....

Printing Options ....

Starting With ....

Ending With ....

Age Accounts (y/n)? ....

Dunning Message:

  Current ....

  31-60 Days ....

  61-90 Days ....

  91-120 Days ....

  120 Days and Over ....

Statement Message ....

Special Message ....

Prepare Bills (y/n)? ....

Trial Bill (y/n)? ....

Print Statements (y/n)? ....

Worksheet 3: Process Patient Statements

COMPETENCY

Prepare and print patient statements.

GUIDELINES

To prepare and print patient statements, you must enter specifications as to who is to be billed, and when, and how it is to be done. This is accomplished by completing the data entry screen illustrated on the opposite page. The Learning Activities will provide you with the necessary information to perform this task.

DOCUMENTATION

Statement Date: Enter the date the statements are being sent. The date entered will appear on each statement generated.

Finance Charge (y/n)?: Enter whether you wish to charge interest on an overdue account. Finance charges are calculated on the balance forward minus any payments made since the date of the last billing. Finance charges may be a percentage of the overdue balance, or they may be a fixed dollar amount for all overdue accounts.

Skip Insurance (y/n)?: A "y" response means that the patient is not billed until an insurance claim has been filed and some response has been received from the carrier. An"n" response tells the computer to bill all patients with non-zero balances regardless of insurance claims submission.

Minimum Balance: Enter the minimum balance that the account must have in order to be included in the billing run. An account would have to have a balance equal to or greater than the amount entered in this field in order to be included in the billing run.

Printing Sequence: The printing sequence allows you to specify the order by which statements are to be printed. Enter the printing sequence code desired (A, N, or Z).

A: Accounts with a balance due are sorted and printed by patient account numbers.
N: Accounts with a balance due are sorted and printed by guarantor's last name.
Z: Accounts with a balance due are sorted and printed by guarantor's zip code.

Printing Options: The printing option allows you to specify whether all accounts, a range of accounts, or an individual account are to be billed. Enter the printing option code desired (A, R, or I).

A: Directs the computer to prepare and print statements for all accounts with a balance due.
R: Directs the computer to prepare and print a statement for a range of accounts (e.g., A through E). The range option is useful for cycle billing.
I: Directs the computer to prepare and print a statement for an individual account.

(Continued next page)

Starting With: Enter the value (account number, guarantor last name or zip code) you wish to start with for this billing run.

Ending With: Enter the ending value for this billing run (account number, guarantor last name or zip code)

Age Accounts (y/n)?: Enter a "y" response to direct the system to age accounts. An "n" response will tell the computer that the accounts are not to be aged.

Dunning Messages: Dunning messages are designed according to the age of the bill and printed at the bottom of the bill. The message can indicate the severity of the delinquent account.

Statement Message: Statement messages are used to relay information to the patient on submitting payment.

Special Message: This field may be used to enter a customized message on the bill (e.g., Happy Holidays!).

Prepare Bills (y/n)?: A "y" response tells the computer to begin preparing the bills. The cursor remains in this field until all the bills have been prepared. The time will vary based upon the number of bills being processed. Once the bills have been prepared, the cursor automatically moves to the next field (Trial Bill). An "n" response returns you to the Main Menu.

Trial Bill (y/n)?: This option should be used when bills are printed on preprinted forms. A trial statement is a "dummy" patient statement and its purpose is to make sure the billing forms are properly positioned in the printer. A "y" response tells the computer to print one form with x's placed on the form where information normally is filled in. This gives you the opportunity to make sure the printed information will be lined up with the spaces on the patient statement. A trial statement may be generated as many times as necessary for proper alignment of the forms. It is better to waste statement forms than to have the information out of alignment which makes it difficult for the patient to interpret. An "n" response is entered, a trial statement is not printed and the cursor automatically moves to the next field (Print Statements). This response is entered when the bills are being printed on plain white continuous paper, in which case, alignment is not required.

Print Statements (y/n)?: A "y" response results in the printing of the entire batch of billing statements specified for this billing run. An "n" response returns you to the Main Menu.

LEARNING ACTIVITIES

1. Prepare and print patient statements following the guidelines below. Enter this information on the Process Patient Statements data entry screen on page 248.

   Statement Date: Enter today's date.
   Finance Charge: Your office does not add a finance charge to overdue accounts.
   Skip Insurance: Patients coming to your medical office are not billed until an insurance claim has been filed and a response received from the carrier.
   Minimum Balance: The account must have a $5.00 minimum balance in order for a bill to be generated.
   Printing Sequence: The bills are to be printed by patient account number.
   Printing Options: A range of accounts are to be billed.
   Starting With: This billing run should start with account number 0001.
   Ending With: This billing run should end with account number 1500.
   Age Accounts: The accounts should be aged.
   Dunning Messages: The following dunning messages should be entered:
      Current (0-30 days): All bills must be paid within 30 days of receipt.
      31-60 days: Your account is 30 days past due. Prompt payment is appreciated.
      61-90: Your account is 60 days past due. Please remit!
      91-120 days: Your account is 90 days past due. Please remit to protect your credit rating.
      120 days and over: Your account must be paid in 30 days or it will be turned over to a collection agency.
   Statement Message: Enter the following statement message: Please return the top portion of this statement with your payment.
   Special Message: Enter a special message of your choosing.
   Prepare Bills: Enter "y" to tell the computer to begin preparing bills.
   Trial Bill: The bills are to be printed on preprinted forms. Therefore, a trial bill must be printed to make sure the forms are properly positioned in the printer.
   Print Statements: Enter "y" to tell the computer to begin printing the bills.

2. The first statement is included on the following page to provide you with a sample bill.

3. After completing the Process Patient Statements data entry screen, proceed to Chapter 9.

STATEMENT

PATIENT NAME	
Clare Henderson	
ACCOUNT NUMBER	STATEMENT DATE
0001	*(Today's Date)*

PLEASE MAKE CHECKS PAYABLE TO:

Riverside Family Practice Clinic
400 Broad Street
Norman, Oklahoma 73070

(405) 360-7444

Clare Henderson
501 Florence Drive
Norman, Oklahoma 73070

TOTAL BALANCE DUE

$20.00

PLEASE RETURN THE TOP PORTION OF THIS STATEMENT WITH YOUR PAYMENT

DATE	PHYSICIAN	DESCRIPTION	PROC CODE	DIAG CODE	CHARGES	PAYMENTS
6/10/91	Howe	Intermediate-Est. Patient	90060	789.0	25.00	
6/10/91	Howe	Pelvic Exam	58999	789.0	20.00	
6/12/91		Insurance Filed to BC				
6/29/91		Insurance Payment - BC				-30.00
7/15/91		Patient Payment - CHECK				-15.00
8/8/91	Howe	Limited-Established Patient	90050	034	20.00	
8/8/91	Howe	Throat Culture	87060	034	10.00	
8/12/91		Insurance Filed to BC				
8/20/91		Insurance Payment - BC				-10.00

DATE OF LAST PAYMENT	CURRENT 0 - 30 DAYS	BALANCE OVER 30 DAYS	BALANCE OVER 60 DAYS	BALANCE OVER 90 DAYS	BALANCE OVER 120 DAYS	TOTAL NEW CHARGES	TOTAL PAYMENTS
8/20/91	$20.00					$30.00	$10.00

ALL BILLS MUST BE PAID WITHIN 30 DAYS OF RECEIPT

PLEASE PAY THIS AMOUNT →

BALANCE DUE
$20.00

9 INSURANCE BILLING

COMPETENCY

After completing this chapter, you should be able to perform the following.

Prepare and print insurance claims.

LEARNING OBJECTIVES

After completing this chapter, you should be able to:

1. Describe the insurance billing routine.
2. Identify the name of the form used most often to submit insurance claims.
3. List three sequences that can be used to print out insurance forms.
4. List and describe the criteria which must exist in order to submit claims electronically.
5. Explain the general procedure for electronic claims submission.
6. Explain the function of each of the following insurance billing options: Print Insurance Claims, Insurance Labels, Electronic Claims Submission, Claim Summary Report, Insurance Claim Tracking.

Introduction

Insurance claims processing has placed a tremendous burden on the medical office of today. This is due not only to the increase in the number of individuals covered by health insurance but also to the increase in the amount of information required on the claim forms. In addition, the completion of these forms has become even more complicated than it was before. Thus, a large portion of front office responsibility is often devoted to preparing and submitting insurance claims. Computers provide much assistance in this area because they are able to prepare and process claims in a short period of time. As procedures and diagnoses are entered into the computer during posting transactions, they are stored in the medical practice database. Later on, this information is available when needed to prepare insurance claims. From the information stored in the database, the computer is able to automatically fill out every major portion of the claim form.

The Insurance Billing Routine

The function of the Insurance Billing System is to prepare and generate insurance claims. Insurance claims are processed in two stages similar to the stages previously described in the patient billing routine. The first stage is to prepare the insurance claims following specifications entered by the user. In preparing the claims, the system first scans the medical practice database and gathers all the necessary information to complete each data item on the claim form. Examples of information required on the claim form include the patient's name and address, the patient's date of birth, the subscriber ID number and group number, the date of service, the diagnosis code(s) and description(s), the procedure code(s) and description(s), and the provider's name and address. If required information is lacking for a particular claim, the computer will not be able to prepare that claim. When this occurs the computer displays a message on the screen of the monitor indicating the patient account number and the information that is missing (e.g., subscriber ID number, diagnosis code). A summary report is subsequently printed which lists all the claims which have incomplete information. To process these claims, the required information must be added to the database.

During the preparation stage, the computer arranges the claim forms in groups by insurance carrier (e.g., Medicare, Blue Cross, Blue Shield, CHAMPUS and so on). This in turn results in the forms being printed out by insurance carrier, thus making it easier to group the forms together for mailing to the appropriate carriers. As in patient billing, it appears as if the computer is doing nothing while the insurance claims are being prepared. However, the computer is working very hard accessing all of the necessary information from the medical practice database. The amount of time this takes depends upon the number of insurance claims being prepared.

Once the insurance claims have been prepared, the computer moves on to the second stage of the insurance billing routine which is the generation of the insurance claims. Insurance claims can be generated in two ways: a) by printing them out in hardcopy form or b) by transmitting them electronically over the phone lines directly to the insurance carrier. These methods are described in more detail on the following pages.

Printed Insurance Claims (Paper Claims)

Using a computer system to print insurance claims is much more convenient and less time-consuming than typing each claim individually. The insurance claims are printed out on a tractor feed printer using continuous preprinted claim forms.

The form used most often to submit insurance claims is the Health Insurance Claim Form which is often referred to as the HCFA-1500 form. The abbreviation HCFA stands for Health Care Financing Administration which is a division of the federal government responsible for overseeing Medicare. The Health Insurance Claim Form is a standard claim form approved by the AMA and accepted by nearly all general insurance carriers including Medicare and CHAMPUS. Because of its widespread use in submitting claims for many different insurance carriers, the Health Insurance Claim Form has come to be called the *Universal Claim Form*.

The Health Insurance Claim Form is available for use with a computer system using continuous preprinted claim forms on a tractor feed printer. The Health Insurance Claim Form can be purchased either as a continuous single or multiple-part form in boxes of 1000 forms. The multiple-part form consists of an original and one copy which permits the medical office to mail the original to the insurance carrier and retain the copy for reference.

The insurance claim forms are printed out in groups by insurance carrier. Within each "carrier group", the claims can be arranged in various sequences based on the needs of the practice. Examples include a) in numerical order by account number, b) in alphabetical order by account name and c) by zip code. Insurance forms are printed in sequence—one right after another until they have all been printed. Once the forms have been printed, they must be separated at their perforations and mailed to the appropriate insurance carriers.

Electronic Claims Submission

Electronic Claims Submission (ECS) involves the transmission of insurance claim information directly to an insurance carrier from one computer to another over the telephone lines. This method of generating insurance claims is often termed the *paperless* processing of insurance claims because it takes place without the use of a hardcopy. Because mailing time is eliminated, electronic claims submission usually results in a faster turnaround time by insurance carriers. The medical office generally receives reimbursements within ten days to two weeks after submission, which is about half the time it takes to receive payment with paper claims.

In order to process claims electronically, several criteria must exist. First, the medical management program must have an electronic claims submission option. The option may have already been included when the medical management program was purchased or it may be available for purchase as an "add-on" option. In addition, the insurance carrier must be a *cooperating insurance carrier,* which is one that allows claims to be sent to them electronically. In order to transmit the claims across the telephone lines, the computer must be connected to a modem. A *modem* is a device that changes data into a form that can be transmitted over telephone lines. At the other end, it must be changed back by another modem to a form that can be utilized by the computer at the insurance carrier site.

The general procedure for electronic claims submission is as follows. The claims are first prepared by the computer in the manner previously described on page 254. Once prepared, the computer displays a message on the screen of the terminal to indicate that the claims are ready for transmission. The cooperating insurance carrier is then notified and the claims are transmitted over the telephone lines from the medical office computer to the insurance carrier computer. During this time interval, a message is displayed on the user's screen indicating the transmission process is taking place. While the claims are being transmitted, that particular terminal cannot be used to perform other tasks. When all the claims have been transmitted, a final message appears on the screen to let the user know the process has been successfully completed. At this time, the process may be repeated with another cooperating insurance carrier, and so on, until all the electronic claims have been transmitted to their appropriate carriers.

Insurance Billing System Options

The *Medical Practice Manager* includes four options within the Insurance Billing System. Each of these options is used to perform specific functions which are listed and described below.

Print Insurance Claims: The Print Insurance Claims option is used to process paper claims. This option provides you with a data entry screen for specifying information needed to process the claims.

Insurance Labels: This option is used to print mailing labels for sending paper claims to insurance carriers. When this option is selected, mailing labels are printed for all carriers included in the current insurance billing run.

Electronic Claims Submission: This Electronic Claims Submission option is used to submit insurance claims directly to an insurance carrier over the telephone lines. This option provides you with a data entry screen for specifying information needed to prepare and transmit the claims.

Claim Summary Report: This option is used to print a reference list of the paper and/or electronic claims generated during each billing run. The Claim Summary Report includes the claim number, the carrier's name, the patient's and insurer's name, each claim amount, the total number of claims submitted to each carrier, the total dollar amount of all claims, and the total number of claims generated for the billing run. A Claim Summary Report should be printed after each insurance billing run. Due to the paperless nature of electronic claims, it is of particular importance to permanently retain the Electronic Claim Summary Report as documentation of claims submitted.

Insurance Claim Tracking: This option is used to access information regarding the status of insurance claims in order to answer inquiries regarding insurance claims. The information is available for on-screen display or for printing and includes the following data: when the claim was submitted, for what patient, to what carrier, and for what amount. The Insurance Claim Tracking option is often used to look up information when patients have questions regarding their insurance claims.

CHECKPOINT

1. How are computers able to prepare insurance claims in such a short period of time?

2. What occurs during the first stage of the insurance billing routine?

3. What occurs during the second stage of the insurance billing routine?

4. What is the name of the form used most often to submit insurance claims?

5. What is electronic claims submission?

6. What are the advantages of electronic claims submission?

7. What criteria must exist before forms can be submitted electronically?

8. What is the function of the Insurance Claim Tracking option?

MEDICAL PRACTICE MANAGER

Main Menu

1. Patient Registration
2. Posting Transactions
3. Patient Billing
4. Insurance Billing
5. Reports
6. File Maintenance

Enter Selection? ....

Worksheet 1: Insurance Billing System

COMPETENCY

Access the Insurance Billing System

GUIDELINES

You are responsible for entering the necessary information to prepare and print insurance claims for your medical practice. In order to do this, you must first make the appropriate selection from the main menu.

LEARNING ACTIVITIES

1. What is the function of the Insurance Billing System? ____________________

   ____

2. What number should you select to move to this system?

   ____

3. a. Make this selection of the screen in the space entitled *Enter Selection.*

   b. Turn the page to move to the next screen.

INSURANCE BILLING SYSTEM

Menu Options

1. Print Insurance Claims
2. Insurance Labels
3. Electronic Claims Submission
4. Claim Summary Report
5. Insurance Claim Tracking

ESC: Return to Main Menu

Enter Selection? ________________

Worksheet 2: Processing Insurance Claims

COMPETENCY

Access the Print Insurance Claims option.

GUIDELINES

There are five options included within the Insurance Billing System as illustrated on the menu screen on the opposite page. Make sure you are familiar with the function of each of these options by reviewing the information on page 256 followed by completion of the Learning Activities presented below.

LEARNING ACTIVITIES

1. What option (by name and number) would you select to perform the following tasks?

   a. To print mailing labels for sending paper claims to insurance carriers

   ____

   b. To submit insurance claims electronically to Medicare

   ____

   c. To look up the date that an insurance claim was submitted for Saralyn Griggs

   ____

   d. To print an insurance claim summary report

   ____

   e. To determine which insurance companies have not yet sent reimbursement for claims submitted

   ____

2. a. You are now ready to prepare and print insurance claims. What number should you select to move to this option?

   ____

   b. Make this selection on the screen in the space entitled *Enter Selection.*

   c. Turn the page to move to the next screen.

PRINT INSURANCE CLAIMS

Data Entry Screen

Claim End Date ....

Bill Range/Order ....

Special Message ....

Prepare Insurance Claims (y/n)? ....

Form Alignment (y/n)? ....

Print Insurance Claims (y/n)? ....

Worksheet 3: Print Insurance Claims

COMPETENCY

Prepare and print insurance claims.

GUIDELINES

To prepare and print insurance claims, you must enter specifications as to how this should be done. This is accomplished by completing the data entry screen on the opposite page. The Learning Activities at the end of this worksheet will provide you with the necessary information to perform this task.

DOCUMENTATION

Claim End Date: This date represents the cutoff date for printing transactions on the insurance claims. In other words, any transactions occurring after this date are not included in this billing run. The system prints all claims not billed since the last billing run. This prevents claims from being submitted more than once for the same bill.

Bill Range/Order: This field allows you to specify the range and order for printing insurance claims. Enter the range/order code desired (I, A, N, or Z).

- I: Directs the computer to print a form for an individual account. Selecting this code results in a prompt asking you to specify the patient account number.
- A: Directs the computer to print claim forms for all accounts in account order.
- N: Directs the computer to print claim forms for all accounts in name order.
- Z: Directs the computer to print claim forms for all accounts in zip code order.

Special Message: This field may be used to enter a one-line special message that will be included on the bottom of all forms printed during this run (e.g., Prepared by Jane Smith).

Prepare Insurance Claims (y/n)?: A "y" response tells the computer to begin preparing the claims. The cursor remains in this field until all the claims have been prepared. The time will vary based on the number of claims being prepared. Once the claims have been prepared, the cursor automatically moves to the next field (Form Alignment). An "n" response returns you to the Main menu.

Form Alignment (y/n)?: The Insurance Billing System has been programed to print claims using the Health Insurance Claim Form. A "y" response tells the computer to place x's on the form where information is normally filled in. This gives you the opportunity to make sure that the printed information will be lined up with the spaces on the insurance form. If you print an alignment form and are not satisfied, adjust the alignment and then answer "y" when this question appears again. When your claims are properly aligned, answer "n" to indicate that you do not wish to print another alignment form.

Print Insurance Claims (y/n)?: A "y" response results in the printing of the entire batch of insurance claims specified for this billing run. An "n" response returns you to the Main Menu.

LEARNING ACTIVITIES

1. What is the claim end date? ______________________________

____

2. What is the purpose of the Form Alignment field? ______________________

____

3. Prepare and print insurance claims following the guidelines presented below. Enter this information on the Print Insurance Claims data entry screen on page 262.

   Claim End Date: Enter yesterday's date to tell the computer that all transactions through this date should be included on the insurance claim forms.

   Bill Range/Order: Print forms for all accounts in account order

   Special Message: Enter the following message in this field: Prepared by (your name).

   Prepare Insurance Claims: Enter "y" to tell the computer to begin preparing the claims.

   Form Alignment: Enter "y" to make sure the forms are properly aligned in the printer.

   Print Insurance Claims: Enter "y" to tell the computer to begin printing the insurance claim forms.

4. After completing the Print Insurance Claims data entry screen, proceed to Chapter 10.

10 REPORTS

LEARNING OBJECTIVES

After completing this chapter, you should be able to:

1. Describe the following categories of reports: patient demographic reports, accounting reports, practice analysis reports, standard reports.
2. Describe and identify the use of each of the following types of patient demographic reports: Account Name, Last Name, Age, Zip Code.
3. Describe and identify the use of each of the following types of accounting reports: Daily Report, Aged Accounts Receivable, Outstanding Insurance Carriers.
4. Describe and identify the use of each of the following types of practice analysis reports: Procedure Analysis, Diagnosis Analysis, Referral Analysis.
5. Identify the information contained in each of the following types of standard reports: Diagnosis Table, Procedure Table, Provider Table, Insurance Carrier Table, Place of Service Table, Referral Table.

Introduction

One of the most useful features of a medical management program is its ability to create a variety of reports on almost every aspect of the medical practice. These reports allow the medical practice to review and analyze many business and practice activities. This, in turn, assists the physician in making informed decisions regarding the medical practice based on the interpretation of statistical data.

The information contained in the reports is accessed by the computer from the medical practice database. The number and type of reports available for review depend on the medical management program in use. Most medical software programs have the capability of generating a multitude of reports, however the degree and frequency to which these reports are run depend on the needs of each individual medical office. For example, some reports are generated by the office on a daily basis, others on a monthly basis, and still others on a yearly basis. There are some reports which may not be generated at all because the office does not have a current use for the information they contain. Hence, each office determines the reports that are most beneficial to the efficient running of their medical practice.

Categories of Reports

Reports can be divided into four general categories: patient demographic reports, accounting reports, practice analysis reports, and standard reports. Each category is described in more detail in the following paragraphs.

Patient Demographic Reports: These types of reports are used to categorize patients. Examples of these categories include account number, last name, age, and zip code.

Accounting Reports: These types of reports are used to audit the financial activity of the medical practice. Audits check for accuracy and detect errors so that steps can be taken to correct them. Overall accounting reports help to manage the practice more effectively by helping to control cash flow, monitor patient and insurance payments, and by providing indicators of the profitability of the practice.

Practice Analysis Reports: These types of reports provide assistance in making managerial decisions about the practice. They provide data that can help the physician make salary and bonus determinations, decide whether to add staff or additional physicians, or whether to purchase additional equipment.

Standard Reports: These types of reports include tables of information that are used as a reference in day-to-day front office operations. For example, the Procedure Table is a list of all procedures stored in the medical practice database and is used as a reference to look up procedure codes and/or descriptions. As you probably remember, the information included in standard reports is entered into the medical practice database during the completion of start-up tasks (Refer to Chapter 5: File Maintenance System).

CHECKPOINT

1. What functions are served by generating reports? ______

2. Where does the computer access the information contained in each report?

3. Describe the function of each of the following categories of reports.

   a. Patient Demographic Reports ______

   b. Accounting Reports ______

   c. Practice Analysis Reports ______

   d. Standard Reports ______

REPORTS SYSTEM

Menu Options

Patient Demographic Reports
1. Account Number
2. Last Name
3. Age
4. Zip Code

Accounting Reports
5. Daily Report
6. Aged Accounts Receivables
7. Outstanding Insurance Claims

Practice Analysis Reports
8. Provider Analysis
9. Procedure Analysis
10. Diagnosis Analysis
11. Referral Analysis

Standard Reports
12. Diagnosis Table
13. Procedure Table
14. Provider Table
15. Insurance Carrier Table
16. Place of Service Table
17. Referral Table

ESC: Return to Main Menu

Enter Selection? ________________

Worksheet 1: Reports

COMPETENCY

Identify the appropriate selection for generating medical practice reports.

GUIDELINES

The *Medical Practice Manager* is capable of generating the reports included in the menu illustrated on the opposite page. Each report includes the practice name and the title of the report at the top of the page (e.g., Riverside Family Practice Clinic: Provider Analysis Report).

LEARNING ACTIVITIES

1. Which option (by number) would you select to generate the following reports?

   a. Patient Demographic Report by account number ________________

   b. Daily Report ________________

   c. Procedure Analysis Report ________________

   d. Procedure Table ________________

   e. Diagnosis Analysis Report ________________

   f. Aged Accounts Receivable Report ________________

   g. Patient Demographic Report by last name________________

   h. Insurance Carrier Table ________________

   i. Provider Analysis Report ________________

   j. Diagnosis Table ________________

2. The remaining sections provide a detailed explanation of the reports included in the *Medical Practice Manager*. Turn the page to begin these competencies.

Worksheet 2: Patient Demographic Reports

COMPETENCY

Identify the use of patient demographic reports in the medical office.

GUIDELINES

Listed below are the patient demographic reports generated by the *Medical Practice Manager* including a description of the report, information included in the report and use of the report.

Patient Demographic Reports:

Account Number: This report is a list of all patients in the practice organized by patient account number. It is used as a reference to look up the patient's name when only the account number is known.

Last Name: This report is a list of all patients in the practice organized alphabetically by last name. It also includes the patient's account number, address and home and work telephone numbers. This report is used as a reference to look up patient information by last name.

Age: This report categorizes all patients in the practice by age. It includes the total number and percent of patients in each age category. This report can be used to determine the age distribution of the patients in the practice.

Zip Code: This report categorizes all patients in the practice by the zip code of their home address. It includes the total number and percent of patients living in each zip code area. This report can be used to define geographic area served by the medical practice.

LEARNING ACTIVITIES

1. Indicate the report you would use to accomplish each of the following tasks:

   a. To determine the geographic area served by the medical practice.

   ____

   b. To look up the home phone number of Henry Clark.

   ____

   c. To determine what percent of the practice is made up of pediatric patients.

   ____

   d. To look up the patient's name with the account number of 850.

   ____

   e. To determine how many patients in the practice are 40 years of age or older.

   ____

   f. To look up the patient account number of Betsy Gribble.

   ____

2. Turn the page to begin completion of the next competency.

Worksheet 3: Accounting Reports

COMPETENCY

Identify the use of accounting reports in the medical office.

GUIDELINES

Listed below are the accounting reports generated by the *Medical Practice Manager* including a description of the report, information included in the report and use of the report.

Accounting Reports:

Daily Report: The daily report is a detailed report of all transactions that have occurred for the current day. It includes all charges, payments, adjustments and write-offs posted that day, and organized by patient and account number. The daily report should be run at the end of each working day. It is used to provide a printed record of the day's financial activities, to reconcile total charges and cash receipts, to prepare the bank deposit slip, and to provide a complete and detailed audit trail of all transactions for that day.

Aged Accounts Receivable: This report lists all accounts receivable by patient name and account number showing the aging distribution categories for the current period (less than 30 days), 31-60 days, 61 to 90 days, 91 to 120 days and 120 days and over. It also includes the name, address, and phone number of the responsible party, and the total account balance. The Aged Accounts Receivable report is used to identify outstanding patient accounts in order to follow up on delinquent accounts.

Outstanding Insurance Claims: This report lists all outstanding insurance claims submitted to insurance carriers including the date the claim was filed, the name and phone number of the insurance carrier, the name of the insured party, patient's name and the amount of the claim. This report is used to follow-up on outstanding insurance claims.

LEARNING ACTIVITIES

1. Indicate the report you would use to accomplish each of the following tasks:

   a. To look up the patients who have outstanding balances over 120 days for the purpose of turning them over to a collection agency.

   ____

   b. To review the payments made for the current day.

   ____

   c. To determine which insurance claims have not yet been paid by insurance carriers.

   ____

   d. To determine which accounts have outstanding balances that are 91-120 days overdue for the purpose of calling these patients regarding payment.

   ____

   e. To review all charges for the current day.

   ____

2. Turn the page to begin completion of the next competency.

Worksheet 4: Practice Analysis Reports

COMPETENCY

Identify the use of practice analysis reports in the medical office.

GUIDELINES

Listed below are the practice analysis reports generated by the *Medical Practice Manger* including a description of each report, information included in the report and uses of each report.

Practice Analysis Reports:

Provider Analysis: This report lists the revenue generated by each provider in the practice. It is used to analyze the productivity of each provider in the medical practice and to determine profit distribution among providers.

Procedure Analysis: This report lists all the procedures performed during a specified time period and includes the number of times each procedure was performed, the total charges for each procedure, and the percentage of the total revenue provided by each procedure. The Procedure Analysis Report is used to determine which procedures are performed the most, how much revenue is generated by each procedure, and to assist in making decisions on new equipment purchases.

Diagnosis Analysis: This report lists all diagnoses on file in the medical practice database including the number of times each diagnosis was used. This report is used to determine what types of patients are being seen and can also help determine areas in which the physician may want to seek appropriate continuing medical education (CME).

Referral Analysis: This report provides a list of each referring source (by name, address, and referral code) and includes the total number of patients referred along with the dollar amount of charges performed on these patients. The Referral Analysis Report is used to determine the number of new patients generated by physician referrals to the office. It is also used to determine the revenue generated by physician referrals.

LEARNING ACTIVITIES

1. Indicate the report you would use to accomplish each of the following tasks:

   a. To determine how many times a diagnosis of otitis media was made for the current month.

   ____

   b. To determine the total revenue generated by each provider in the practice for the current day.

   ____

   c. To determine how many patients were referred to the practice by Shirley Pearce, M.D.

   ____

   d. To determine how many electrocardiograms were run for the current month.

   ____

2. Turn the page to begin completion of the next competency.

Worksheet 5: Standard Reports

COMPETENCY

Identify the use of standard reports in the medical office.

GUIDELINES

Listed below are the standard reports generated by the *Medical Practice Manager,* including a description of the report and information included in the report.

Standard Reports:

Diagnosis Table: The Diagnosis Table is a list of all the diagnoses on file in the medical practice database. It includes the office code, ICDA code and description next to each diagnosis listed in the report.

Procedure Table: The Procedure Table is a list of all the procedures on file in the medical practice database. It includes the office code, CPT code and description, and standard charge next to each procedure listed in the report.

Provider Table: The Provider Table is a list of all providers in the medical practice. It includes the provider code, name and address and identification numbers next to each provider listed in the report.

Insurance Carrier Table: The Insurance Carrier Table is a list of all insurance carriers on file in the medical practice database. It includes the insurance carrier code, name, address, and phone number next to each carrier listed in the report.

Place of Service Table: The Place of Service Table is a list of all the place of service locations on file in the medical practice database. It includes the facility code, name, address, and phone number next to each place of service listed in the report.

Referral Table: The Referral Table is a list of all referring physicians on file in the medical practice database. It includes the referral's code, name, address, and phone number next to each referring physician listed in the report.

LEARNING ACTIVITIES

1. Indicate the report you would use to accomplish each of the following tasks:

   a. To look up the telephone number of Blue Cross.

   ____

   b. To look up the referral code for Ryan Gassaway, MD.

   ____

   c. To look up the office code for congestive heart failure.

   ____

   d. To look up the address of the Aetna Insurance Company.

   ____

   e. To look up the CPT code for an allergy injection.

   ____

   f. To look up the social security number for Henry Clark.

   ____

Congratulations!

You have completed the Medical Practice Manager

____

Your Signature

Glossary

alpha-numeric field—A field which allows the entry of both letters and numbers including special characters.

ALU (arithmetic/logic unit)—The part of the CPU that executes the program's instructions by performing mathematical computations and logical operations.

application software —Software designed to accomplish a specific task (e.g., word processing). Also called application program and software program.

backup copy—A duplicate copy of a program or data kept for reference in case the original is damaged, lost, or destroyed.

block—A group of characters such as a sentence or paragraph.

byte—A unit of computer storage capacity. One byte is approximately equal to one character.

computer—An electronic machine which has the ability to process data according to a program in order to produce a desired result.

computerphobia—The fear of computers.

control unit—The part of the CPU that coordinates the entire computer system.

CPU (central processing unit)—The "heart" of the computer housed in the main unit. The CPU consists of the control unit, the ALU, and primary storage.

CRT (cathode ray tube)—A monitor similar to a television screen that permits the visual display of input and output.

cursor—A position marker which indicates where the next character entered will be displayed on the screen.

data—Raw, unorganized facts about subject matter presented to the computer for processing.

data disk—A disk that has been formatted and prepared to receive and store data from an application program.

data entry—The input of data into the computer.

data entry screen—A screen used to enter data into the computer.

data field (field)—A single item of information (example: Name). A field consists of a title followed by a space for entering the data.

data processing—The changing of raw facts or data into usable information following a three part sequence: input, processing, output.

database—A large collection of data organized in a manner which allows for retrieval and use of that data.

database management—The task of storing data in a database and retrieving information from that data.

directory—A special area on a disk which contains the names and location of all the items stored on the disk. The computer uses the directory to locate items on the disk.

disk drive—A mechanical device which rotates a floppy disk and uses a read/write head for the purpose of data transmission.

document—Any single piece of writing that you work on, such as a letter, memo, or report. Another name for a document is a file.

documentation—A written set of instructions accompanying an application program, designed to assist the user in understanding how to operate the program. Examples include the user manual, help screens and reference cards.

DOS (Disk Operating System)—A term commonly used to refer to the following operating systems: PC-DOS and MS-DOS.

double-density disk—A disk that can hold twice as much information as a single-density disk.

double-sided disk—A disk that can store information on both sides of the disk.

edit—To revise the text in a document.

file—A complete collection of records (example: patient registration file).

filename—The name you give a document when you create it.

floppy disk—A secondary storage device consisting of flexible mylar plastic coated with iron oxide and encased in a square jacket.

formatting (initializing)—The process of marking track and sector numbers on a disk so that it can be used by the computer to store and retrieve information. Formatting erases any information previously stored on the disk.

hard disk—A secondary storage device consisting of one or more rigid, nonflexible magnetic platters encased in a permanently sealed, air-tight container.

hardcopy—Printed output from a computer.

hardware—The physical devices making up the computer system (e.g., CPU, keyboard, monitor, printer).

impact printer—A type of printer that forms characters using a print element that strikes an inked ribbon against the paper (e.g., dot-matrix, daisywheel).

information—Data that has been processed into a usable form by the computer.

input—1. (noun) Data that has been entered into the computer. 2. (verb) The transfer of data to the computer for processing.

input device—A device for entering data into the computer (e.g., keyboard, scanner, mouse).

K (kilobyte)—A unit of computer storage capacity. Once kilobyte is equal to 1024 bytes (characters).

keyboard (computer)—An input device which converts data into an electronic code for processing by the computer.

letter quality (LQ)—Print that is characterized by sharp, crisp, high-quality, fully formed characters similar to the characters produced by a typewriter.

load—The process of transferring information into computer memory from a secondary storage device such as a hard disk or floppy disk.

main menu—A menu which lists the primary functions performed by an application program.

magnetic tape—A secondary storage device consisting of a thin, plastic material which has a magnetic surface for storing data. Magnetic tape is most often used to back up a hard disk.

MB (megabyte)—A unit of computer storage capacity. One megabyte is equal to a little over one million bytes.

medical office management software program—A program which provides instructions to the computer for performing medical office management procedures. (Also termed medical management program).

menu—A list of the tasks or functions which can be performed by an application program. The user selects the function desired from this list of choices.

menu screen—A type of screen which displays a menu. Menu screens are used to move from one part of an application program to another.

multiuser computer system—A computer system consisting of one CPU that is shared by two or more terminals. In a multiuser system, one or more terminals can be used at the same time and these terminals can be doing different tasks simultaneously.

near-letter quality (NLQ)—Print that is of a slightly lesser quality than that of letter quality print.

nonimpact printer—A type of printer that forms characters without making a striking motion against the paper, but rather through the use of laser beams, ink-jet spraying, or heat (e.g., laser printer, ink-jet printer, thermal printer).

numeric field—A field which only allows the entry of digits and special characters associated with digits.

operating system—A group of programs which serve as a manager to control computer operations not controlled by ROM.

output—1. (noun) Information that has been generated by the computer. 2. (verb) The transfer of processed data back to the user.

primary storage—The part of the CPU that is responsible for temporarily storing information until it is needed for processing by the computer. Primary storage in a microcomputer is known as RAM.

printer—An output device that produces hardcopy output.

processing—The manipulation and reorganization of data according to the instructions in a program.

program—A set of instructions organized in a logical step-by-step sequence which tells the computer how to perform a specific function.

program disk—A floppy disk that contains an application program.

RAM (random-access memory)—Primary storage in a microcomputer which is used to temporarily store items until needed by the computer. Also known as computer memory.

read—The transfer of information from a storage medium, such as a floppy disk or a hard disk, to computer memory.

record—A set of fields pertaining to the same thing (example: patient registration record).

resolution—The sharpness of the image displayed on the screen of a computer monitor.

ROM (read-only memory)—A type of memory found in microcomputers which can only be read. ROM is permanently installed by the manufacturer and holds instructions that the computer needs to manage itself.

saving (a document)—The process of transferring a copy of the text that has been entered into the computer to a secondary storage device.

screen—Information displayed on the computer monitor.

secondary storage device—A storage device used to permanently store information for later retrieval by the computer.

single-sided disk—A disk which can store information on only one side of the disk.

softcopy—The visual display of information on the display screen of a computer monitor.

software—A general term for the programs or instructions that tell a computer what to do.

source document—An original document from which data is extracted for input into the computer.

submenu—A menu which further defines a function listed in the main menu. A submenu lists the specific tasks that can be performed within each main menu option.

system disk—A floppy disk that contains an operating system.

terminal—An input-output device consisting of a monitor and a keyboard.

text—The words, numbers, and punctuation that make up a word processing document.

text formatting—The arrangement or layout of text on paper.

user—The individual using the computer.

user manual (program)—A manual that describes how to use an application program.

word processing—The manipulation of words using (an electronic device such as) a computer.

write—The transfer of information from computer memory to a storage medium such as a floppy disk or hard disk.

write-protect—To protect the information on a disk. When a disk is write-protected, the computer cannot make changes to information, erase any information or write new information on the disk.

Index

H

I

K

L

M

N

O

P

R